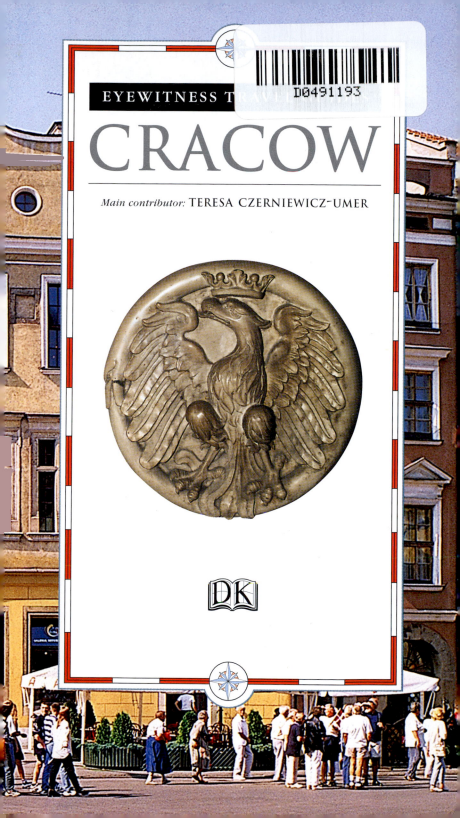

EYEWITNESS TRAVEL GUIDES

CRACOW

Main contributor: TERESA CZERNIEWICZ-UMER

DK

LONDON, NEW YORK,
MELBOURNE, MUNICH AND DELHI
www.dk.com

Produced by Wydawnictwo Wiedza i Życie, Warsaw

MANAGING EDITOR Ewa Szwagrzyk
SERIES EDITOR Joanna Egert
DTP DESIGNER Paweł Pasternak
CONSULTANT Jan Ostrowski
PRODUCTION Anna Kożurno-Królikowska

CONTRIBUTORS
Teresa Czerniewicz-Umer, Andrzej Betlej, Piotr Krasny,
Robert Makłowicz

PHOTOGRAPHERS
Andrzej Chęć, Wojciech Czerniewicz, Piotr Jamski,
Dorota and Mariusz Jarymowicz

ILLUSTRATORS
Andrzej Wielgosz, Piotr Zybrzycki, Paweł Mistewicz

Printed and bound by South China Printing Co. Ltd., China

First published in Great Britain in 2000
by Dorling Kindersley Limited
80 Strand, London WC2R 0RL
Reprinted with revisions 2003

Copyright 2000, 2003 © Dorling Kindersley Limited, London
A Penguin Company

ISBN 0 7513 4822 8

◁ **Houses around Cracow's Market Square**

CONTENTS

HOW TO USE THIS GUIDE 6

The side arcade of Cloth Hall

INTRODUCING CRACOW

PUTTING CRACOW ON THE MAP 10

THE HISTORY OF CRACOW 16

CRACOW AT A GLANCE 36

CRACOW THROUGH THE YEAR 52

**Icon of the Virgin of the Rosary
in the Dominican Church**

Cloth Hall (Sukiennice) by night

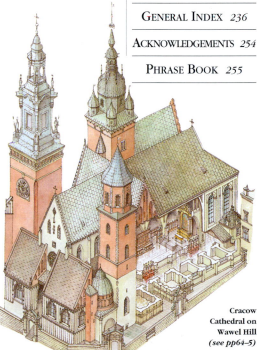

Musicians wearing regional Cracow costumes

A room on the first floor of the Royal Castle

Cracow Cathedral on Wawel Hill
(see pp64–5)

HOW TO USE THIS GUIDE

THIS Dorling Kindersley guide is intended to help you make the most of your stay in Cracow. It provides detailed practical information and expert recommendations. *Introducing Cracow* tells you about the geographical location of the city, establishes Cracow in its historical context and guides you through the succession of cultural events. The section on *Cracow at a Glance* takes you through the tourist attractions in the city. *Cracow Area by Area*

describes the most important sights with photographs, maps and illustrations. It recommends short excursions out of Cracow and offers three walks around the city. Information about hotels, restaurants, shops and markets as well as cafés, bars, entertainment and sport can be found in the section called *Travellers' Needs*. The section headed *Survival Guide* has advice on everything from posting a letter to using public transport to getting medical assistance.

HOW TO USE THE KEY INDICATORS

Each of the six quarters has been colour coded for your convenience. Each section gives an introduction to the area, its history and character. The *Street by Street* map shows the

most interesting parts of the quarter. Finding your way round is made easy by the numbering system. This follows the order in which the descriptions are presented.

Each area has its colour coded thumb tabs.

1 Area Map
For ease of reference, sights in each area are located and numbered on the area map. Sights of particular interest are listed together: churches, museums and galleries, streets and squares, historic buildings, parks and monuments.

Locator map

A locator map places you in relation to the surrounding area.

A suggested route takes you through the most interesting streets in the area.

2 Street-by-Street Map
The most interesting part of each sightseeing area is given from a bird's-eye view. On the area map the most interesting sights are indicated and given a full description on the following pages.

Stars indicate the features that no visitors should miss.

CRACOW AREA MAP

This colour-coded map (*see pages 14–15*) indicates the six main sightseeing quarters described in this guide. Each of these quarters is more fully covered in the *Area by Area* section (*pages 56–149*). In *Cracow at a Glance* this same colour coding allows you to locate the most interesting places. You will also be able to orientate yourself during the three suggested walks (*page 158*).

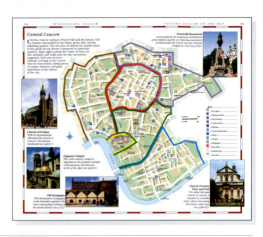

Numbered circles locate the listed sights on the area map and within the descriptive section.

Practical information provides everything you need to know to visit each sight. Map references pinpoint the sight's location on the *Street Finder* map (*see pp226–235*).

3 Detailed Information
Each of the most interesting sights are described in depth. You will find them listed in order following the numbering on the area map. Practical information, including map references, opening hours and telephone numbers is also provided.

The visitors' checklist provides useful information you may need to plan your visit.

The boxes contain detailed information on a particular subject relating to the sight.

Stars indicate the most interesting sights as well as architectural details and the most important works of art.

4 Cracow's Main Sights
Historic buildings are dissected to reveal their interiors. Museums and galleries have colour-coded floor plans enabling you to find important exhibits.

A timeline indicates important dates in the history of the building.

KRAKÓW, ULICA JÓZEFA 38
Tel/fax +48 12/430-65-40
e-mail: pkzkrakow@onet.pl

THE HIGH SYNAGOGUE
OPEN: MONDAY-SUNDAY 9:00-19:00

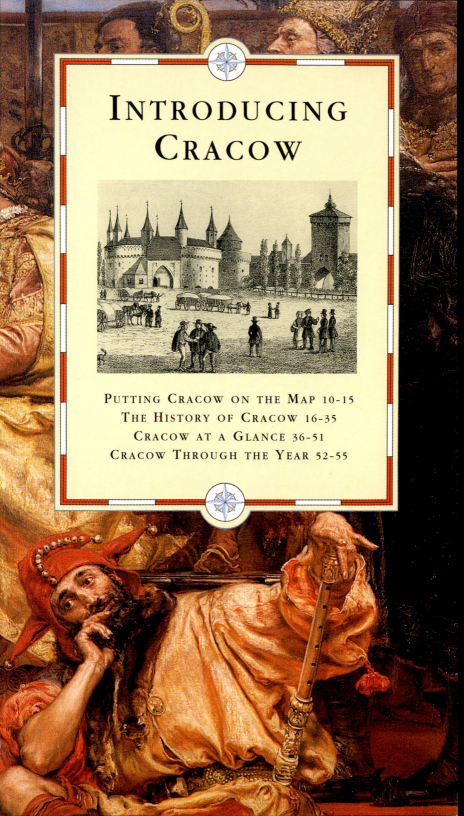

INTRODUCING CRACOW

Putting Cracow on the Map

THE OLD PART OF CRACOW (Kraków), with the Royal Castle on Wawel Hill, is regarded as a fascinating historic town rich in heritage. The historic quarters constitute only a small part of present-day Cracow, the largest urban development in the Lesser Poland (Małopolska) region. The geographical position makes Cracow an ideal base for excursions to the Polish mountains or the picturesque Cracow-Częstochowa Valley. The town is also well positioned for international connections to Prague, Brno, Bratislava, Vienna, Košice and L'viv.

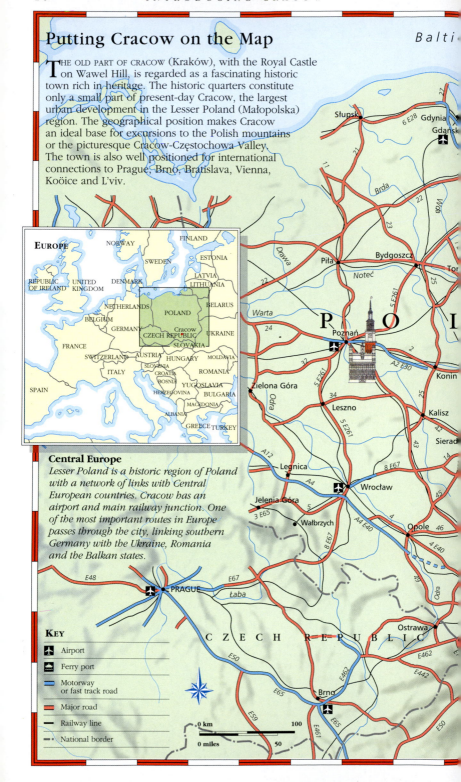

EUROPE

NORWAY · FINLAND · SWEDEN · ESTONIA · REPUBLIC OF IRELAND · UNITED KINGDOM · DENMARK · LATVIA · LITHUANIA · NETHERLANDS · BELARUS · BELGIUM · GERMANY · POLAND · UKRAINE · CZECH REPUBLIC · Cracow · FRANCE · SLOVAKIA · SWITZERLAND · AUSTRIA · HUNGARY · MOLDAVIA · SLOVENIA · CROATIA · ROMANIA · ITALY · BOSNIA · HERZEGOVINA · YUGOSLAVIA · BULGARIA · SPAIN · MACEDONIA · ALBANIA · GREECE · TURKEY

Central Europe

Lesser Poland is a historic region of Poland with a network of links with Central European countries. Cracow has an airport and main railway junction. One of the most important routes in Europe passes through the city, linking southern Germany with the Ukraine, Romania and the Balkan states.

KEY

- ✈ Airport
- ⛴ Ferry port
- ▬ Motorway or fast track road
- ▬ Major road
- ▬ Railway line
- ·—·— National border

0 km   100
0 miles   50

Balti...

Słupsk · 6 E28 · Gdynia · Gdańsk

Piła · Bydgoszcz · Tor...

Notéć · Drawa · Brda · Wda

POZNAŃ · P O I

Zielona Góra · Odra · Warta · Leszno · Konin · Kalisz · Sierad

Legnica · A12 · A4 · Wrocław · 8 E67 · Opole · 46

Jelenia Góra · 3 E65 · Wałbrzych · 8 E67 · A4 E40 · 4 E40

E48 · E67 · PRAGUE · Łaba

C Z E C H   R E P U B L I C · Ostrawa · E462 · E442

E50 · E65 · Brno · E59 · E461 · E50

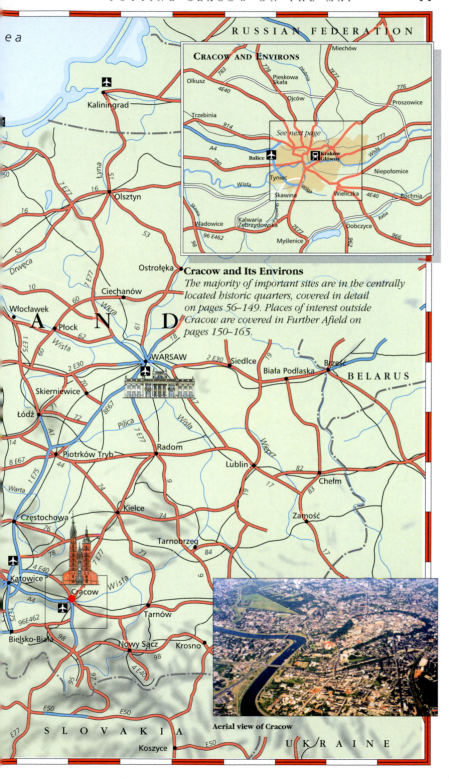

Cracow and Its Environs

The majority of important sites are in the centrally located historic quarters, covered in detail on pages 56–149. Places of interest outside Cracow are covered in Further Afield on pages 150–165.

Cracow and Environs

Miechów
Olkusz
783
778
Dłubnia
7E77
Pieskowa Skała
4E40
Ojców
776
Trzebinia
914
Proszowice
See next page
A4
777
780
Wisła
Balice
Kraków Główny
Niepołomice
Tyniec
Wieliczka
4E40
Bochnia
Wisła
Skawina
Raba
Wadowice
Dobczyce
966
Kalwaria Zebrzydowska
296
96 E462
7E77
98
Myślenice

Aerial view of Cracow

RUSSIAN FEDERATION

Kaliningrad
Łyna
50
16
7E77
15
Olsztyn
16
53
52
Drwęca
Ostrołęka
10
60
Ciechanów
Włocławek
Wkra
61
Płock
62
18
A N D
Wisła
1 E75
69
WARSAW
2 E30
Siedlce
19
Brześć
2 E30
Biała Podlaska
Skierniewice
70
BELARUS
Łódź
71
72
Pilica
7 E77
Wisła
8E67
14
Radom
Wieprz
A1
44
Piotrków Tryb
8 E67
1 E75
74
6
Lublin
82
Chełm
Warta
17
83
Kielce
19
74
Zamość
Częstochowa
76
Tarnobrzeg
17
78
73
84
4 E40
7 E77
9
Katowice
Wisła
A4
Cracow
96E462
Tarnów
1 E75
98
Bielsko-Biała
Nowy Sącz
Krosno
98
95
97
4 E40
E50
E50
E77
SLOVAKIA
UKRAINE
Koszyce
E50

Cracow and Its Environs

UNTIL the early 20th century the conurbation of Cracow occupied a relatively small area on the banks of the Vistula (Wisła) River and was made up of several small towns (Kleparz, Kazimierz, Garbary and Podgórze). Greater Cracow was established in 1910 after the incorporation of the extensive lands of Rakowice, Prądnik, Czarna Wieś, Krowodrza, Bielany, Dębnik, Płaszów and Prokocim. A new industrial district of Nowa Huta was constructed outside Cracow after World War II. Long walks in Cracow are always interesting as all the historic quarters have their own unique character.

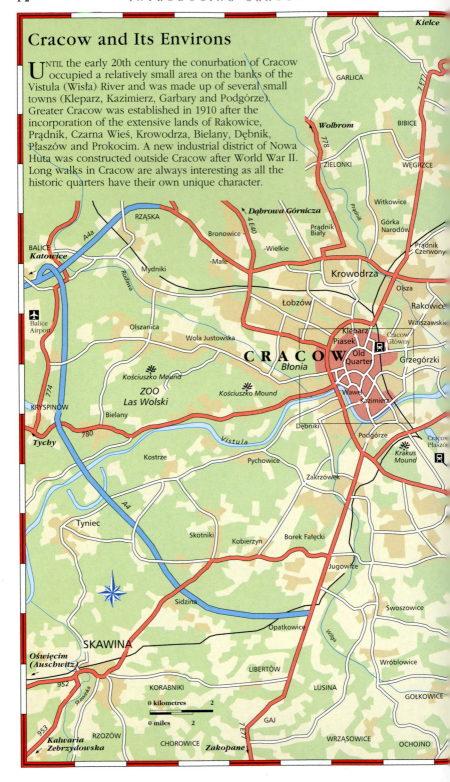

Kielce

GARLICA

Wolbrom

BIBICE

ZIELONKI

WĘGRZCE

Witkowice

Dąbrowa Górnicza

Górka Narodów

RZĄSKA

Bronowice -

Prądnik Biały

Prądnik Czerwony

BALICE
Katowice

-Wielkie

-Małe

Mydniki

Krowodrza

Olsza

Łobzów

Rakowice

Balice Airport

Olszanica

Wola Justowska

Warszawskie

Kleparz
Piasek

Cracow Główny

CRACOW
Błonia

Old Quarter

Grzegórzki

Kościuszko Mound

ZOO
Las Wolski

Kościuszko Mound

Wawel

Kazimierz

KRYSPINÓW

Bielany

Dębniki

Podgórze

Cracow Płaszó

Tychy

780

Vistula

Krakus Mound

Kostrze

Pychowice

Zakrzówek

A4

Tyniec

Skotniki

Kobierzyn

Borek Fałęcki

Jugowice

Swoszowice

Sidzina

Opatkowice

Wilga

SKAWINA

LIBERTÓW

Wróblowice

*Oświęcim
(Auschwitz)*

952

KORABNIKI

LUSINA

GOŁKOWICE

0 kilometres   2

0 miles   2

953

RZOZÓW

CHOROWICE *Zakopane*

GAJ

WRZĄSOWICE

OCHOJNO

*Kalwaria
Zebrzydowska*

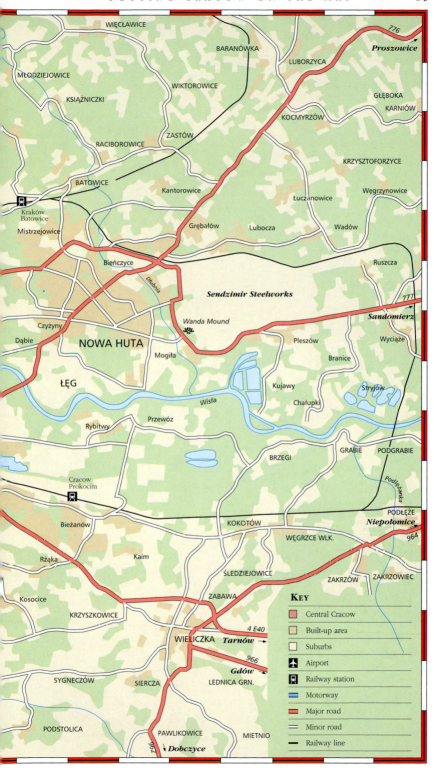

WIĘCŁAWICE

BARANÓWKA

776

Proszowice

LUBORZYCA

MŁODZIEJOWICE

WIKTOROWICE

GŁĘBOKA

KSIĄŻNICZKI

KARNIÓW

KOCMYRZÓW

ZASTÓW

RACIBOROWICE

KRZYSZTOFORZYCE

BATOWICE

Kantorowice

Węgrzynowice

Łuczanowice

Kraków
Batowice

Mistrzejowice

Grębałów   Lubocza   Wadów

Bieńczyce

Ruszcza

Dłubnia

Sendzimir Steelworks

777

Sandomierz

Czyżyny

Wanda Mound

Dąbie

Pleszów   Wyciąże

NOWA HUTA

Mogiła   Branice

ŁĘG   Kujawy

Stryjów

Wisła   Chałupki

Rybitwy   Przewóz

BRZEGI   GRABIE   PODGRABIE

Podłężanka

Cracow
Prokocim

PODŁĘŻE

Bieżanów   KOKOTÓW

Niepołomice

WĘGRZCE WLK.   964

Rząka   Kaim

ŚLEDZIEJOWICE

ZAKRZÓW   ZAKRZOWIEC

Kosocice   ZABAWA

KRZYSZKOWICE

KEY

WIELICZKA   *Tarnów*   4 E40
                                                Central Cracow

966
                                                Built-up area
Gdów

SYGNECZÓW   LEDNICA GRN.
SIERCZA   Suburbs

                                        ✈ Airport

                                        🚉 Railway station

PODSTOLICA   Motorway

PAWLIKOWICE   MIETNIO   Major road

964   ↓ *Dobczyce*   Minor road

                                            Railway line

Central Cracow

CENTRAL Cracow embraces Wawel Hill and the historic Old Quarter surrounded by the Planty green belt, and the adjoining quarters. The six areas of interest for tourists listed in this guide do not always correspond to particular quarters. Major sights outside the centre of town are also included, and walks and one-day excursions suggested. Each area receives separate coverage in the Cracow Area by Area section, listing places of unique character and great importance in the history of the city.

Church of St Mary
With its asymmetrical silhouette this church is Cracow's best known landmark (see pp94-7).

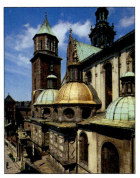

Zygmunt Chapel
This 16th-century chapel is regarded as the greatest example of Renaissance architecture north of the Alps (see pp65-6).

Old Synagogue
This Renaissance synagogue in the Kazimierz quarter is the most outstanding building of the Jewish district (see p122).

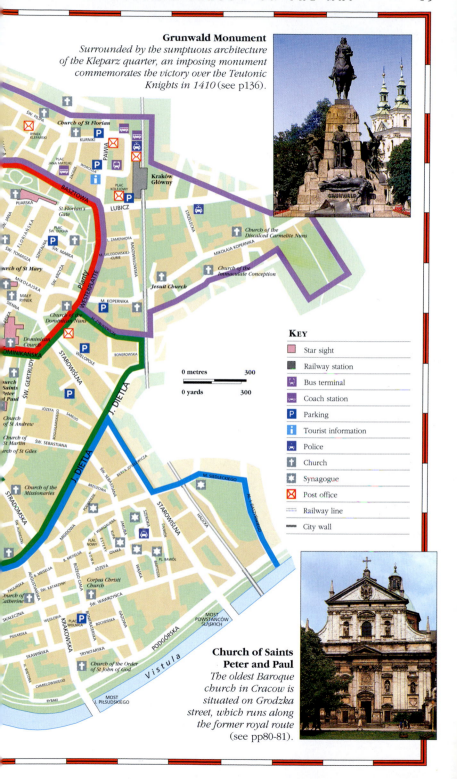

Grunwald Monument
Surrounded by the sumptuous architecture of the Kleparz quarter, an imposing monument commemorates the victory over the Teutonic Knights in 1410 (see p136).

Church of St Florian
RYNEK KLEPARSKI
SW. FILIPA
KURNIKI
PLAC JANA MATEJKI
ZACISZE WORCELLA
PAWIA
Kraków Główny
PIJARSKA
BASZTOWA
St Florian's Gate
PLAC KOLEJOWY
LUBICZ
PLAC SW. DUCHA
SW. MARKA
SW. TOMASZA
SW. JANA
FLORIAŃSKA
SZPITALNA
SW. KRZYŻA
SW. KRZYŻA
L. ZAMENHOFA
L. SKŁODOWSKIEJ-CURIE
RADZIWIŁŁOWSKA
STRZELECKA
Church of the Discalced Carmelite Nuns
MIKOŁAJA KOPERNIKA
Church of the Immaculate Conception
urch of St Mary
MIKOŁAJSKA
MAŁY RYNEK
SIENNA
PLANTY
WESTERPLATTE
M. KOPERNIKA
Jesuit Church
Church of the Dominican Nuns
AL. STRADOMA
Dominican Church
DOMINIKAŃSKA
WIELOPOLE
BONEROWSKA
SW. GERTRUDY
STAROWIŚLNA
urch Saints Peter and Paul
JÓZEFA
SAREGO
BOGUSŁAWSKIEGO
Church of St Andrew
Church of St Martin
urch of St Giles
J. DIETLA
J. DIETLA
SW. SEBASTIANA
BRZOZOWA
SW. SEBASTIANA
BERKA JOSELEWICZA
JAKUBA
M. SIEDLECKIEGO
HALICKA
AL. PŁASZOWSKA
Church of the Missionaries
STRADOMSKA
SW. AGNIESZKI
SW. WAWRZYŃCA
SZEROKA
CIUMOR
STAROWIŚLNA
MIODOWA
PODBRZEZIE
ESTERY
KUPA
PLAC NOWY
JÓZEFA
IZAAKA
WĄSKA
PL. BAWÓŁ
Corpus Christi Church
PAULIŃSKA
AUGUSTIAŃSKA
SW. MEDESLSA
B. MEDESLSA
BOŻEGO CIAŁA
SW. KATARZYNY
JÓZEFA
SW. WAWRZYŃCA
GAZOWA
urch of atherine
SKAŁECZNA
WĘGŁOWA
KRAKOWSKA
BOCHEŃSKA
MOSTOWA
DIETLOWSKA
PIEKARSKA
SKAWIŃSKA
TRYNITARSKA
MOST POWSTAŃCÓW ŚLĄSKICH
PODGÓRSKA
Church of the Order of St John of God
H. WIETORA
CHMIELOWSKIEGO
RYBAKI
MOST J. PIŁSUDSKIEGO
Vistula

KEY

▢	Star sight
▢	Railway station
▢	Bus terminal
▢	Coach station
P	Parking
i	Tourist information
▢	Police
✝	Church
✡	Synagogue
⊠	Post office
⸺	Railway line
▬	City wall

0 metres   300
0 yards   300

Church of Saints Peter and Paul
The oldest Baroque church in Cracow is situated on Grodzka street, which runs along the former royal route (see pp80–81).

THE HISTORY OF CRACOW

FOR MANY centuries Cracow was the capital of Poland and the country's largest city. Polish rulers resided at Wawel Castle. The royal court moved to Warsaw in 1609, after parliamentary sessions and the election of kings began to take place there. Until the collapse of the First Republic, however, Cracow continued to be regarded as the official capital. Deprived of her former status Cracow suffered a deep crisis in the 18th and 19th centuries.

The coat of arms of Cracow

Despite all the past upheavals, Cracow has retained her magnificence. It is more than 400 years since Cracow ceased to be the seat of national government, and yet she maintains her leading role in preserving Polish national identity. Wawel, the seat of Polish kings, the Cathedral that bore witness to their coronations and houses their tombs, as well as the Paulite Church "On the Rock" in whose crypt prominent Poles are buried, belong to the most treasured national heritage. The 600-year-old Jagiellonian University, formerly known as the Academy of Cracow, is the oldest and one of the most important universities in the country and a pillar of Polish culture.

Bearing in mind the small population of Cracow (approximately 715,000), visitors may be surprised by the great number of theatres, cabarets, concert halls and art galleries, which are always popular with regular audiences.

Polish historic cities suffered badly during World War II. Luckily, Cracow's losses were minimal. For those interested in old Polish art, Cracow, with her rich heritage, is certainly the place to go. For many years Cracow's architectural treasures were in a state of neglect, hidden beneath peeling plaster, cracking paint and layers of dirt caused by pollution. In recent years, however, many buildings have been renovated and returned to their former splendour.

Cracow is different from some other large European towns in which historic inner cities have been transformed into open-air museums. The medieval Market Square remains at the heart of today's city. It is the venue for some of the most important events and the traditional meeting place for locals and visitors alike, all of whom enjoy Cracow's unique atmosphere and heritage.

View of Cracow with the Kościuszko Mound (in the foreground), a 19th-century lithograph, Museum of Cracow

◁ *Tadeusz Kościuszko Taking the Oath on Market Square* by Michał Stachowicz (detail), Museum of Cracow

Cracow's Origins

CRACOW is one of the oldest cities in Poland. The archaeological findings provide evidence of a Palaeolithic settlement, as well as those from the Neolithic period, and the Bronze and Iron Ages. The Celtic people and invaders from the east, namely the Scythians and Huns, also left important artefacts. In the early centuries AD Cracow and Lesser Poland bordered and traded with the Roman Empire. Written accounts date only from the 9th century and pertain to the Vistulan settlers who, by the end of the same century, came under the rule of the Great Moravian Empire. The Polish rulers from the House of Piast regained power only at the end of the rule of Mieszko I (around 992).

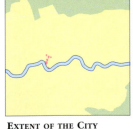

EXTENT OF THE CITY

🟥 *AD 1000*   🟨 *Today*

An imaginary view of Wawel Castle

The cave in Wawel Hill

THE DRAGON OF WAWEL
This woodcut comes from Sebastian Münster's *Cosmographia universalis* of 1544 and shows the legendary dragon and his slayer, the cobbler Skuba, below of Wawel Castle.

King Krak
The legendary founder of Cracow is believed to have lived in the early 8th century.

Earthenware with String Ornaments
These earthenware containers were among the 1st-century artefacts excavated at Nowa Huta while constructing the new town.

TIMELINE

c. 200,000 BC Earliest evidence of settlements in the Cracow area	**c. 1300 BC** Lusatian culture flourishes in Lesser Poland		*Palaeolithic stone tool*
200, 000 BC	**2000**	**0**	**AD 200**
	c. 50,000 BC Evidence of a settlement on Wawel Hill	**1st – 4th century AD** Cracow settlers trade with the Roman Empire	

Saints Cyril and Methodius

Methodius and his brother Cyril are two of the three Patrons of Europe. The former failed in his attempt to convert the prince of the Vistulans from paganism to Christianity. Soon after, their land was conquered by the Great Moravian Empire.

Wawel means a hill surrounded by marshes

WHERE TO SEE PREHISTORIC CRACOW

Very little has survived from prehistoric times in Cracow. There are, however, two mounds worth a visit: the Krak Mound dominating the southern quarters, and the Wanda Mound near Mogiła village. The Archaeological Museum (*see p83*) houses many interesting artefacts from southern Poland, and the Cracow region in particular. The figure of the four-faced pagan idol Światowid is of special interest.

The Krak Mound contains, according to legend, a tomb of Krak, the ancient ruler of Cracow. In reality it was more likely to have been used as a religious site of the Celts.

Światowid

This statue represents a four-faced idol holding a cornucopia. Evidence of ancient pagan cults has been found at the Wawel and other sites.

Iron Treasures

Iron objects in the form of elongated axes found at Wawel Hill were used as a form of payment in the 11th century.

600–1000 Vistulans establish their state, possibly with Cracow as the capital

965 Ibrahim Ibn Yaqub, an Arab traveller, comments on Cracow as a Czech city

400	600	800	1000

Early medieval earthenware vase

before 885 The Vistulans' state loses its independence. Cracow becomes part of the Great Moravian Empire

before 992 Mieszko I adds the former state of the Vistulans to his other territories

Cracow in the Early Middle Ages

Romanesque capital

FOLLOWING the establishment of the bishopric in 1000 and the construction of the cathedral, Cracow became one of the most important centres of the Polish state. After the destruction of other centres in Greater Poland (Wielkopolska) by the Czechs in the first half of the 11th century, Kazimierz the Restorer and his successors made Cracow their main seat. Following the death of Bolesław the Wrymouthed Poland was divided into duchies, and the Dukes of Cracow gained suzerain position. From 1138 to 1320 the dukes aimed to unite the remaining provinces. Despite the Tatar invasion in 1241, this period saw Cracow flourish.

EXTENT OF THE CITY

▦ *1253*	▢ *Today*

Bishop Stanisław in prayer

Szczerbiec
According to legend this is the sword of Bolesław the Brave with which he struck the Golden Gate of Kiev on entering the city in 1018. The sword was actually made in the 13th century. Today it is housed in the Crown Treasury as one of the most treasured regalia.

Denarius of Bolesław the Brave
Following the establishment of Cracow's bishopric in 1000, Bolesław made this city one of his seats.

TIMELINE

c. 1038 Kazimierz the Restorer makes Cracow the capital of Poland

1079–98 Construction of St Andrew's Church

1090–1142 Construction of second Cathedral at Wawel

1000 Bishopric of Cracow established

c. 1044 Benedictine Abbey at Tyniec is established

1000	1025	1050	1075	1100

1020 Construction of first Cathedral in Cracow begins

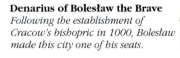

1079 Martyrdom of St Stanisław

Coat of Arms of the Chapter of Cracow

The Supposed Mitre of St Stanisław
*This ornate 13th-century mitre
decorated with pearls, sapphires
and rubies testifies to the riches
of metropolitan Cracow, one
of the most important bishoprics
in medieval Poland.*

WHERE TO SEE ROMANESQUE CRACOW

Cracow is rich in Romanesque architecture. Most buildings have survived in their original form, though they have often been enlarged and refurnished. The Church of St Andrew *(see pp78–9)* dates from this period, as does St Adalbert's *(see p93)* and the remains of the earliest buildings at Wawel, including the Rotunda of St Mary's *(see p63)* and the little church of the Most Holy Redeemer *(see p162).*

King Bolesław the Bold

**Kazimierz the Restorer
after Jan Matejko**
*It can be said that Cracow
owes her capital status to this
ruler, who settled here
around 1038 and established
a central administration.*

The Church of St Adalbert
*was, according to legend,
consecrated by Adalbert before
his missionary journey to
Prussia in 997.*

THE DEATH OF BISHOP STANISŁAW

The conflict between Bishop Stanisław of Szczepanów (later canonized) and Bolesław the Bold ended with the murder of the bishop in 1079 and the exile of the king. Both events contributed to the weakening of Poland. The cult of St Stanisław began in the 15th century. This scene decorates a 16th-century chasuble (priest's vestment) commissioned by Piotr Kmita.

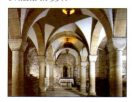

The Crypt of St Leonard
*is a remnant of Cracow's
second cathedral. It was
built by Władysław
Herman between 1090
and 1142.*

1138 Bolesław the Wrymouthed grants Cracow the status of a capital of the suzerain province

1173 Bolesław the Curly is the first Piast to be buried at Wawel

Cloister at the Dominican Church

1241 Tatars led by Batuhan destroy Cracow

1150	1175	1200	1225	1250

1141–1320 Polish dukes fight for Cracow

1250 Consecration of the Dominican Church

Benedictine Abbey at Tyniec

Gothic Cracow

THE CHARTER granted to Cracow in 1257 facilitated urban development and allowed for a new and more structured plan. A Gothic defence wall surrounded the city, and Cracow began to flourish anew following the coronation of Władysław the Short in 1320. The new satellite towns of Kazimierz and Kleparz both received municipal charters. The architectural panorama of

Detail of the high altar at St Mary's

Cracow was substantially transformed by the building of many new churches and the Cathedral in the 14th and 15th centuries. The foundation of the Cracow Academy, and its subsequent renewal, contributed greatly to the development of culture and intellectual activities. The ideas of Italian humanism were known in Cracow early on.

EXTENT OF THE CITY

🟥 *1370*	🟨 *Today*

The coat of arms of the Piasts

The Diptych Reliquary
A double leaf Gothic reliquary containing the relics of saints is decorated with the image of the Virgin Mary and that of Christ.

Saints Stanisław and Wacław
shown standing on the battlement walls are patron saints of Cracow's Cathedral and the Kingdom of Poland.

A View of Late Gothic Cracow, 1493
This townscape from the 15th century World Chronicle *by Hartmann Schedel is the earliest known view of Cracow.*

TIMELINE

Coat of Arms of Kazimierz

1285 Construction of Cracow's defence walls begins

1312 Revolt of German burghers, led by Albert

1364 Cracow Academy founded by Kazimierz the Great

1340 Construction of Corpus Christi Church begins

1250	1275	1300	1325	1350

1257 Duke Bolesław the Chaste grants Cracow her Charter on 5 June

Crown of Kazimierz the Great (replica)

1335 Kazimierz the Great grants Kazimierz its Charter

1366 Kleparz (Florencja) receives its Charter

Cracow's Charter
The municipal status granted to Cracow was modelled on the Magdeburg law and contributed to uniform urban development.

The Coats of Arms shown on both sides of the gate are those of Bolesław the Chaste who granted Cracow its Charter.

Krużlowa Madonna
This beautiful Madonna with Child is an interesting example of the influence of International Gothic on wood sculpture of Lesser Poland in the 15th century.

SEAL OF THE ROYAL CITY OF CRACOW

The 14th-century Great Seal of Cracow (shown here with the image reversed) features the emblem of Poland, thus stressing the role of Cracow as its capital.

WHERE TO SEE GOTHIC CRACOW

Some of the biggest attractions in Cracow are the Gothic buildings, such as the Barbican (*see p114*), Florian's Gate (*see p111*), the Collegium Maius (*see pp106–7*), and large churches such as St Mary's (*see pp94–5*), the Dominican Church (*see pp116–7*), St Catherine's (*see p124*) and Corpus Christi (*see p123*). Some smaller churches, such as the Holy Cross (*see p115*), are equally interesting. The works by Veit Stoss are gems of Gothic art.

The Cathedral (see pp64–9) *is the burial place of kings and the seat of the local archbishop.*

The Church of the Holy Cross *has a single nave whose interior is covered with palm vaulting.*

1386 Grand Duke Jogaila of Lithuania becomes King Władysław II Jagiełło of Poland

Mace of the rector of the Academy of Cracow

1473 First Polish printing house of Łukasz Straube issues a calendar

1400	1425	1450	1475	1500

re 1400
ollegium
Maius is
ablished

1400 Władysław Jagiełło re-establishes the Cracow Academy

1477–89 Veit Stoss works on the high altar at St Mary's

Coat of Arms of the Jagiellons

1492 Kazimierz Jagiellończyk dies

Renaissance Cracow

Eagle on the cover of Anna Jagiellonka prayer book

CRACOW, the capital city, rapidly developed economically and began to change in appearance. The Cloth Hall, the city landmark, was remodelled in the Renaissance style, and the rich merchants of Cracow also began to modernize their houses. The art and culture of the Italian Renaissance was assimilated by the royal courts of King Aleksander and King Zygmunt the Old and his second wife Bona Sforza. Bartolomeo Berrecci, Giovanni Maria Padovano and other outstanding Italian masters established their workshops in Cracow during this time.

EXTENT OF THE CITY

☐ *1572*   ☐ *Today*

Shield with the Polish eagle

Royal orb   **Royal sceptre**

"The Sword Makers" from the Baltazar Behem Codex
This Codex of 1505 contains laws and privileges of the town guilds and is illustrated with 27 illuminations showing craftsmen at work.

A Tapestry with Satyrs
This is one of 160 tapestries commissioned in the 16th century by Zygmunt August for the Wawel Collection.

TIMELINE

1502–5 Erection of King Jan Olbracht's monument, the first work of Renaissance art in Poland

1505 Baltazar Behem Codex made

Head in the Hall of Deputies

1525 Prussian Homage to the Polish king at the Market Square on 10 April

1543 The treatise *De revolutionibus* by Copernicus is published

1500	1510	1520	1530	1540

1504 Rebuilding of the Wawel Castle starts

1513 First Polish book in print from the Ungler House

1521 Zygmunt's Bell is hung

1519 Bartolomeo Berrecci begins work on Zygmunt's Chapel in the Cathedral

NICOLAI CO
PERNICI TORINENSIS
DE REVOLVTIONIBVS ORBI
um ecclestium, Libri VI.

Detail of the title page from Copernicus's treatise

A Renaissance Portal

The first post office in 16th-century Poland, serving the Cracow-Venice route, was situated in the house of Prospero Provana. Today the building houses the Hotel Pod Różą.

Cock of the Marksmen's Brotherhood

This gilt masterpiece, made in 1565, belonged to the members of the Brotherhood whose aim was to support soldiers responsible for the defence of the town.

Oval recess with Renaissance decoration

MONUMENT OF ZYGMUNT AUGUST

King Zygmunt August was a patron of the arts. It was through his commissions that the Royal Castle at Wawel was enriched with an outstanding collection of tapestries. The king's monument was made by Santi Gucci between 1574 and 1575, in Hungarian red marble.

WHERE TO SEE RENAISSANCE CRACOW

Renaissance architecture was introduced by Italian masters during the rebuilding of the Royal Castle at Wawel in the early 16th century. The Zygmunt Chapel *(see pp64–9)*, the Montelupis Monument at St Mary's Church *(see pp94–5)* and a number of houses at Kanonicza Street *(see p79)* are among the finest examples of Renaissance art and architecture in the city.

The arcaded courtyard *at the Royal Castle at Wawel is one of the most beautiful in Europe* (see pp70–71).

The Renaissance Cloth Hall (see pp102–3), *topped with a characteristic parapet, displayed the prosperity of Jagiellonian Cracow.*

after 1550 Santi Gucci comes to Poland

Tomb of Stefan Batory

1595 Santi Gucci works on the tomb of King Stefan Batory

1550	1560	1570	1580	1590

1569 Polish-Lithuanian commonwealth established

1586 First secular secondary school is opened

1595 Archconfraternity of The Passion established

1556–1559 Giovanni Maria Padovano rebuilds the Cloth Hall

1574 Coronation of the first elected king, Henri de Valois

1596 Royal court moves from Cracow to Warsaw

Baroque Cracow

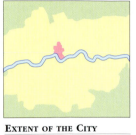

THE 17TH and 18th centuries saw the decline of Cracow. After the king had moved his residence to Warsaw, he was followed by the noblemen who held high office. Foreign incursions and occupations, wars and the First Partition of Poland in 1772 all added to the city's woes. Despite a number of attempts at reform towards the end of the rule of Stanisław August Poniatowski, Cracow became a provincial, under-developed frontier town, though the atmosphere was enlivened by royal coronations and funerals. The failure of the Kościuszko Insurrection of 1794 and the subsequent Third Partition of Poland in 1795 brought an end to Cracow's prominence.

Coat of Arms of the House of Vaza

EXTENT OF THE CITY

◼ *1700*   ◻ *Today*

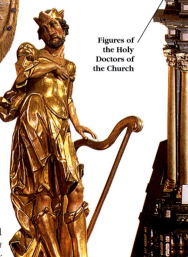

The Evangelists with their symbols: eagle, angel, lion and ox.

Figures of the Holy Doctors of the Church

Hood of the 1669 Coronation Cape
The eagle (the emblem of the Commonwealth) on the cappa magna of Bishop Tomicki, made for the coronation of Michał Wiśniowiecki, was embroidered with pearls and sapphires.

Epitaph of King Władysław IV
The monumental and sombre interior of the Vaza Chapel in the Cathedral is decorated with black marble and features splendid memorial plaques of the Vaza dynasty.

King David
This late Baroque dancing figure in the Corpus Christi Church was made by Anton Gegenbaur in the second half of the 18th century.

TIMELINE

1626–9 Canopy of St Stanisław is erected in the Cathedral

1619 Church of Saints Peter and Paul is completed

1661 First Polish newspaper "Merkuriusz Polski" published by Jan Alexander Gorczyn's Press

Title page of "Merkuriusz Polski"

1600	1620	1640	1660	1680

Zygmunt III Vaza

1609 Zygmunt III Vaza finally abandons his Cracow residence in favour of Warsaw on 25 May

1655–7 Swedish, then Transylvanian, armies occupy Cracow

1676 University Press is established after the Academy buys Piotrowczyks' Press

1664–76 Vaza Chapel in the Cathedral is completed

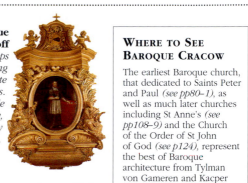

Memorial Plaque of Bishop Denhoff

Memorial plaques of bishops in the cloister adjoining the Franciscan Church date from different periods. This plaque was made in the early 18th century, probably to a design by Baldassare Fontana.

A silver sarcophagus with the Bishop's mitre and crozier is a reliquary of St Stanisław.

Kołłątaj's Panoramic Map of Cracow

Hugo Kołłątaj led the reform of the University. In 1785 he also created this precise map of Cracow, which shows all the land owned by the city.

CANOPY OF ST STANISŁAW

This canopy in the Wawel Cathedral was inspired by a number of unexecuted designs for the great baldachin in St Peter's in the Vatican.

WHERE TO SEE BAROQUE CRACOW

The earliest Baroque church, that dedicated to Saints Peter and Paul *(see pp80–1)*, as well as much later churches including St Anne's *(see pp108–9)* and the Church of the Order of St John of God *(see p124)*, represent the best of Baroque architecture from Tylman von Gameren and Kacper Bażanka, among others.

The Church of Saints Peter and Paul *is one of the finest early Baroque churches in Central Europe.*

The façade of the Church of the Missionaries *was inspired by Roman Baroque architecture (see p85).*

Medal of Virtuti Militari

1734 Coronation of August III Wettin, the last to take place in Cracow, on 17 January

1791 Kazimierz and Kleparz are incorporated into Cracow

1768–72 Confederates of Bar fight for Cracow

1794 Tadeusz Kościuszko takes his oath in Market Square on 24 March

1720	1740	1760	1780	1800

1705 St Anne's Church is consecrated

1702–05 Cracow is invaded several times by the Swedes

Hugo Kołłątaj

1777–8 Hugo Kołłątaj reforms the Cracow Academy

1788 Astronomical Observatory established

1798 First permanent theatre building established in Cracow

Cracow in Galicia

In 1772 Austria occupied the southern part of Poland, called Galicia. After a period of Austrian occupation, Cracow was briefly incorporated into the Duchy of Warsaw. The Russian occupation followed. In 1815 the Republic of Cracow, which included the area round the city, was established, but by 1846 Cracow was under Austrian rule again. After a period of suppression, Galicia received extensive autonomy from the 1860s onwards. During the 19th century Cracow was the only Polish territory to enjoy relative freedom. It embarked upon a mission of safeguarding traditions and past historic successes, thus becoming the spiritual capital of Poland.

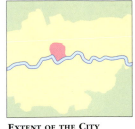

EXTENT OF THE CITY

■ *1818*   □ *Today*

Sarcophagus of Prince Józef Poniatowski
Of all the famous Poles who died abroad, Józef Poniatowski was the first to have his body brought back to receive a solemn funeral, which transformed itself into a patriotic demonstration.

A beggar woman receiving alms

Emperor Franz Joseph

The Opening of the Sarcophagus of Kazimierz the Great by Jan Matejko
An accidental discovery of the remains of the king prompted his second funeral in 1869, which became an event on a national scale, reminiscent of the glorious past.

THE ENTRY OF EMPEROR FRANZ JOSEPH IN 1880

Franz Joseph was a popular ruler with the people of Cracow. He was believed to be behind the development of the city and its autonomy. A series of watercolours by Juliusz Kossak (1824–99), such as this one, depicts his stay in Cracow.

TIMELINE

1800 Royal Castle at Wawel made into army barracks

1813–15 Cracow occupied by the Austrians

Ruins of the fire-damaged Dominican Church

1846 Cracow Uprising Cracow becomes par of Austria

1800	1810	1820	1830	1840

1809 Cracow incorporated into the Duchy of Warsaw

1810–14 City walls demolished

1820–3 Kościuszko Mound constructed

1815 "Free, independent and strictly neutral city of Cracow" and her region established as the Republic of Cracow

Coat of arms of Galicia

House of Jan Matejko
Jan Matejko, whose particular genre of history painting imprinted in the nation's mind an image of its past, lived in this house.

Inhabitants of Cracow greeting the Emperor

Design for the Mickiewicz Monument
This model by Antoni Kurzawa was never fully executed. It is held at the National Museum.

The Cracow Uprising
The uprising of 1846 was intended to spark a revolt in all parts of partitioned Poland, but was suppressed by the Austrians.

WHERE TO SEE 19TH CENTURY CRACOW

The architecture of Cracow in the 19th century was eclectic. The Renaissance Revival style predominated (for example the Academy of Fine Arts, *see p136*), and was often influenced by the monumental architecture of Vienna, the place where many of Cracow's architects trained. The University buildings are a good example of Gothic Revival in which the historic style is blended with vernacular features.

The Church of the Felician Sisters *is one of the few buildings in the Romanesque Revival style (see p142).*

The Collegium Novum *is a prestigious Gothic Revival building designed by Feliks Księżarski (see p104).*

1866 Local government established in Cracow with Józef Dietl as Mayor

1854 Society of Friends of Fine Arts established

1872 Academy of Skills established

1876 Czartoryski Collection opens to the public

1883–7 Collegium Novum built

1850	1860	1870	1880	1890

1850 Great fire of Cracow

Apparatus for condensing oxygen

1883 Two Cracow scientists, Z. Wróblewski and K. Olszewski, condense oxygen

1893 Słowacki Theatre opens

Modernist Cracow

Bust of Wyspiański decorating the Palace of Art

A**T THE** turn of the 19th century Greater Cracow was established and became a place of mass excursions from other parts of occupied Poland. People came to see the newly re-established University and the repossessed Wawel, which was then undergoing restoration. It was the period of "art for art's sake", and Cracow became an oasis for Polish artists. Modern life concentrated around artistic cafés, such as the Paon and the Jama Michalika, which were also venues for cabarets. The latter café housed the Zielony Balonik Cabaret. The ambience in Cracow was that of melancholy and decadence but life, permeated by patriotic Neo-Romantic symbolism, was lived here to the full. The outbreak of World War I put an end to this unique bohemian era.

EXTENT OF THE CITY

🟥 *1900*   ⬜ *Today*

The Cathedral

House of Deputies of the new Parliament

Academies and museums

Stańczyk
This painting by Leon Wyczółkowski portrays the court jester, Stańczyk, in pensive mood, playing with marionettes of historic Polish characters.

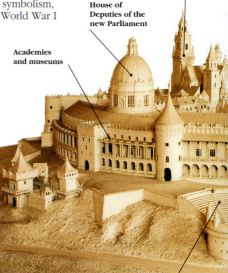

An amphitheatre modelled on the Barbican in Cracow

"Życie"
This is the vignette of the magazine of the Polish Modernist movement. The contributors were the leading authors of the time.

TIMELINE

1897 "Życie" weekly is established

1898 Stanisław Przybyszewski arrives in Cracow

1901 Palace of Art, the seat of the Society of Friends of the Fine Arts, is built

1903–5 Old Theatre (Teatr Stary) rebuilt in the Art Nouveau style

1895	1897	1899	1901	1903	19

1895 Adam Mickiewicz's statue is unveiled

1898–1900 Stanisław Wyspiański decorates the Franciscan Church with murals and stained glass

1901 Premiere of *The Wedding* by Stanisław Wyspiański

Wyspiański's Art Nouveau murals in the Franciscan Church

Poster by Stanisław Wyspiański
This poster announces a lecture by S. Przybyszewski followed by a play by M. Maeterlinck.

WHERE TO SEE MODERNIST CRACOW

Modernist Cracow was, above all, a city of literature and painting. Architecture from this period is scarce. There are, however, some magnificent buildings, such as the House "Pod pająkiem" *(see p149)* and the Palace of Art *(see p105)*. Art Nouveau interiors of exceptional beauty can be found at the Franciscan Church with its stained glass and murals, designed by Wyspiański *(see pp86–7)*, the Society of Physicians building *(see p130)* and the prestigious Chamber of Commerce and Industry *(see p137)*.

Marionettes from the Zielony Balonik Cabaret
This cabaret and New Year's satirical show, staged by Karol Frycz, ridiculed the narrow-mindedness and hypocrisy of the Cracovians.

Reconstructed churches of St George and St Michael

Stadium modelled on Roman architecture

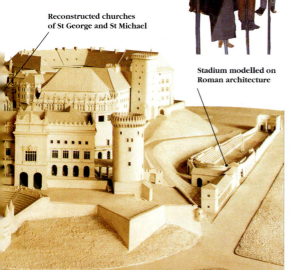

During the rebuilding of the Old Theatre (Teatr Stary) in the Art Nouveau style its façade was decorated with a stucco floral frieze (see p105).

The façade of the Church of the Discalced Carmelite Nuns, with its elaborate decoration, is in sharp contrast to its austere interior.

POLISH ACROPOLIS BY STANISŁAW WYSPIAŃSKI

The idea behind this design for the rebuilding of the entire Wawel Hill was to transform the Royal Castle into a political, social, academic and cultural centre of the liberated Poland. Its architecture was intended to reflect a synthesis of Polish history.

1906 Cracow sports clubs, Wisła and Cracovia, established

1907 Stanisław Wyspiański dies

1910 Riflemen's Union formed by Józef Piłsudski

1912 First cinema opens in Cracow

A late 19th-century armchair

1907	1909	1911	1913	1915

1906 Building of the Chamber of Commerce and Industry completed

1910 Grunwald Monument unveiled

The sphere at the top of the Chamber of Commerce and Industry Building

1914 First Cadre Brigade of the Polish Legions marches out of Cracow on 6 August

Cracow in the Years 1918–1945

W HEN World War I ended in 1918, Poland regained her independence after 146 years of foreign occupation. In the period between the two World Wars Cracow became a source for political, administrative and army staff for the whole of the Republic of Poland. Above all the city was a cultural and academic centre. The Modernist traditions were still present in the arts but soon gave way to a new generation of artists, such as the Formists, Capists (the Polish variant of Post-Impressionists), the avant-garde Cracow Group and the Cricot Theatre. During World War II the German Governor General had his headquarters in Cracow, and this was reason enough for the city to be spared destruction.

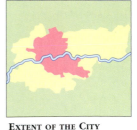

EXTENT OF THE CITY

■ *1938*	☐ *Today*

Józef Piłsudski
The Commander *by Konrad Krzyżanowski portrays well the personality and character of this uncompromising Polish soldier and politician.*

Portrait of Nena Stachurska
This portrait is by S.I. Witkiewicz, who was one of the most unconventional artists of the 20th century. He called for the utopian ideal of "pure art".

Kościuszko Mound

Marshal Józef Piłsudski

Tribune

Figures decorating the Academy of Mines and Metallurgy Building
The first school of its type in liberated Poland was established to educate specialists for the industry in Silesia.

TIMELINE

1918 Austrian Army disarmed in Cracow. Polish Liquidation Commission created on 31 October

1925 Tomb of the Unknown Soldier blessed

1923 Workers' unrest in Cracow

Jagiellonian Library

1918	1921	1924	1927	1930

1919 Academy of Mines and Metallurgy established

1921 Jesuit Church at Wesoła consecrated

Banner which was raised in liberated Cracow

1927 Juliusz Słowacki's remains brought to Cracow and buried at Wawel

1930–9 Jagiellonian Library completed

Funeral of Marshal Piłsudski
The funeral of the Commander, who was buried at Wawel in 1935, was the biggest state event in interwar Poland.

Demolition of Mickiewicz's Statue
During the German occupation all monuments of importance were demolished, including those of Mickiewicz, Kościuszko and Grunwald.

A military band gallops at the head of the troops.

THE CAVALRY PARADE

The parade of the cavalry of the Second Republic took place at Błonie on 6 October 1933. Wojciech Kossak, member of a distinguished Cracow family of artists, painted this grand event.

AUSCHWITZ (OŚWIĘCIM)

The name Oświęcim may have little meaning for most foreigners but the German name, Auschwitz, raises the spectre of death. During World War II the Nazis established Auschwitz and the nearby Birkenau (Brzezinka) concentration camps. Nearly 1.5 million people were put to death in these camps. The Auschwitz camp was set up in 1940 to subject Poles to terror and extermination. Before long the Nazis rounded up and transported people from the whole of Europe, and from 1942 Auschwitz and Birkenau became the largest extermination camps for Jews. A cynical inscription over the gate leading into the Auschwitz camp reads *"Arbeit macht frei"* ("work makes you free").

It was in the Auschwitz Death Block that Maksymilian Kolbe, a Franciscan priest, gave up his life for another inmate. Kolbe (who was later canonized) was sentenced to death by starvation.

In the old barracks of Auschwitz there is an exhibition telling the history of the camp. Temporary displays are also organized. In Brzezinka, 3 km (1.8 miles) away, only some of the original 300 barracks remain. The loading platform elicits a harrowing impression. It was here that prisoners from railway wagons were unloaded and segregated.

1933 Cricot, the Artists' Theatre, is established

1935 Piłsudski is given a state funeral at Wawel

1938 Dietl's statue erected

1939 Outbreak of World War II on 1 September

1943 Jewish ghetto liquidated

1945 Soviet troops enter Cracow on 18 January

1933	1936	1939	1942	1945

1937 Teaching commences at the Academy of Mines and Metallurgy

1941 Jewish ghetto established

1939 Cracow occupied by the Nazis on 6 September

Statue of Józef Dietl

Cracow after 1945

Statue of Cardinal Adam Sapieha

A[FTER] World War II ended Cracow did not willingly accept the new Soviet-imposed regime. In 1946 the celebrations of the 3 May Constitution turned into clashes with tragic consequences. Soon after the famous referendum was rejected. In order to "punish" Cracow, a new industrial suburb of Nowa Huta was established with immense steel mills. The intention was to counterbalance "the reactionist social classes" of the old Cracow. The style of Socialist Realism was adopted for the new architecture. While local authorities struggled to preserve historic buildings, pollution caused by this vast industry damaged many monuments in Cracow, and still remains a major problem.

Tadeusz Sendzimir Steelworks
Formerly known as the Lenin Steelworks, the mills were expected to become a bastion of the Communist proletariat. Paradoxically, they became one of the main seats of opposition.

Banner of the Vatican

Papal high altar

HOLY MASS DURING THE POPE'S VISIT

The political transformation of Poland which took place after 1989 was welcomed in Cracow. The Mass celebrated in 1991 by Pope John Paul II in Market Square attracted unprecedented numbers of worshippers.

Mistrzejowice Church
Built between 1976 and 1983, the church was decorated with sculptures by Gustaw Zemła.

TIMELINE

1946 Bloody suppression of 3 May celebrations

Builders' Brigade *by H. Krajewska*

1956 Piwnica pod Baranami Cabaret established

1967 Construction of the Ark of God Church in Nowa Huta begins

1945	1950	1955	1960	1965	1970

1949 Construction of Nowa Huta begins

1950 Nowa Huta becomes a borough of Cracow

1956 Cricot 2 Theatre established

1957 Celebrations of the city of Cracow's 700th anniversary

1964 600th anniversary of the Academy of Cracow

Demonstrations in Nowa Huta
During the period of martial law, street demonstrations in the workers' suburb of Nowa Huta often ended in riots.

EXTENT OF THE CITY

☐ *1945*   ☐ *Today*

Nobel Prize for Wisława Szymborska
The Cracow poet was awarded the 1996 Nobel Prize for Literature.

St Mary's Church

Polish banner

WHERE TO SEE MODERN CRACOW

Very few postwar buildings in Cracow deserve notice. However, some examples of ecclesiastical architecture, namely the Abbey of the Fathers of the Resurrection designed by Dariusz Kozłowski, and two churches in Nowa Huta – the Ark of God and Mistrzejowice Church, are exceptional. In recent years an extensive programme of building renovation in old Cracow has been undertaken and many new projects started, including the Japanese Centre of Art and Technology.

The Ark of God Church in Nowa Huta (see p152) *is an example of modern ecclesiastical architecture, rich in impressive forms and symbolic content.*

Sculpture Decorating the Tomb of Tadeusz Kantor
The theatre of Tadeusz Kantor (1915–90) had a Polish, as well as a European, dimension. This sculpture on his tomb was originally designed for his play Wielopole, Wielopole.

1978 Committee for the Renovation of Cracow's Monuments is established	**1978** Cracow included in the UNESCO World Heritage List		**1991** International Cultural Centre established		
	1980 Solidarity established		**1992** European Month of Culture celebrations take place in Cracow in June	**1996** Wisława Szymborska is awarded the Nobel Prize for Literature	
	1981 Martial law declared in Poland on 13 December (lifted on 21 July 1983)				

1975	**1980**	**1985**	**1990**	**1995**	**2000**

	1981 Citizens Committee for the Rescue of Cracow established	**1993** Czesław Miłosz, the winner of the Nobel Prize for Literature, becomes an honorary citizen of Cracow	
	1978 Karol Wojtyła, the Metropolitan of Cracow, elected as Pope John Paul II		
John Paul II	**1990** Tadeusz Kantor dies	*A book by Czesław Miłosz*	

MIŁOSZ
Widzenia nad Zatoką San Francisco

CRACOW AT A GLANCE

Cracow was one of the few Polish cities to be saved from major destruction during many wars which devastated the country. The city has preserved not only her monuments but also her specific "antiquarian" atmosphere. Already in the 19th century Cracow was a destination for tourists, from other countries as well as different parts of Poland. Cracow and Wieliczka were included on the very first UNESCO World Heritage List. The section *Cracow Area by Area* describes many places of interest. To help make the most of your stay, the following 14 pages are a guide to the best Cracow has to offer. Each sight has a cross reference to its own full entry. Below are the top ten tourist attractions to start you off. Take a journey back in time and enjoy sites of historic interest and beauty.

CRACOW'S TOP TEN TOURIST ATTRACTIONS

Royal Castle at Wawel
See pp70 – 73.

Cathedral
See pp64 – 9.

Kościuszko Mound
See pp162 – 3.

Church of St Mary
See pp94 – 7.

Market Square
See pp98 – 101.

Church of St Anne
See pp108 – 9.

Planty
See pp160 – 61.

Collegium Maius
See pp106 – 7.

Remu'h Cemetery
See pp122 – 3.

Cloth Hall
See pp102 – 3.

◁ **Zygmunt's Chapel at Wawel**

Cracow's Best: Museums and Galleries

Cracow has dozens of museums, which are very varied in character. The Royal Castle at Wawel is the best known, offering visitors the chance to see collections housed in the royal chambers which date from the time when the Polish kings resided here. The Czartoryski Museum is the best place for Western art. The National Museum has rich collections of Polish art housed in a number of branches in the city centre.

Piasek and Nowy Świat

National Museum Main Building
One of the best collections of modern art in Poland is housed here. The collection of Modernist art is particularly rich, and includes excellent sculptures by Konstanty Laszczka.

Museum of Cracow
This museum is devoted to the history of the city. Cracow is famous for her portable Christmas cribs and the collection housed here is of great beauty.

Wawel Hill

VISTULA

Japanese Centre of Art and Technology
This modern building houses a collection of works from the Far East, much of which was donated by Feliks Manggha Jasieński. The netsuke *(a kind of button) shown takes the form of a tiger.*

Archaeological Museum
Many archaeological findings from the Lesser Poland area, as well as Egyptian mummies, are displayed here.

```
0 metres        500
0 yards         500
```

Czartoryski Museum

This karacena *which belonged to Stanisław Jabłonowski, one of the leaders in the Battle of Vienna in 1683, is one of the exhibits recalling Poland's once glorious past.*

House of Matejko

In the family house of Jan Matejko, some of his works, including this study for Joan of Arc, as well as his extraordinary collection of "antiquities", are brought together.

Wesoła, Kleparz and Biskupie

Old Quarter

Okół and Stradom Quarters

Cloth Hall Gallery of 19th-Century Art

In 1879 Henryk Siemiradzki presented the National Museum with its first gift, his painting The Torches of Nero.

Kazimierz Quarter

Jewish Museum

A collection of Judaica, one of the best in Central Europe, is housed in this Renaissance synagogue.

Royal Castle in Wawel

This royal residence houses an outstanding art collection which includes paintings, sculptures, gold work, arms and Oriental art. Tapestries are of particular interest.

Exploring Cracow's Museums and Galleries

Eagle on a 1918 banner, Museum of Cracow

CRACOW'S museum collections tell the history of the city and Polish culture in great detail. There are also a few specialized foreign collections. A visit to all the many museums would require several weeks but it is possible to concentrate on just the most important collections and still get to know the city well. Many Galleries, including the Starmach Gallery and Mleczko Gallery, display contemporary art.

St Stanisław's Reliquary, Cathedral Museum *(see p62)*

THE HISTORY OF POLAND AND CRACOW

THE FORMER residence of Polish rulers, the **Royal Castle** at Wawel, is the best known of Cracow's museums. Outstanding tapestries and paintings are among the exhibits. The Armoury and Treasury are also open for visits. The latter houses the coronation sword *Szczerbiec*. Worth a visit is the archaeological display "Lost Wawel", which shows the Rotunda of the Virgin Mary

Saints. A virtual visit to the 1,000-year-old Wawel buildings is also on offer. A computer reconstruction is concerned with major sights. The Gregorian chants sung by the Dominican Friars can be heard while viewing the programme.

The history of the former capital of Poland is told at the **Museum of Cracow**. The collections here include the insignia of municipal governments and those of guilds, seals featuring Cracow's coat of arms and many townscapes showing Cracow in the past.

The Jagiellonian University Museum is housed in the **Collegium Maius**, the oldest of the university's buildings. The museum brings together scientific equipment, of which some items are unique, as well as memorabilia left by former professors. Many rooms have retained their original furnishings.

The borough of Kazimierz was inhabited in the past mostly by Jews. This part

of the city became a centre for their culture. The **Jewish Museum**, with its rich collection of Judaica, including liturgical objects, is dedicated to the Jewish heritage.

The election of the Archbishop of Cracow, Karol Wojtyła, to the pontificate was an important event in the history of the city. A room, recreated in the **Archdiocesan Museum,** commemorates the years spent by Karol Wojtyła in Cracow.

The altar by Jerzy Nowosielski, St Vladimir's Foundation, devoted to the Orthodox Church

POLISH ART

IN 1879 Henryk Siemiradzki presented Cracow with his painting *The Torches of Nero*. He thus initiated the establishment of the **National Museum**. Poland was then still an occupied country and the intention was to raise patriotic awareness and morale of the Poles. Only Polish art and works relating to the history of Poland were collected. As a result the museum has no Western collection. The Polish collections, however, give a good insight into Polish artists and those who worked in Poland. The museum has a number of branches throughout the city. Pride of place in the museum

Deputies' Hall in the Royal Castle at Wawel

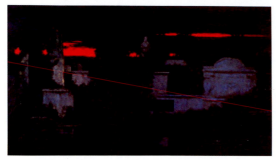

Italian Landscape by Adam Chmielowski, National Museum

goes to the large and outstanding collection of medieval and Renaissance painting and sculpture. This collection will move to 16 Kanonicza Street where a new Museum of Polish Art up to 1794 is being created. Nineteenth-century Polish art, housed at the **Cloth Hall Gallery**, is also of great interest. Twentieth-century painting and sculpture can be admired in the Main Building. The museum has a programme of temporary monographic exhibitions concerned with the life and work of great Cracow artists such as Jan Matejko, Stanisław Wyspiański and Józef Mehoffer. These exhibitions, highlighting the careers of artists who made a great contribution to Polish culture, are always worth a visit.

The **Cricoteka** is a museum of the Cricot 2 Theatre in which works by its founder, Tadeusz Kantor, are displayed.

The collection at **St Vladimir's Foundation** is devoted to the culture of the Orthodox Church among whose faithful were the Ruthenians who lived in the eastern borderlands of Poland. The collection features parts of iconostases and single icons from the 16th to 20th centuries.

Contemporary art can be seen not only at the National Museum but also in a number of galleries, including the **Palace of Art**. The **"Bunker of Art"** also runs a programme of interesting exhibitions of Polish and foreign artists.

The **Archdiocesan Museum** has a magnificent collection of Polish sacred art.

The museum also organizes exhibitions of works on loan from leading church treasuries throughout the country as well as other countries.

FOREIGN ART

THOSE interested in Western art should visit the **Czartoryski Museum**. *The Lady with an Ermine* by Leonardo da Vinci and the *Landscape with the Good Samaritan* by Rembrandt are two celebrated masterpieces, but there are many other fine works here too. Romanesque gold work from the Maas region, Italian Renaissance majolica, and porcelain from the Meissen factory are also in the museum's collections.

The Manggha **Japanese Centre of Art and Technology** covers Japanese art. A bequest of objects from the Far East presented by Feliks Manggha Jasieński constitutes the core of the collection, which also includes works by contemporary artists.

Tin-glazed majolica plate (c. 1545) from the collection of the Czartoryski Museum

MATERIAL CULTURE AND NATURAL HISTORY

THE **Archaeological Museum** displays important objects found in the 19th century in Galicia *(see p28)*, which was then under Austrian occupation. One of them is the statue of Światowid fished out from the Zbrucz River. Other objects found during the construction of Nowa Huta and renovation works at Kanonicza Street were added to the collection. There is also a notable collection of Egyptian mummies.

The **Ethnographic Museum** houses a large collection of folk art from the Lesser Poland region. Temporary exhibitions, which take place at the Krakowska Street branch, are always of interest.

An extremely well preserved rhinoceros *(coelodonta antiquitatis)* from the Ice Age is a highlight of the **Natural History Museum**.

Skull of *coelodonta antiquitatis*, Natural History Museum

Cracow's Best: Churches

THE SKYLINE of Cracow is dominated by churches. There are some 40 churches within the historic centre alone. It must be remembered, however, that a number of churches were destroyed or dismantled in the 19th century. The surviving churches bear witness to the splendour of Cracow. The interiors are surprisingly rich in furnishings and house a variety of works of art in different artistic styles.

Piasek and Nowy Świat

Church of St Anne
This church was created by two outstanding artists at the turn of the 17th century – the architect Tylman van Gameren and the sculptor Baldassare Fontana.

Franciscan Church
Magnificent murals and stained glass by Stanisław Wyspiański decorate the Gothic interior of this church.

Cathedral
This Cathedral is a place where the history of the Polish state meets that of the Church and national memorabilia are treasured.

Wawel Hill

VISTULA

Church of St Mary
The most important church in the centre of historic Cracow, St Mary's is famous for its retable, made between 1477–1489, and its interior decoration, which dates from later years.

0 metres　　　　　500

0 yards　　　　　　500

Piarist Church
The Rococo façade of this church is flat but is richly decorated.

Old Quarter

Wesoła, Kleparz and Biskupie

Dominican Church
This memorial plaque of Callimachus (Italian humanist, secretary to the Royal court), made after 1496 to the design of Veit Stoss, is to be found here. The remaining furnishings are mostly Neo-Gothic.

Okół and Stradom Quarters

Kazimierz Quarter

Church of Saints Peter and Paul
This is the finest early Baroque church in Poland, one which can easily rival Roman architecture from the leading architects of the late 16th century.

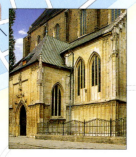

St Catherine's Church
While visiting this church one should not miss the south porch decorated with stonework and tracery.

Exploring Cracow's Churches

CRACOW'S churches represent many different styles, from the Romanesque and Gothic through Baroque and later eclecticism to the modern. Fortunately the majority of churches were saved from wartime destruction and have not been damaged. Today their splendid interiors impress visitors. However, Cracow's churches are not only tourist attractions but also places of pilgrimage. The relics of a number of saints and blessed, as well as many pious figures who enjoy a local cult, are laid to rest in the city's many churches.

Statue of St Peter

Gothic vault in the nave of the Corpus Christi Church

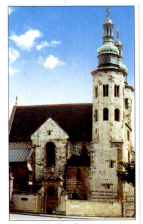

St Andrew's Church

PRE-ROMANESQUE AND ROMANESQUE

THE EARLIEST stone churches in Cracow date from the second half of the 10th century. They were built on the site of today's **St Adalbert's Church** and at Wawel, where the remnants of a number of rotundas have been found.

Today the reconstructed Rotunda of the Virgin Mary (see p 63), originally from the late 10th century, can be visited. Built around 1079, **St Andrew's** is exceptional among the Romanesque churches. The **Church of the Holy Redeemer** dates from around the same period. The Crypt of St Leonard beneath the Cathedral is a remnant of the second cathedral built between 1090 and 1142. The remnants of the Church of St Gereon and the Chapel of St Mary of Egypt are also at Wawel.

GOTHIC

SLENDER silhouettes of Gothic churches enhance the city. Some buildings were, however, demolished in the 19th century during the programme of "tidying up" the old architecture. The **Franciscan Church** is the oldest to have survived. Its irregular plan of a Greek cross with an asymmetric nave is unusual. The **Church of the Holy Cross**, begun around 1300, is worth visiting for its palm vaulting supported by a single pillar. **Cracow Cathedral** is certainly a major attraction. This three-aisled basilica with a transept and ambulatory, surrounded by chapels, was constructed between 1320 and 1364. The Monastery, **Church of St Catherine** and the **Corpus Christi** were both founded by Kazimierz the Great, while the **Dominican Church** was rebuilt during his reign. All three churches share the same structural and stylistic characteristics and were probably constructed by the same stonemasons who moved from one site to another. **St Mary's** the city's main civic church, is also Gothic. It was under construction from the end of the 13th century until the late 15th century.

TOWERS, DOMES AND SPIRES IN CRACOW

The outlines of many church domes and spires dominate the skyline of old Cracow. They also bear witness to the historic and artistic changes which the city has undergone. The Gothic spires of St Mary's and Corpus Christi are among the tallest and most picturesque. Baroque domes are more common and include the Church of Saints Peter and Paul, St Anne's and the Cathedral Clock Tower.

Towers of the Church of St Andrew

Slender Gothic spire of St Mary's Church

Baroque dome of St Anne's Church

RENAISSANCE AND MANNERIST

THERE is no complete church in Cracow in either the pure Renaissance or Mannerist styles, but the Zygmunt Chapel, built from 1519 to 1533, is regarded as the greatest example of Italian Renaissance north of the Alps. The chapel, with its spatial design and decoration, provided a model which was followed faithfully throughout Poland for many years.

Renaissance monuments by Jan Michałowicz of Urzędów and Giovanni Maria Mosca ("Il Padovano") can be seen in a number of churches. The career of the Italian Mannerist Santi Gucci, an equally fine artist, spans the last decades of the 16th century.

BAROQUE

ALTHOUGH in the 17th century Polish kings no longer resided in Cracow, many new ecclesiastical foundations were undertaken. The Jesuit **Church of Saints Peter and Paul** was the most magnificent. The

Baroque façade detail of the Church of the Missionaries

church was completed by the royal architect Giovanni Battista Trevano in 1609–1619. The imposing Zbaraski Chapel in the **Dominican Church**, built between 1629 and 1631, is another fine example of early Baroque. The Canopy of St Stanisław and the Waza Chapel, both in the Wawel **Cathedral**, exemplify the best of the High Baroque style. In the first half of the 17th century the interiors of a number of Gothic churches, such as St Mark's *(see p110)* were remodelled in the Baroque style. The century that followed brought about further architectural masterpieces, including **St Anne's Church**. A mention must also be made of the **Church of the Missionaries** whose exterior and interior were both modelled on Roman architecture, the **Piarist Church** with its airy façade, and the **Church of the Order of St John of God** whose façade displays dynamic articulation.

NEO-CLASSICAL AND ECLECTIC

THE LATE 18th-century choir and the high altar in the Church of the Norbertine Nuns are the only examples of ecclesiastical Neo-Classicism in Cracow. No building activity was undertaken until Galicia became autonomous, and new churches were only constructed in the second half of the 19th and first half of the 20th centuries. The **Church of the Felician Nuns** was built between 1882 and 1884 to designs by Feliks Księżarski, and the **St Joseph's Church**

Decoration of the porch of the Jesuit Church

(1905–1909) was designed by Jan Sas Zubrzycki. The **Jesuit Church** designed by Franciszek Mączyński and decorated with sculptures by Xawery Dunikowski and Karol Hukan, is an outstanding example of 20th-century architecture.

MODERN

A VARIETY of designs were applied to modern churches of the second half of the 20th century. Interesting are the **Ark of God** in Nowa Huta (architect Wojciech Pietrzyk, 1967–1977), the Church of St Maksymilian Kolbe in Mistrzejowice (architect Józef Dutkiewicz, 1976–1983) and the Church of St Jan Kanty at Bronowice Nowe.

Late Baroque Clock Tower of the Cathedral

Neo-Gothic spire of St Joseph's Church at Podgórze

Modern spire of the Ark of God Church in Nowa Huta

Cracow's Best: Cemeteries

THE VENERATION of tombs of prominent Poles who left their mark on the history of the nation is an important element of Polish national identity. In the 19th century Cracow was a destination for pilgrims from the whole country. They came primarily to visit the Wawel crypt. The crypt within the Paulite Church "On the Rock" is another mausoleum of eminent Poles. The communal cemeteries established in the 19th century are embellished with many fine sculptures and resemble parks.

Zwierzyniecki Cemetery

This quiet 19th-century cemetery has a pleasant location. Many famous artists are buried here.

Piasek and Nowy Świat

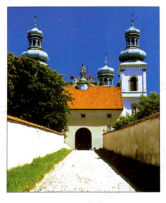

Camaldolese Catacombs

The niches in the crypt beneath the Camaldolese Church in Bielany house the deceased monks and benefactors of the Order.

Wawel Hill

VISTULA

0 metres	500
0 yards	500

The Cathedral

Polish kings were buried in Wawel Cathedral from the time of Władysław the Short until the decline of the Polish-Lithuanian Commonwealth. From the 19th century onwards national heroes and prominent literary figures were buried here.

Rakowicki Cemetery
A resting place for many distinguished citizens of Cracow, this cemetery may be regarded as a kind of chronicle of Cracow's life and a museum of sepulchral sculpture.

Old Quarter

Wesoła, Kleparz and Biskupie

Church of St Mary
The cemetery by this church (see p 48) was the largest in the city until the late 18th century. Many tombs and wall epitaphs from the 16th to 18th centuries have survived.

Okół and Stradom Quarters

Remu'h Cemetery
Established in 1533, the cemetery by the Remu'h Synagogue in Kazimierz is one of the oldest Jewish cemeteries in Europe.

Kazimierz Quarter

Crypt in the Paulite Church "On the Rock"
In 1480 the eminent chronicler Jan Długosz was buried in this crypt. From the 19th century onwards those who had made important contributions to Polish culture were also interred here.

Exploring Cracow's Cemeteries

Tomb in the Church of St Barbara

ALL OVER Europe the cult of commemoration of the dead resulted in the establishment of many large cemeteries, with beautiful sculptures often decorating the tombs. Cracow is no different in this respect. Numerous cemeteries and mausolea in church crypts have been established here over the years. They were already regarded as tourist attractions in the 19th century and continue to be visited by tourists to the city.

The Jerzmanowski Mausoleum, Rakowicki Cemetery

CHRISTIAN CEMETERIES

AT THE END of the 18th century a Cracovian noted that "Every time one looks through the window one cannot but see graves and crosses in the centre of the city". At that time the cemeteries used to be located near the churches. The one at St Mary's was the largest. It was relocated at the turn of the 18th century and the original burial site transformed into the Mariacki Square. Many tombstones and epitaphs, often medieval, which commemorate those who died centuries ago, have survived on the exterior walls of the churches of St Mary and St Barbara. A number of mausolea, built as chapels by the patrician families of Cracow, also survive on the former site of St Mary's Cemetery.

The **Rakowicki Cemetery** was established outside the city in 1803 and is the oldest cemetery in use. It occupies a vast plot and its layout is transparent. Many old trees give the place a park-like appearance. Some tombstones, especially those made around 1900 by the best Polish sculptors of the time, are true works of art.

In 1920 a **Military Cemetery** was set up by the Rakowicki Cemetery (they have since merged). Polish soldiers who fell in the years 1914–1920 and in September 1939, as well as British airmen who lost their lives in World War II, all rest here.

The **Zwierzyniecki Cemetery** is a far more modest place with no great monuments, but rather smaller tombstones decorated with small-scale but nevertheless interesting bas-reliefs. It is, however, a lovely place, picturesquely situated on a high hill and rich in varied fauna. One of the best times of year to visit Cracow's cemeteries is a few days either side of 1 November, when they glow under candlelight at night.

The graves of British airmen, Military Cemetery

JEWISH CEMETERIES

FOR MANY centuries Jews constituted a substantial part of the population of Kazimierz, the so-called

---

MONUMENTS AND TOMBS

The monuments in Cracow's cemeteries show different ways in which people wished to commemorate the deceased. The medieval monuments show a stiff figure lying on a death bed placed under a canopy. The canopy symbolizes Heaven awaiting the soul. Elements glorifying the deceased were introduced into Baroque monuments. Female figures with attributes personified the virtues. Neo-Classical monuments were influenced by ancient sculpture. Fine sculptures and symbolic content are characteristic of the monuments in the Art Nouveau style.

Monument of Kazimierz the Great (died 1370) in the Cathedral

Sarcophagus of Kościuszko in the Cathedral crypt (1818)

Sarcophagus of Jan III Sobieski in the Cathedral (1760)

Jewish city. They were interred at the **Remu'h Cemetery**, established in 1533. This small plot, squeezed between buildings, has many layers of tombs which have been placed here over hundreds of years. The tombstones are engraved with Hebrew inscriptions and symbolic images that identify the religion and social rank of the deceased. The dense accumulation of tombstones within a tiny and bare space contributes to the unique character of this Jewish cemetery.

The **New Jewish Cemetery** is different. It was established in the 19th century and given, like other cemeteries, a park-like appearance. Tombstones are scattered randomly and surrounded by luxuriant vegetation. This is one of a few Jewish cemeteries in Poland which is still in use.

View of Remu'h Cemetery

CRYPTS WITH TOMBS OF GREAT POLES

D URING the Partitions period (1795–1918) a number of celebrated Poles received state

The Angel of Vengeance on the Monument to Victims of the 1848 Bombardment of Cracow (1913)

The Waza Crypt in the Cathedral

funerals. These events were intended to raise the patriotic feelings of the Polish people.

Church crypts were open to the public and transformed into pantheons of Poland's greatest men. The **Cathedral's Crypt** contains the most solemn royal tombs of all. The crypt is divided into galleries in which Polish rulers, leading poets and national heroes rest. Tadeusz Kościuszko and Prince Józef Poniatowski were interred here during the occupation of Poland. The funerals of Józef Piłsudski and Władysław Sikorski took place in the 20th century.

The **Crypt in the Paulite Church "On the Rock"** is a resting place for those who made great contributions to the arts and sciences. The eminent historian Jan Długosz was buried here in the 15th century.

MONASTIC CEMETERIES

T HE CRYPTS beneath monastic churches are unique to Cracow. Their character reflects the unusual burial practices of particular religious orders.

The corpses in the **Crypt in the Church of the Reformed Franciscans** have been mummified naturally owing to the crypt's construction and ventilation. One can see here the corpses of poor friars lying on sand with their heads resting on a stone, as well as lay people in rich clothes resting in elaborate coffins.

The **Camaldolese Catacombs beneath the church** in Bielany are different. Here, the corpses are laid at first in niches cut out in a wall and then bricked up. Some years later the bones are removed and placed in an ossarium with the exception of the skull, which is taken by one of the monks for the purposes of contemplation. The Camaldolese crypt strikingly shows that in the face of death all are equal.

Mummified monks in the Crypt of the Church of the Reformed Franciscans

Cracow's Best: Personalities

MANY leading personalities of Polish academic, cultural and public life were born in Cracow. Eminent scholars were educated at or drawn to the Jagiellonian University, which was sometimes called "a gem of all knowledge". Famous artists and writers chose to live here, attracted by the unique atmosphere of the place enlivened by old traditions. The cult of such great figures as Adam Mickiewicz, Juliusz Słowacki, Tadeusz Kościuszko and Józef Piłsudski, all buried in Cracow, is still alive.

Andrzej Wajda (born 1926)
A leading film and theatre director, Wajda was educated in Cracow. He was the main instigator of the Japanese Centre of Art and Technology, one of the city's best museums. Wajda won an Oscar for Lifetime Achievement in 2000.

Piasek and Nowy Świat

Helena Modrzejewska (1840–1909)
This famous actress began her career at the Old Theatre (Teatr Stary) She is buried in Cracow.

Krzysztof Penderecki (born 1933)
World renowned composer and conductor, Penderecki was educated in Cracow. He was a Professor and Rector of the Music Academy.

Wawel Hill

VISTULA

Stanisław Lem (born 1921)
One of the most widely read science-fiction authors in the world, Lem is also an essayist and critic.

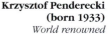

Wisława Szymborska (born 1923)
A prominent poet who was awarded the 1996 Nobel Prize for Literature, Szymborska's links with Cracow span over 50 years.

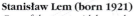

| 0 metres | 500 |
| 0 yards | 500 |

Jan Matejko (1838–93)
The most renowned Polish painter of the 19th century, Matejko's vision of Polish history has influenced many generations.

Sławomir Mrożek (born 1930)
An outstanding playwright and satirist, Mrożek began his career in Cracow as a journalist. After many years abroad, he returned and settled here in 1996.

Wesoła, Kleparz and Biskupie

Old Quarter

Czesław Miłosz (born 1911)
A poet, translator, Nobel Prize winner and honorary doctor of the Jagiellonian University, Miłosz was made an honorary citizen of Cracow in 1993.

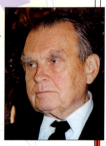

Tadeusz Kantor (1915–90)
One of the foremost European artists and theatre directors, Kantor established the world famous Cricot 2 Theatre.

Okół and Stradom Quarters

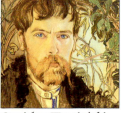

Kazimierz Quarter

Stanisław Wyspiański (1869–1907)
Best known for his play The Wedding, *Wyspiański was a dramatist, painter, and designer. His great artistic visions are embedded in the Polish perception of national identity.*

John Paul II (born 1920)
Before his elevation to the papacy, Karol Wojtyła was Suffragan Bishop, then Archbishop of Cracow from 1963 to 1978.

CRACOW THROUGH THE YEAR

BEAUTIFUL and magical, Cracow is a city where old traditions are maintained. The bugle call played at hourly intervals from the tower of St Mary's Church sets the rhythm of life. And life is lived here slowly, for one should not hurry when surrounded by stones a thousand years old. Embraced by the Planty, which had replaced the medieval walls,

Gingerbread heart from a church fair

the old quarter remains at the heart of the city. It is not an open-air museum that visitors vacate at night. Although no longer the capital of Poland, Cracow is a cultural centre and one of the oldest university cities in Europe. There is something for everyone here. Press listings and other local media, as well as tourist agencies, are good sources of information.

The Emmaus Fair in Zwierzyniec on Easter Monday

SPRING

IN PODHALE, the region at the foothills of the Tatra Mountains, vast fields of crocuses announce the arrival of spring. In Cracow, the opening of street cafés and people spilling onto the pavements herald the new season.

MARCH

International Festival of Alternative Theatre, Rotunda Club. The oldest event of its kind in which alternative theatres and fans of theatre are brought together.
Jazz Juniors, Rotunda Club. This international jazz festival for young musicians.
Festival of Organ Music *(Mar–Apr)*.

EASTER

Palm Sunday *(Sun before Easter)*. The blessing of palms in churches. A competition for the largest and best decorated palm takes place in Lipnica Murawana village, 41 km (25.6 miles) east of Cracow.
Holy Saturday is a day when baskets with food are taken to the church for a blessing, and symbolic tombs of Christ are venerated.
Easter Sunday is the most important Catholic feast.
Easter Monday. The Emmaus Fair takes place in Zwierzyniec and people are splashed with water *(Śmigus-dyngus)* throughout the city.

APRIL

Paka Cabaret Festival. Amateur and professional satirical performers, Polish and foreign, all take part.

MAY

3 May Constitution Day celebrates the first Polish Constitution of 1791 with a Mass said in the Cathedral followed by the laying of wreaths at the Tomb of the Unknown Soldier. Afterwards, there are fairs and picnics.
Procession from Wawel to the Paulite Church "On the Rock" *(first Sun after 8 May, Feast of St Stanisław)*. The Primate and bishops lead the procession and carry the relics of the patron saints of Poland, joined by the faithful in regional costumes.
Juvenalia. Cracow is ruled by students for a couple of days.
International Short Film Festival *(May–Jun)*. The oldest film festival in the country.
Cracow Spring Ballet Festival Słowacki Theatre, *(May–Jun)*. Leading ballet companies of the world take part.

ARCHCONFRATERNITY OF THE PASSION

Since 1595 the Good Friday processions of the Archconfraternity of The Passion have taken place in the Franciscan Church. The Brothers wear black habits with hoods covering the face. The ritual has remained unchanged for centuries. The Archconfraternity had the right to pardon those condemned to death.

Brothers in Procession

AVERAGE DAILY HOURS OF SUNSHINE

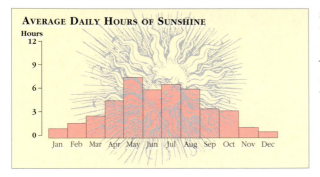

Hours
12
9
6
3
0

Jan Feb Mar Apr May Jun Jul Aug Sep Oct Nov Dec

Sunshine Chart
May is the sunniest month of the year in Cracow, but June, July and August are usually also sunny. December is the gloomiest month.

SUMMER

SUMMER heat may be difficult to bear in Cracow. This is because of the city's location in a valley and its humid microclimate. Many bars, cafés and restaurants in the Old Quarter are open and busy till the early hours of the morning. Crowds of tourists are attracted not only by the heritage but also the nightlife and cultural events. Organ Recitals at the Benedictine Abbey at Tyniec are among the most famous events.

JUNE

Corpus Christi (Boże Ciało)
(Thu in May or June). A great procession proceeds from Wawel to the Market Square. On Thursday a week after Corpus Christi *Lajkonik* (the Khan) canters around the town *(see p92)*.
Enthronement of the "King" Marksman, Market Square. The Marksmen's Brotherhood has existed since

the Middle Ages. Its members are burghers who are members of craftsmen guilds. Their leader is the winner of the annual shooting competition. The outgoing leader passes the silver cock to the new "king" during a colourful ceremony.
Midsummer's Eve (Wianki) Sat preceding the eve of St John's Feast *(24 Jun)*. Candle wreaths are set adrift on the Vistula by Wawel and there are fireworks displays.
International Music Festival of Military Bands features gala shows of drill, parades in period uniforms and many concerts.

JULY

Summer Early Music Festival. Concerts are held in historic houses.
Summer Opera and Operetta Festival.
Cracow Jazz Festival (Stary Jazz w Krakowie), *(Jul–Aug)*. A real treat for fans of traditional jazz.
Jewish Culture Festival *(early Jul)*, Kazimierz.

Poster announcing events during the Jewish Culture Festival

Outstanding Jewish performers from all over the world take part in this festival.

AUGUST

The Assumption of the Virgin Mary (Święto Wniebowzięcia Matki Boskiej) *(15 Aug)*. A Solemn Mass is said in the Cathedral. This is also the national holiday of the Polish Soldier, commemorating the 1920 victory over the Bolshevik Army. There is a military guard of Honour by the Tomb of the Unknown Soldier.
International Festival of Music in Old Cracow *(15–31 Aug)*. One of the most prestigious events in Cracow, with recitals and concerts of orchestral and chamber music in the magnificent historic buildings of the Old Quarter.
The Highlander Folk Festival (Folklor Górali Świata), Market Square. Concerts given by the world's leading groups after taking part in the Zakopane Festival.

Enthronement of the "king" Marksman in the Market Square

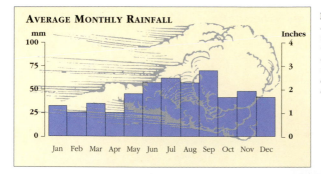

AVERAGE MONTHLY RAINFALL

Rainfall
September is the wettest month in Cracow. Storms and cloudbursts may occur in summer. February and April are the driest months.

AUTUMN

ON DRY and sunny autumn days Cracow is beautifully shrouded in colours; the Planty chestnut trees turn golden and market stalls display baskets full of wild mushrooms from the woodlands of the mountain foothills.

Students return to Cracow by the end of September to take part in the inaugural celebrations of the new academic year. The hymn *Gaudeamus Igitur* can be heard sung at many colleges, and in particular at the Jagiellonian University, Poland's oldest university, established in 1364.

Inauguration of the academic year at the Jagiellonian University

SEPTEMBER

Folk Art Fair (Targi Sztuki Ludowej), Market Square. Demonstrations and sale of local art and craft.

OCTOBER

"Etude" International Film Festival (Międzynarodowy Festiwal Filmowy Etiuda). Short films by students of art and film schools from all over the world.
International Festival of Forgotten Music (Międzynarodowy Festiwal Muzyka Utracona) is dedicated to archaic songs of the Slavs and people from the Baltic regions, performed by country folk groups. Seminars and

All Saints' Day

workshops also take place.
Early Music Festival (Festiwal Muzyki Dawnej) *(Oct–Nov)*. Organized simultaneously in a number of cities, the festival presents mainly the music of the Renaissance and Baroque performed on old instruments.
International Biennial of Architecture (Międzynarodowe Biennale Architektury).

NOVEMBER

All Saints' Day (Dzień Wszystkich Świętych), *(1 Nov)*. Many Cracovians visit cemeteries to lay flowers and light candles on the graves. The views of the old Rakowicki Cemetery or of the beautifully located cemetery on the Hill of the Holy Redeemer (św. Salwator) are unforgettable. It is an old custom of Cracow to be able to buy, on this day only, so-called Turkish honey (caramelized sugar with walnuts or pistachios) at the entrance to cemeteries. Children, especially, look forward to this event.
Independence Day (Święto Niepodległości), *(11 Nov)*. After a Mass at the Wawel Cathedral, wreaths are laid at the Tomb of the Unknown Soldier by the Grunwald Monument in Matejko Square.

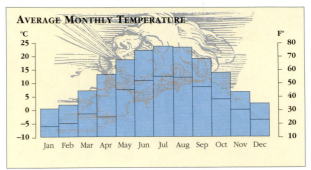

AVERAGE MONTHLY TEMPERATURE

Temperature
July and August are the hottest months with the temperature often exceeding 20 °C, sometimes even reaching 30 °C. Winter is cold and damp. The average temperature in January is -5 °C.

All Souls Jazz Festival
(Krakowskie Zaduszki Jazzowe). Oldest jazz festival in post-communist Europe, with concerts in the Philharmonic hall and jazz clubs.

WINTER

CRACOW under a blanket of snow is a wonderful sight, but winter also brings misty and bitingly cold days.

Every year on the first Thursday of December a competition for the best Christmas crib *(szopka)* takes place by the Mickiewicz Monument in Market Square. The winning cribs are later displayed at the Museum of Cracow. The tradition of making Christmas cribs, unique to Cracow, goes back to medieval Christmas plays.

Nativity scenes at churches are also worth visiting. The one outside the Franciscan Church, with real people and animals, is best known. It can be seen only on Christmas Eve and Christmas Day.

Stalls selling hand-made Christmas decorations and traditional delicacies fill the Market Square during the Christmas Fair.

Nativity play being staged at the Franciscan Church

DECEMBER

Christmas Eve (Wigilia), *(24 Dec)*. The evening begins with a meat-free meal. Midnight Masses are said and the Zygmunt Bell rings at Wawel.
Christmas (Święto Bożego Narodzenia) *(25 and 26 Dec)* and the day after are public holidays. Masses are celebrated in all churches.
New Year's Eve (Sylwester), *(31 Dec)*. A crowd, several thousand strong, gathers in Market Square to see in the New Year. The Wielopolski Palace, the seat of local government, is the venue for one of the grandest balls in Poland. Distinguished guests arrive from all over the world, and the proceeds go to charity.

JANUARY

New Year's Day (Nowy Rok) *(1 Jan)*. Public holiday. A month of balls and parties begins on this day.

FEBRUARY

"Fat Thursday" (Tłusty czwartek), *(Last Thu before Lent)*. Everybody eats doughnuts. The *Gazeta w Krakowie*, the local supplement to the *Gazeta Wyborcza*, rates the bakeries to help people choose the best doughnuts in Cracow.
Shrovetide (Ostatki), *(last Sat and Tue of the Carnival season, before Ash Wednesday)*. This is a time of parties before Lent.

Christmas decoration

Carol singers in traditional costume in Floriańska Street at Christmas time

PUBLIC HOLIDAYS

New Year's Day (1 Jan)
Easter Monday (Mar/Apr)
Labour Day (1 May)
Constitution Day (3 May)
Corpus Christi (Thu 8 weeks after Easter)
Assumption (15 Aug)
All Saints' Day (1 Nov)
Independence Day (11 Nov)
Christmas (25 & 26 Dec)

CRACOW AREA BY AREA

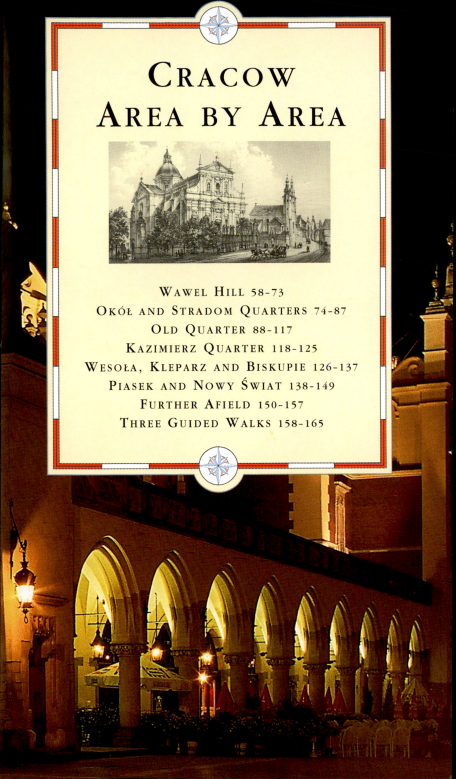

WAWEL HILL

Wawel hill was inhabited by the Vistulan (Wiślanie) people in ancient times. The settlement came to prominence during the reigns of Bolesław the Brave and Kazimierz the Restorer. The latter made Wawel the seat of his political power. In the late medieval period, from the 14th century onwards, the royal residence and a new cathedral were built. The Cathedral houses the relics of St Stanisław, patron saint of Poland. The last rulers of the Jagiellonian dynasty transformed the Gothic castle into one of the most magnificent Renaissance royal residences in Central Europe.

The eagle in the Zygmunt Chapel

They also endowed the Cathedral with important works of art and architecture. Although the capital of Poland was moved from Cracow to Warsaw at the end of 16th century, royal coronations and funeral ceremonies continued to take place in Cracow. A series of events in the 17th and 18th centuries led to the dilapidation of the Castle. The Austrian army was in garrison here from 1795 until the early 20th century. The Castle and Cathedral have both regained their former magnificence through an intensive restoration programme. Fortunately Wawel was saved from destruction in both World Wars.

SIGHTS AT A GLANCE

Churches
Cracow Cathedral pp64–9 ❸

Historic Sights, Buildings and Monuments
Archaeological Site ❼
Dragon's Lair ❽
Fortifications and Towers ❶
Statue of Tadeusz
  Kościuszko ❷

Museums
Cathedral
  Museum ❹

"Lost Wawel" Exhibition ❻
Royal Castle pp70–3 ❺

KEY

▨	Street-by-Street map *pp60–1*
▬	Fortifications

GETTING THERE

Bus routes 103, 124 and 502 pass along the Planty green belt and Straszewski Street. Get off there and walk. You can also use tram, routes 6, 8, 10, 18 travel to the Wawel, with the nearest stop by the Royal Hotel on St Gertrude Street.

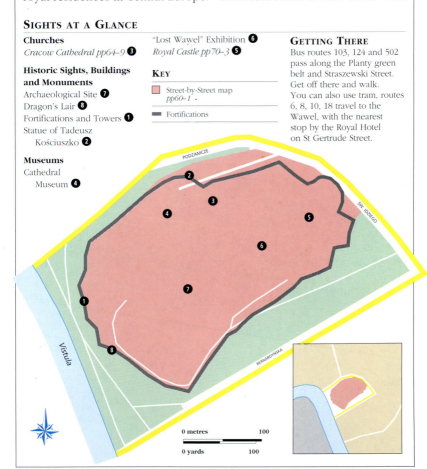

◁ **The arcaded courtyard of the Royal Castle on Wawel Hill**

Street-by-Street: Wawel Hill

THE WAWEL is exceptional because of its first-class collections and its unique atmosphere. To savour it unhindered by large crowds you should plan an early morning visit when the Cathedral and Castle courtyard are nearly deserted. Groups of tourists from every corner of the world gather here before noon, thereby enlivening the place. A trip to the Cathedral, where a variety of styles intermingle, as well as to the Royal Castle, is a must for visitors to Cracow.

Statue of Tadeusz Kościuszko
The statue of Kościuszko stands at the entrance to Wawel Castle. Kościuszko was the general who led the Insurrection of 1794 against the Russian army. His ashes rest in the Cathedral crypt ❷

The Coat of Arms Gate

Cathedral Museum
The museum houses a collection of sacred art, as well as a selection of insignia and memorabilia of the Polish kings, including the coronation robe of Stanisław August Poniatowski ❹

Dragon's Lair
This cave, consisting of a number of interconnecting chambers, and a sculpture of a fire-belching dragon is a much loved attraction. It is particularly popular with children ❽

KEY

- - - Suggested route

Fortifications and Towers
The compact but varied defence system on Wawel Hill was constructed from the 15th to the 19th centuries ❶

★ Royal Castle
A visit to the Castle includes the interior with its display of 16th-century tapestries, regalia, gold treasures and lavish Oriental objects ❺

LOCATOR MAP
See Street Finder maps 3, 5 & 6

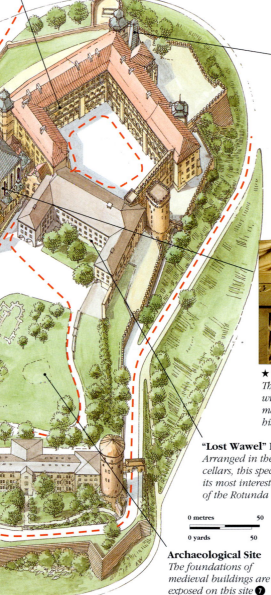

The "Hen's Claw" Wing (Kurza Stopka) is the most prominent remnant of the medieval castle. It was erected during the reign of Jadwiga and Władysław II Jagiełło.

★ Cracow Cathedral
The 19th-century sarcophagus of St Jadwiga, the Queen of Poland, is among many monuments associated with the history of the Church and Nation ❸

"Lost Wawel" Exhibition
Arranged in the former royal kitchen in the cellars, this special exhibition includes among its most interesting exhibits a reconstruction of the Rotunda of the Virgin Mary ❻

0 metres 50
0 yards 50

Archaeological Site
The foundations of medieval buildings are exposed on this site ❼

STAR SIGHTS
★ Cracow Cathedral
★ Royal Castle

Fortifications and Towers ❶

Wawel Hill. **Map** 3 C1 (5 C5). 🚌 *103, 124, 502.* 🚊 *6, 8, 10, 18.*

THE FORTIFICATIONS surrounding Wawel Hill date from different periods. Three massive towers – the Thief's Tower (Złodziejska), Sandomierz and Senator's Towers (the latter also called Lubranka) are dominant features of the architectural silhouette of the Wawel. They date from the second half of the 15th and early 16th centuries, when the royal residence was rebuilt by the Jagiellonians. New, mainly earth fortifications designed by Jan Pleitner were erected under Władysław IV between 1644 and 1646 on the Castle's northern terrace. The southeast bastion and redan (fortification of two parapets) were constructed in the early 18th century for King August II. Later in the century star-shaped fortifications designed by Bakałowicz and Mehler were built on the side of the Vistula River. The Austrians expanded the system between 1849 and 1852. Two round towers, forming part of the Austrian additions, have survived. The Wawel Castle was thus transformed into a citadel surrounded by a complex defence system.

The Coat of Arms Gate and part of fortifications surrounding Wawel Hill

The Sandomierz Tower, one of the three Wawel defence towers

Statue of Tadeusz Kościuszko ❷

Wawel Hill. **Map** 3 C1 (5 C5). 🚌 *103, 124, 502.* 🚊 *6, 8, 10, 18.*

THE STATUE of Tadeusz Kościuszko, general and main leader of the 1794 Uprising in Poland (see p27) and a participant in the American Revolution, was erected in 1921. It was designed by Leonard Marconi and completed by Antoni Popiel. The statue was destroyed by the Germans in 1940. The present reconstruction was donated in 1960. When approaching the Władysław bastion, where the statue stands, you can see a number of plaques mounted in the brick wall. These commemorate the donors who contributed to the restoration works carried out within the Castle during the inter-war years. Also of interest is the Coat of Arms Gate by Adolf Szyszko-Bohusz.

Stirrup that belonged to the Grand Vizier Kara Mustafa, Cathedral Museum

Cracow Cathedral ❸

See pp64–69.

Cathedral Museum ❹

Wawel 3. **Map** 3 C1 (5 C5). 🕾 *422 51 55 ext. 396.* 🚌 *103, 124, 502.* 🚊 *6, 8, 10, 18.* ⏰ *10am–3pm Tue–Sun.* 📷

THE CATHEDRAL MUSEUM was established in September 1978 by the then Archbishop Karol Wojtyła, the Metropoli-tan of Cracow. The display consists of objects from the Cathedral treasury. Among the exhibits are a sword, which was purposely broken in two places at the funeral of the last Jagiellonian king, Zygmunt August; the coronation robe of Stanisław August Poniatowski; the replica of the royal insignia found inside the royal coffins buried beneath the cathedral, and the stirrup of the Grand Vizier Kara Mustafa which was presented to the Cathedral by King Jan III Sobieski following his victory at the Battle of Vienna (1683). The outstanding collection of reliquaries, church vessels and vestments includes objects found in the tomb of Bishop Maur, as well as rational (a breast ornament) of the Bishops of Cracow, and memorabilia of John Paul II.

Royal Castle ❺

See pp70–73.

"Lost Wawel" Exhibition ❻

Wawel Hill 5. **Map** 3 C1 (5 D5). 🕾 *422 16 97.* 🚌 *103, 124, 502.* 🚊 *6, 8, 10, 18.* ⏰ *9:30am–3pm Mon, Wed, Thu, Sat; 9:30am–4pm Fri; 10am–3pm Sun.* ● *16–30 Mar.* 📷 *Free Sun.* ⓦ *www.wawel.krakow.pl*

THIS SPECIAL exhibition, arranged in the basement of the former royal kitchen (now occupied by the administration office), will appeal to those interested in the medieval history of Wawel. There were possibly ten churches on Wawel Hill in the past. The Rotunda of the Virgin Mary (Sts Felix and Adauctus), unearthed in 1917 during excavations carried out by Adolf Szyszko-Bohusz, is of great interest. The remnants of a man's body with some articles of jewellery were discovered nearby. It is believed that the circular rotunda formed part of the first palatium (the seat of the first ruler of Wawel), and was built in the late 10th or early 11th century. Its plan resembles a quatrefoil, with strong evidence of Czech influences in the design of the structure. The rotunda was almost completely destroyed in the 19th century.

A virtual computer model of the Wawel architecture is a recent addition to the exhibition, enabling visitors to travel into the past to the early 10th century. The computer reconstruction of the medieval buildings shows the state of current research into the early history of Wawel. The models of the so-called Rotunda B, the Rotunda of the Virgin Mary and other buildings, including the palatium, the Church of St Gereon and the Cathedral, are all included.

The Archaeological Site

Archaeological Site ❼

Wawel Hill. **Map** 3 C1 (5 C5). 🚌 *103, 124, 502.* 🚋 *6, 8, 10, 18.*

T HE ARCHAEOLOGICAL site is an open area where foundations of medieval buildings can be seen. The buildings were numerous and once formed a small town. A vicarage in the Renaissance style was among them. All the buildings were demolished by the Austrians in 1803–1804 and replaced by a drill ground. The lower parts of the walls of St Nicholas, the small Romanesque church rebuilt in the Gothic style during the reign of Kazimierz the Great, are of particular note. This church was an interesting example of a single nave church, supported on one central column. The plan of the small church of St George is also easy to discern.

Dragon's Lair ❽

Wawel Hill. **Map** 3 C1 (5 C5). 🚌 *103, 124, 502.* 🚋 *6, 8, 10, 18.* 🔲 *May–Oct: 10am–5pm daily.*

W ITHIN WAWEL HILL there are a number of rock caves. The earliest records of these caves date from the 16th century and are thought to be concerned with crimes. A pub and a brothel were here in the 18th century. In the 19th century the Austrians sealed the entrance when constructing the fortification walls.

The Lair is open during the summer months only. Some 135 spiral steps lead down into the den, and there are 145 m (476 ft) of tunnels in total, of which only a part can be visited. The bronze statue of the Dragon, designed by Bronisław Chromy, which stands at the entrance, was made in 1972.

According to an old legend the inhabitants of ancient Cracow were terrorized by a dragon until one day a brave shoemaker, Skuba by name, cheated the monster with a sheep stuffed with sulphur. The dragon swallowed the bait. When the fire heated its gut, the dragon drank so much water from the Vistula that its body burst. To reward the shoemaker King Krak gave him the hand of his daughter in marriage.

The metal monster belches fire and is always regarded as a major attraction by little visitors, both local and from further afield.

The Rotunda of the Virgin Mary at the "Lost Wawel" Exhibition

Cracow Cathedral ❸

The Eagle in Zygmunt Chapel

No other building is so strongly associated with the history of Cracow, and the whole nation, as the Cathedral. The existing building is the third to have been built on this site. The Cathedral was built by Władysław the Short to house the relics of St Stanisław, who was much venerated by the Poles. The basilica consists of nave with single aisles, non-projecting transept, and a choir with ambulatory. There are also three towers. Many chapels adjoin the aisles. The chapels date from different periods and have been remodelled many times. The internal structure of the Gothic cathedral is now obscure because of later additions. Today the interior displays a variety of styles. Despite this eclecticism the layout of the interior is straightforward.

Baroque spire from the first half of the 18th century

Exterior of the Cathedral
Although dating from different periods, all the distinct parts of the Cathedral make a unique and picturesque ensemble.

Clock Tower
The top of the tallest tower is decorated with four statues of the patron saints of the Kingdom of Poland and the Cathedral: Wacław, Adalbert, Stanisław and Kazimierz (Casimir).

Bell tower

Entrance
The bones of an "ancient creature" hang above the entrance. According to legend the end of the world will come when they fall. The letter K on the door is the initial of Kazimierz the Great, during whose reign the Cathedral was completed.

STAR SIGHTS

★ **Zygmunt Chapel**

★ **Zygmunt Tower**

★ Zygmunt Tower

The Zygmunt bell in the tower, cast in 1520, is the largest in Poland. It weighs nearly 11 tons and is more than 2 m (6.5 ft) in diameter.

High Altar

The high altar was commissioned in 1649 by Piotr Gembicki, one of the most powerful bishops of 17th-century Cracow.

Załuski Chapel

★ Zygmunt Chapel

This chapel is a mausoleum of the rulers of the Jagiellonian dynasty. Surmounted by a gilt dome, it is a Renaissance masterpiece.

Potocki Chapel

Remodelled in the 19th century, this chapel features The Crucifixion *by the 17th-century Bolognese artist Giovanni Francesco Barbieri, "Il Guercino".*

TIMELINE

1020 Laying of the foundation stone of the Cathedral

1521 The Zygmunt bell hung

1626–9 St Stanisław's Canopy erected

1320–64 Third Cathedral built

1664–76 Waza Chapel built

1000	1250	1500	1750

1090–1142 Second (so-called Herman) Cathedral built

1519–33 Zygmunt Chapel built by Bartolomeo Berrecci

1758–66 Bishop Załuski's Chapel built

Clock on the Clock Tower

Interior of the Cathedral

Bust of Bishop Piotr Gembicki from his monument

T HE CATHEDRAL of Cracow is exceptional not only for the works of art which are housed here, but also because it bore witness to many historic events such as coronations, royal weddings and funerals, as well as thanksgiving ceremonies. The Cathedral enjoys not only high sacred status but it also acquired symbolic importance during the occupation of Poland when it became a treasury of objects commemorating national glory. The Cathedral was chosen by the great Polish playwright Stanisław Wyspiański as a dramatic setting for his *Deliverance*. The Cathedral reflects the past and continues to exert much influence.

Poets' Crypt
Adam Mickiewicz and Juliusz Słowacki, the two foremost Polish poets, are buried here. The remains of Mickiewicz were laid here in 1890 and those of Słowacki in 1929 ❷

Zygmunt Chapel
The splendid double Monument of King Zygmunt the Old (top; by Santi Gucci, 1574–75) and his son, King Zygmunt August (below; by Bartolomeo Berrecci, 1530s) is the outstanding artistic feature of the Cathedral ❼

Entrance to the Crypt

Czartoryski Chapel

The Cathedral Crypt
houses the tombs of kings and distinguished Poles.

Chapel of the Holy Trinity

Sarcophagus of King Kazimierz Jagiellończyk
One of the most expressive works of Veit Stoss, this was made in 1492, the year of the king's death ❽

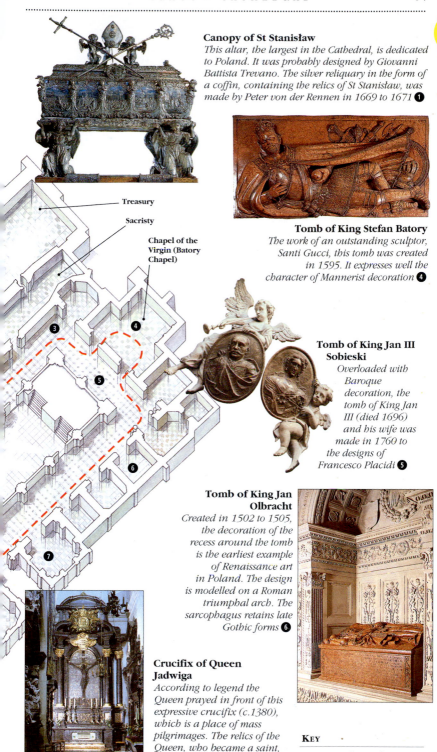

Canopy of St Stanisław

This altar, the largest in the Cathedral, is dedicated to Poland. It was probably designed by Giovanni Battista Trevano. The silver reliquary in the form of a coffin, containing the relics of St Stanisław, was made by Peter von der Rennen in 1669 to 1671 ❶

Treasury

Sacristy

Chapel of the Virgin (Batory Chapel)

Tomb of King Stefan Batory

The work of an outstanding sculptor, Santi Gucci, this tomb was created in 1595. It expresses well the character of Mannerist decoration ❹

Tomb of King Jan III Sobieski

Overloaded with Baroque decoration, the tomb of King Jan III (died 1696) and his wife was made in 1760 to the designs of Francesco Placidi ❺

Tomb of King Jan Olbracht

Created in 1502 to 1505, the decoration of the recess around the tomb is the earliest example of Renaissance art in Poland. The design is modelled on a Roman triumphal arch. The sarcophagus retains late Gothic forms ❻

Crucifix of Queen Jadwiga

According to legend the Queen prayed in front of this expressive crucifix (c.1380), which is a place of mass pilgrimages. The relics of the Queen, who became a saint, rest in the altar ❸

KEY

- - - - Suggested route

A Guided Tour of Cracow Cathedral

A Renaissance tondo by Giovanni Maria Mosca

CRACOW CATHEDRAL requires more than one visit to do justice to the magnificent building. Its interior with its variety of styles, from medieval to modern, is simply overwhelming. It is worth returning here for a careful visit to all the chapels in the aisles, and to the monuments and tombs of the kings and prominent people in the crypt.

It is also possible to look at works in chronological order. The artistic backdrop adds to the spirituality of the Cathedral, which is above all else used for worship. To avoid crowds, the best time to visit is in the early morning or just before closing time.

CHAPELS

THE CHAPEL of the Holy Cross, erected on the initiative of King Kazimierz Jagiellończyk and his wife Elisabeth von Habsburg, has retained much of its medieval character. The cycle of old Russian wall paintings is one of the largest ensembles to have survived. It is of the Pskov School. Two triptychs of the Holy Trinity and the Virgin Mary of Sorrows both date from the second half of the 15th century. The most interesting furnishing is the tomb of Kazimierz made by Veit Stoss with Huber of Passau. The king is shown in majestic resplendence. It is also a dignified image of death. The stained-glass windows were designed by Józef Mehoffer in the Art Nouveau style.

The Zygmunt Chapel (1519–33), designed by Bartolomeo Berrecci, is of exceptional beauty. The chapel is considered as one of the purest examples of the Italian Renaissance outside Italy. The chapel was modelled on the best Italian architectural and decorative works. The silver altar was made between 1531 and 1538 in Nuremberg by Melchior Baier to the designs of Peter Flötner. The royal tombs are equally interesting. The interior is peaceful and majestic and conveys the spirit of 16th-century humanism. Bishop

Tomicki's Chapel is also Renaissance in style. Remodelled by Bartolomeo Berrecci in 1526 to 1535, the chapel played an important role as a model for mausolea for the nobility and gentry. The Chapel of the Virgin Mary (King Stefan Batory's Chapel) houses a 17th-century Baroque tabernacle with the Holy Eucharist. The tomb of Batory and the royal stalls were designed by Santi Gucci.

The Waza Chapel, probably also designed by the same architect, exemplifies a 17th-century interior: monumental, heavy forms executed in black marble with large epitaphs. It acts as a reminder of the fragility and transcience of earthly life.

Among the chapels constructed in the 18th century, two are of particular interest. The Lipski Chapel (1743–7), designed by Francesco Placidi, displays light-catching and shadow effects. The decoration of Bishop Załuski's Chapel (1758–66) employs the allegory of the passage through the gate (note the enlarged entrance).

The *Crucifixion* by Guercino and the statue of the Risen Christ by Bertel Thorvaldsen are to be seen in the Chapel of Bishop Filip Padniewski. This Renaissance chapel was remodelled in the 19th century for the Potocki family. The statue of Włodzimierz Potocki in the Holy Trinity Chapel is also by Thorvaldsen.

The altar in the Zygmunt Chapel

Intricately carved stalls in the choir of the Cathedral

FURNISHINGS

As well as the canopy of St Stanisław, particularly noteworthy are the epitaphs of the bishops of Cracow placed on the pillars, and decorated with busts of the deceased. Marcin Szyszkowski, Piotr Gembicki, Jan Mała-chowski and Kazimierz Łu-bieński all rest here, providing eternal company for the relics of St Stanisław. The Baroque stalls in the choir were made around 1620; additions were made in the 19th century. The low relief epitaph of Cardinal Fryderyk Jagiellończyk shows superb craftsmanship. It was made after 1503 in the Vischer workshop in Nuremberg. The throne of Bishop Piotr Gembicki has splendid Baroque decoration. The organ loft, made around 1758 to the design of Francesco Placidi, is also of much interest.

SARCOPHAGI AND TOMBS

The cathedral is a resting place for Polish rulers, and all its medieval tombs follow a particular model. They show a figure laying in state on a massive sarcophagus, decorated with allegorical figures of the king's subjects lamenting the death of their sovereign. A dog, symbolizing fidelity, is usually placed at the king's feet, and the head of the ruler rests on a lion, the symbol of power. A stone canopy is suspended over the tomb. The tomb of Władysław the Short, dating from the mid-14th century is the earliest sarcophagus of this type. Kazimierz Jagiellończyk was the last to have such a monument erected.

Two tombs of much later date were inspired by this early type of sepulchre. The beautiful and majestic tomb of Queen Jadwiga is one of them. It was executed with great delicacy in white Carrara marble by Antoni Madeyski in 1902. The tomb is one of the most visited places of pilgrimage in the Cathedral. The other sarcophagus, also by Madeyski, was erected in 1906. It is a cenotaph (tomb without a corpse) commemorating King Władysław III Warneńczyk, who was killed in 1444 at the

The tomb of Władysław Jagiełło

Battle of Varna against the Turks. His body was never found, giving rise to stories about his miraculous salvation.

ROYAL TOMBS

The royal tombs were placed in the crypt following the construction of the Zygmunt Chapel, which is a mausoleum. Zygmunt the Old and his sons are buried in the crypt under the chapel. Earlier rulers were buried in the Cathedral, except Bolesław the Brave, Bolesław the Bold, Przemy-sław II, Louis of Anjou, Władysław III Warneńczyk and Aleksander Jagiellończyk. A crypt was also constructed for the Waza dynasty. Later rulers were buried beneath the Chapel of the Holy Cross and in St Leonard's crypt. In 1783 the last Polish king, Stanisław August Poniatowski, commissioned a grandiose sarcophagus for Jan III Sobieski. The elected kings Henri de Valois, August II of Saxony and Stanisław August Poniatowski do not rest in the Wawel. The national heroes, Kościuszko and Prince Józef Poniatowski, were laid here during the Partitions of Poland. State funerals of Piłsudski and General Sikorski took place in the Cathedral in the 20th century.

The sarcophagi of the Vaza kings

Royal Castle ❺

Head in the Deputies' Hall

Lᴵᴛᴛʟᴇ ɪs ᴋɴᴏᴡɴ about the earliest Wawel residence. The Romanesque palatium was probably built by Kazimierz the Restorer; later Władysław the Short started to construct a new building but it was only completed by Kazimierz the Great. The present Renaissance castle was constructed in the first half of the 16th century. At the turn of the 17th century the apartments in the north wing were remodelled in the early Baroque style. After the royal court moved from Cracow to Warsaw, the castle fell into ruin. Further devastation was caused by the occupying foreign powers. Early in the 20th century the castle was given back to Cracow, and restoration was begun.

The Confusion of Speech
This is one of the tapestries in the series The Building of the Tower of Babel *that decorates the Senators' Hall.*

Senators' Staircase

First floor

CASTLE GUIDE

The Crown Treasury and Armoury, each with a separate entrance, are situated on the ground floor together with a number of state rooms. The remaining state rooms and other apartments are on the first and second floors. After leaving the Senators' Hall a visit to the "Orient in the Wawel Collections" exhibition on the first and second floors in the west wing is recommended.

"Orient in the Wawel Collections" Exhibition
Turkish military spoils taken in Vienna in 1683 are the highlights of the Wawel's Oriental collection.

Crown Treasury and Armoury
This 11th-century chalice belonged to the Abbots of Tyniec and is now in the Treasury. Adjacent to the Treasury is the Armoury with its rich collection.

KEY

- ▢ Royal Apartments
- ▢ Treasury
- ▢ Armoury
- ▢ "Orient in the Wawel Collections" Exhibition
- ▢ Non-exhibition area

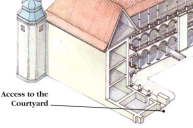

Access to the Courtyard

Entrance to the Crown Treasury and Armoury

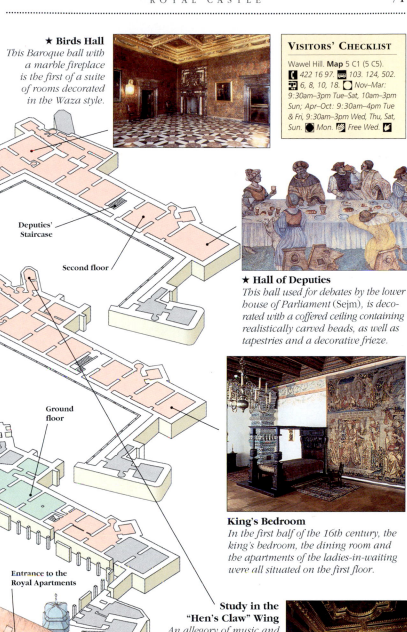

★ Birds Hall
This Baroque hall with a marble fireplace is the first of a suite of rooms decorated in the Waza style.

VISITORS' CHECKLIST

Wawel Hill. **Map** 5 C1 (5 C5).
📞 *422 16 97*. 🚌 *103. 124, 502.*
🚋 *6, 8, 10, 18.* 🕐 *Nov–Mar:
9:30am–3pm Tue–Sat, 10am–3pm
Sun; Apr–Oct: 9:30am–4pm Tue
& Fri, 9:30am–3pm Wed, Thu, Sat,
Sun.* ● *Mon.* 🎫 *Free Wed.* 📷

Deputies' Staircase

Second floor

★ Hall of Deputies
This hall used for debates by the lower house of Parliament (Sejm), is decorated with a coffered ceiling containing realistically carved heads, as well as tapestries and a decorative frieze.

Ground floor

King's Bedroom
In the first half of the 16th century, the king's bedroom, the dining room and the apartments of the ladies-in-waiting were all situated on the first floor.

Entrance to the Royal Apartments

Study in the "Hen's Claw" Wing
An allegory of music and putti, surrounded by musical instruments, can be admired on the ceiling here.

STAR SIGHTS

★ **Hall of Deputies**

★ **Birds Hall**

Exploring the Royal Castle

THE ROYAL APARTMENTS are the main reason for visiting Wawel Castle. The present interior decoration is, for the most part, a reflection of the artistic tastes of the last Jagiellonians. Some of the rooms are in the Waza style and display portraits of the elected kings. There is a separate exhibition entitled "Orient in the Wawel Collections", where Turkish military tents and lavishly decorated Oriental arms can be seen. The Crown Treasury and Armoury, which are visited separately, each display many precious objects.

A room on the first floor

ROYAL APARTMENTS

THE HOUSE OF THE LORD (one of the highest offices at the royal court) is the name given to the suite of rooms on the ground floor. The offices were situated here in the 16th century. The ornate door architraves, made by Master Benedict, are noteworthy. They represent the Renaissance and yet show a strong Gothic influence. Equally interesting are the larch wood ceilings as well as the paintings, such as *The Adoration of the Magi*, executed in the first quarter of the 16th century by a follower of Hans Suess von Kulmbach; the *Holy Family*, painted in the second quarter of the 16th century by Pieter Coecke van Aelst; and the *Virgin and Child* by an unknown artist of the third quarter of the 16th century. The Deputies' Staircase ends this suite of rooms.

The rooms on the first floor which are accessible to visitors are mainly in the south wing. They are decorated with original Renaissance friezes painted on the walls, and polychrome beamed ceilings. Splendid tapestries are among the furnishings. They include *verdures* (tapestries with animal or floral patterns, in which the colour green dominates) and tapestries hung above the windows, which are decorated with coats of arms. There are also tapestries with grotesque ornaments and some with the monogram SA (referring to Zygmunt August) on

The Dutch Study in the Tower of Zygmunt III

a cartouche supported by satyrs. Note also the *Portrait of a Man* by Lucas Cranach the Younger, the allegory of *Charity* by Jan Massys, the *Madonna and Child* by a follower of Sandro Botticelli, and a triptych with the *Last Judgement* inspired by the art of Hieronymus Bosch, all from the second half of the 16th century. At the north end of the east wing of the Castle are a number of rooms used for temporary displays and the apartment of President Ignacy Mościcki. Some rooms are situated in the Hen's Claw Wing and Zygmunt's Tower.

The State Apartments on the second floor were used for official functions and royal audiences. The tour begins with the rooms in the south wing and continues through to the north wing. The names of the rooms often refer to the friezes which decorate the walls. They were painted between 1534 and 1536 by Hans Dürer and Anton of Breslau (now Wrocław) and feature, among other themes, knights jousting. All paintings and furniture (including *cassoni*, or dowry chests) are Italian. Paintings are by Alessandro Allori, Palma Vecchio and Paris Bordone, a pupil of Titian. There are also other works by the school of Titian, as well as that of Andrea del Sarto and Raphael.

The Hall of Deputies ends the tour. This was the place for debates of the *Sejm* (Polish parliament) and royal audiences. It is also known as the Hall of Heads because of the unusual decoration of the ceiling. The coffers were originally decorated with 194 heads carved in the 1530s by Sebastian Tauerbach and Master Hans, both from Breslau. The heads portray kings, knights, burgher women, merchants and possibly also allegorical figures. Unfortunately only 30 heads have survived.

The rooms north of the Deputies' Staircase are also named after wall friezes painted in 1929 to 1933, mostly by Leonard Pękalski. The wall hangings which decorate the rooms illustrate the *Story of the Tower of Babel* and that of

Coffered ceiling in the Hall of Deputies

TAPESTRIES

The first tapestries were imported to the Wawel by Zygmunt the Old. His son, Zygmunt August, enlarged the collection through commissions made in the leading weaving workshops in Brussels, those of Nicholas Leyniers Willem and Jan de Kaempeneer. They were executed after cartoons by Michiel van Coxcie and Jan van Thieghem. The collection contains some 360 tapestries.

They are arranged in series which illustrate Biblical themes such as: *Adam and Eve in Eden*, *The Story of Noah* (The Deluge) and *The Building of the Tower of Babel*. Some 140 *verdures* (see p72), showing fantastic creatures, and tapestries with grotesques, royal monograms and state emblems, constitute a large proportion of the present collection.

The tapestry showing the *Story of Noah*

Noah. Italian paintings from the 15th, 16th and 17th centuries are also of interest.

The rooms that follow are decorated in the Waza style. They are imposing, with dark colour schemes. *The Portrait of Prince Władysław* by Peter Paul Rubens was painted in 1624 during the prince's tour of Europe. The portrait of Władysław IV on horseback, as well as that of his father Zygmunt III, are also of note. Paintings by Dutch and Flemish artists displayed in the small Dutch Study, entirely filling the walls, are equally interesting.

The Senators' Hall was the venue for the Senate's debates, hence the name, and important court ceremonies. The Hall ends the tour. The exit from the royal apartments is by the Senators' Staircase which was constructed early in the 17th century to designs by Trevano.

Tourists and local people alike always gather by a *tchakram* (stone which has special power) in the northwest corner of the courtyard. They lean against the wall to feel the revitalizing power emanating from this stone which is believed to indicate the intersection of cosmic and earthly forces. A wall separates this place from the so-called St Gereon's Church, formerly believed to contain the remnants of the first cathedral and today considered as the royal chapel St Mary of Egypt. This part can only be visited by appointment.

CROWN TREASURY AND ARMOURY

THE CROWN TREASURY and Armoury are situated in the Gothic rooms on the ground floor, in the northeast part of the Castle. The coronation sword of the Polish kings (the Szczerbiec), the royal insignia, including Zygmunt August's banner, the honorary insignia of Jan III Sobieski and rare, precious objects and jewels made by leading European goldsmiths are displayed. A collection of knights' armour includes a number of 17th- and 18th-century hussars winged armour. There are also lavishly decorated horse saddles and trappings, as well as replica banners of the Teutonic Knights captured at the Battle of Grunwald in 1410.

"ORIENT IN THE WAWEL COLLECTIONS" EXHIBITION

AMONG the spoils from the Battle of Vienna of 1683, Turkish tents and banners are of particular importance. There are also tapestries and rugs from Persia. Eastern arms and some interesting pieces of porcelain from Japan and China complete the collection.

Turkish tent seized at Vienna in 1683, "Orient in the Wawel Collections"

OKÓŁ AND STRADOM QUARTERS

OKÓŁ was probably the earliest settlement at the foot of Wawel. Timber-built houses and a palisade enclosure were already here in the 10th century. The settlement developed along the so-called Salt Route which led from Hungary to Greater Poland. The quarter became elitist as a result of its proximity to the Royal Castle and the Cathedral. High-ranking

Heraldic emblem on the house at 32 Grodzka Street

clergy resided here and many churches were built.

The development of Stradom, situated between Okół and Cracow, was hidered by its location on peat marshes and the vicinity of the Wawel fortress. Splendid new churches and palaces were constructed here from the mid-17th century. Stradom developed rapidly at the end of the 19th century.

SIGHTS AT A GLANCE

Churches and Monasteries
Bernardine Church **19**
Church of Saints Peter and Paul pp80–81 **3**
Church of St Andrew **4**
Church of St Giles **7**
Church of St Martin **5**
Church of the Bernardine Nuns **18**
Church of the Missionaries **21**
Franciscan Church pp86–7 **15**

Museums and Galleries
Archaeological Museum **14**
Archdiocesan Museum **10**
Cricothéque **13**
Natural History Museum **22**
St Vladimir's Foundation **11**
Wyspiański Museum **12**

Historic Parks
Dietl Plantations **23**

Historic Monuments and Buildings
Collegium Iuridicum **2**
Częstochowa Seminary **20**
Deanery **9**
Royal Arsenal **6**
Statue of Józef Dietl **17**
Wielopolski Palace **16**

Historic Streets
Grodzka Street **1**
Kanonicza Street **8**

GETTING THERE
Trams 1, 2, 6, 8 and 18 stop at Wszystkich Świętych Square. Alternatively, trams 6, 8, and 10 stop in Św. Gertrudy Street by the Royal Hotel, or in Stradomska Street.

KEY
Street-by-Street map pp76–7
P Parking
Post office

◁ **Vault in the Franciscan Church**

Street-by-Street: Okół

T HE HISTORIC Okół is more or less in line with the southern part of the medieval centre of Cracow. It is a picturesque area. Those who want a change from the regular plan of the Old Quarter will enjoy Okół's curving streets and dead-end mews, lined with some outstanding buildings. Fortunately the great fire of Cracow in 1850 did not damage the buildings in Okół, and much of the original architecture can still be seen here.

Collegium Iuridicum
This sculpture of classical beauty in the courtyard is by Polish-born Igor Mitoraj. It was presented to the Jagiellonian University by the artist, who now lives in Italy **2**

Archaeological Museum
The collections here tell the prehistory of the Polish lands **14**

Cricothéque
The Cricot 2 Theatre and Museum are located in this Gothic house **13**

Wyspiański Museum
Many works by this leading Polish Art Nouveau artist are gathered here **12**

St Vladimir's Foundation
This building houses artefacts explaining the life of the Ruthenas in the Polish-Lithuanian Commonwealth **11**

Archdiocesan Museum
The collection consists of objects from churches in the Cracow Archdiocese which are no longer used in the liturgy **10**

Deanery
The arcaded courtyard of this small house, formerly a canonry, gives the impression of a magnificent Renaissance residence **9**

Kanonicza Street
This quiet street has retained much of the old royal character of Cracow **8**

★ **Church of Saints Peter and Paul**

This early Baroque Jesuit church is a masterpiece of 17th-century Polish architecture. The façade, with its rich sculptural decoration, is remarkable ❸

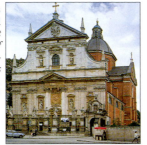

LOCATOR MAP
See Street Finder maps 1, 3 & 6

Grodzka Street
The townhouses situated along one of the oldest streets in Cracow were once palaces ❶

★ **Church of St Andrew**
This is the best preserved example of Romanesque architecture in Cracow ❹

Church of St Martin
This small early Baroque church was transformed into the Augsburg Protestant Church in the early 19th century ❺

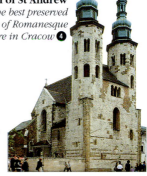

Royal Arsenal
This entrance to the Arsenal is one of the most beautiful 17th-century doorways in Cracow ❻

GRODZKA

Church of St Giles
This is a rather modest Gothic church dating from the first half of the 14th century ❼

0 metres   50
0 yards   50

KEY

– – – Suggested route

STAR SIGHTS

★ **Church of Saints Peter and Paul**

★ **Church of St Andrew**

Children wearing traditional clothing on Grodzka Street

Grodzka Street ❶
Ulica Grodzka

Map 1 C5 (6 D4). 🚃 1, 2, 6, 8, 18.

GRODZKA is one of the oldest streets in Cracow. In the past it formed part of the important Salt Route from Hungary to Greater Poland. As part of the Royal Route it bore witness to coronation and funeral processions of Polish kings.

Grodzka Street was once lined with many palaces and a few churches. These palaces were rebuilt and converted into tenement houses. Grodzka is a lovely street full of character, owing to its irregular plan, varying width and diverse architecture.

Collegium Iuridicum ❷

Grodzka 53. **Map** 1 C5 (6 D4).
📞 422 77 11. 🚃 1, 2, 6, 8, 18.
Courtyard 🕐 7:45am–8pm daily.
Natural History Museum (Muzeum Przyrodnicze UJ) 🕐 10am–6pm
Mon–Fri, 10am–3pm Sat, 11am–3pm Sun.

THE collegium Iuridicum of the Academy of Cracow was founded early in the 15th century through the bequest of Queen Jadwiga. The exca-

vation work carried out at the site has confirmed that the building had replaced a large trade hall, probably built in the 14th century on the orders of Władysław the Short. The remnants of the hall have survived in the basement. The Collegium Iuridicum was rebuilt several times. The works were funded by Bishop Jan Rzeszowski, among others. The elaborate doorway decorated with the University's emblem was made around 1680. The

Two-tier arcaded courtyard of the Collegium Iuridicum

College was entirely rebuilt after a fire in 1719 and the two-tier arcaded courtyard added. The Institute of the History of Art and the Natural History Museum, both part of the Jagiellonian University, are housed here, the latter being located in the basement. A collection of shells and butterflies is of interest.

In the summer months concerts and theatrical performances take place in courtyard, which features a sculpture by Igor Mitoraj.

Church of Saints Peter and Paul ❸
Kościół św. św. Piotra i Pawła

See pp80–81.

Church of St Andrew ❹
Kościół św. Andrzeja

Grodzka 56. **Map** 1 C5 (6 D4).
📞 422 16 12. 🚃 1, 2, 6, 8, 18.
🕐 7:30am–5pm daily and during services.

THE CHURCH of St Andrew in Okół is regarded as one of the finest examples of Romanesque architecture in Poland. It was built between 1079 and 1098 as a foundation of Sieciech, the powerful Palatine to Duke Władysław Herman. It was rebuilt around 1200. The towers and aisles were extended and a transept added. According to the chronicler Jan Długosz this was the only church in Cracow to resist the Tatar invasion of 1241. Around 1702 it was remodelled in the Baroque style to the designs of Baldassare Fontana, who also covered the internal walls and vaulting with stuccowork. Mural paintings by Karl Dankwart complete the decoration. Among furnishings worth noting are the pulpit, in the form of a boat, and the high altar with an imposing ebony tabernacle decorated with silver ornaments.

The treasury in the convent adjoining the church houses some priceless objects, such as a portable mosaic depicting the Virgin Mary from the turn

Church of St Andrew with its two spires

of the 12th century, 14th-century marionettes used in Christmas nativity plays, and early medieval reliquaries.

Church of St Martin ❺

Kościół św. Marcina

Grodzka 58a. **Map** 6 D4. 422 26 65. 6, 8, 10, 18. 10am–1pm Mon–Sat and during services.

THE FIRST church was probably built on this site in the 12th century. In 1612 the Discalced Carmelite Nuns were brought here. The old church was demolished and in 1637–40 the nuns commissioned a new, rather small church in the early Baroque style. After the convent was closed down, the church was taken over by the Protestant community. The interior was converted according to the needs of the Lutheran liturgy. The high altar features a 14th-century crucifix and *Christ Calming the Storm*, painted by Henryk Siemiradzki in 1882.

Royal Arsenal ❻

Arsenał Królewski

Grodzka 64. **Map** 6 D5. 422 47 03. 6, 8, 10, 18. to the public.

IN THE FIRST half of the 16th century Zygmunt the Old built an arsenal and a cannon foundry next to the city wall. They formed part of Cracow's fortifications. The present building is a result of the remodelling undertaken in 1927. The architect, Stanisław Filipkiewicz, juxtaposed the Baroque structure of the arsenal with an austere, modern extension thus achieving an interesting effect.

Church of St Giles ❼

Kościół św. Idziego

Św. Idziego 1. **Map** 6 D5. 6, 8, 10, 18. during services only.

ACCORDING to historic evidence made popular by a song by Ewa Demarczyk (of the Piwnica pod Baranami Cabaret), this church was "built in 1082 by Władysław Herman and his wife Judith, after they bore a child through the intervention of St Giles". The present church was built in the early 14th century. In 1595 the Dominicans took over and soon remodelled it.

Among the furnishings, the stone stalls are particularly interesting. They were made in 1629 by reusing fragments of the Renaissance tomb of St Jacek (otherwise known as St Hyacinth) from the Dominican Church.

Kanonicza Street ❽

Ulica Kanonicza

Map 1 C5 (6 D4). 6, 8, 10, 18.

KANONICZA STREET formed the last stretch of the Royal Route leading towards Wawel. From the 14th century onwards it was lined with the houses of Cracow's canons. The canons were given the use of these houses for life when they took up office in the Chapter of Cracow. Each successive inhabitant tended to modernize the house. As a result Gothic houses acquired arcaded Renaissance courtyards, Baroque doorways or Neo-Classical façades. The canons could afford to spend lavishly on architecture owing to their elite status within the ecclesiastical world.

The great diversity of architectural styles which can be found within the narrow and winding little Kanonicza Street gives it a picturesque character.

Decorative bas-relief plaque of 1480 on the Długosz House, Kanonicza Street

Church of Saints Peter and Paul ❸

Emblem of the Jesuits

T HIS CHURCH, modelled on the Jesuit Church of Il Gesù in Rome, is considered to be one of the most magnificent early Baroque churches in Central Europe. The history of its construction and the name of the architects involved are the subjects of an ongoing debate among architectural historians. The foundation stone was laid in 1596. The leading Jesuit architect, Giovanni de Rosis, contributed the design, and works were carried out by Giuseppe Brizio and Giovanni Maria Bernardoni. In 1605 the church neared its completion but, due to some structural problems, a number of walls had to be dismantled and rebuilt to an altered design. The court architect Giovanni Battista Trevano was put in charge of the second stage.

Cartouche with an Eagle
This exquisitely carved coat of arms belonged to the main founder of the church, King Zygmunt III Waza.

Organ Gallery
The late Baroque organ gallery with a curved balustrade, designed by Kacper Bażanka, is in contrast with the austere and monumental architecture of the Church. It is located inside, just above the main entrance.

Statues of the Apostles
This railing was designed by Kacper Bażanka and is decorated with copies of statues originally carved by David Heel from 1715 to 1722.

Statue of St Ignatius Loyola
The founder of the Society of Jesus is depicted in this late Baroque sculpture by David Heel. The adjoining statues are of Stanisław Kostka, Francis Xavier and Aloysius Gonzaga.

Main entrance

VISITORS' CHECKLIST

Grodzka 38. **Map** 1 C5 (6 D4).
📞 422 65 73. 🚋 1, 2, 6, 8, 10,
18. ⬤ 9am–5pm Mon–Sat,
1pm–5pm Sun and during
services. 📷

Stuccowork (1622–39)
*The stuccowork above the
high altar is by Giovanni
Battista Falconi and includes scenes from the lives of
Saints Peter and Paul,
patrons of the church.*

★ High Altar
*Made in 1726–28 to
Kacper Bażanka's
design, the high altar
was conceived to
convey a call for unity
between the Roman
Catholic and Orthodox
Churches.*

**Entrance
to the
Skarga
Crypt**

**★ Tomb of Bishop
Andrzej Trzebicki**
*The monumental decoration
of this tomb, created in
1695–96, commemorates
the bishop with true
Baroque ostentation.*

Statue of Piotr Skarga
The author of Parliamentary
Sermons *died in 1612
and was buried in the
crypt beneath the high
altar. This statue of
Father Skarga was made
by Oskar Sosnowski
in 1869 and placed in
the church in the early
20th century.*

STAR SIGHTS

★ High Altar

★ Tomb of
    Bishop Andrzej
    Trzebicki

Massive portal of the medieval Deanery

Deanery **9**
Dom Dziekański

Kanonicza 21. **Map** 1 C5 (6 D4).
🚏 *1, 2, 6, 8, 10, 18.*

THIS HOUSE is considered to be the most beautiful of all the canons' houses in Cracow. The medieval house was completely rebuilt in the 1580s, probably by the architect and sculptor Santi Gucci. The arcaded courtyard with its magnificent decoration, carved in stone, the impressive portal and the *sgraffiti* on the façade all date from this period. The statue of St Stanisław in the courtyard was added in the 18th century. In the 1960s this was home to the future Pope and then Suffragan Bishop of Cracow, Karol Wojtyła.

Archdiocesan Museum **10**
Muzeum Archidiecezjalne

Kanonicza 19. **Map** 1 C5 (6 D4).
📞 *421 89 63.* 🚏 *1, 2, 6, 8, 18.*
🕐 *10am–4pm Tue–Fri, 10am–3pm Sat & Sun.* ♿

THIS HOUSE is traditionally associated with the residence of St Stanisław while he was a canon in Cracow, hence the name, St Stanisław's House. It was actually built in the 14th century but entirely remodelled in the late 18th century. The Archdiocesan Museum is now housed here. It runs a programme of temporary exhibitions of sacred art based on loans from church treasuries in the Cracow Archdiocese. Interesting goldwork displays have taken place here.

Part of the Archdiocesan Museum is given over to the room of Karol Wojtyła, who became Pope John Paul II. The room has been faithfully reconstructed here as it stood originally in the adjoining Deanery, where he lived.

St Vladimir's Foundation **11**
Fundacja
św. Włodzimierza

Kanonicza 15. **Map** 1 C5 (6 D4).
📞 *421 99 96.* 🚏 *1, 2, 6, 8, 10, 18.*
🕐 *Apr–Sep: noon–4pm daily; Oct–Mar: noon–4pm Wed–Fri.* ♿

ST VLADIMIR'S FOUNDATION is based in a 14th-century house which displays fine Renaissance decoration. Icons from disused Orthodox churches in the Beskidy, Bieszczady and Tomaszów Lubelski regions, dating mainly from the 17th and 18th centuries, are kept here.

The Greek Catholic Chapel dedicated to the martyr saints Boris and Gleb is decorated with paintings by Jerzy Nowosielski. This contemporary Cracow artist is influenced by Byzantine art but uses modern forms of expression.

The sanctuary features the miraculous icon of the Korczmin Madonna.

Wyspiański Museum **12**
Muzeum Stanisława
Wyspiańskiego

Kanonicza 9. **Map** 1 C5 (6 D4).
📞 *422 83 37.* 🚏 *1, 2, 6, 8, 10, 18.*
🕐 *10am–6pm Tue & Thu, 10am–3.30pm Wed, Fri–Sun.*
♿ *free Sun.*

THIS MUSEUM, established in the 1980s as a branch of the National Museum, is entirely devoted to the life

Karol Wojtyła's room in the Archdiocesan Museum

and work of Stanisław Wyspiański, Cracow's foremost Art Nouveau artist (1869–1907).

The house features an early 19th-century façade and an impressive arcaded courtyard. The collections are displayed in a number of rooms on the first floor. Among the exhibits of particular interest are cartoons for stained glass and stage designs, as well as the model of Wawel Hill transformed into a Polish Acropolis (see pp30–31).

Helenka by Stanisław Wyspiański

Cricothéque ⑬

Kanonicza 5. **Map** 1 C5 (6 D4). ☎ 422 83 32. ⛴ 1, 2, 6, 8, 18. ◷ 10am–4pm Mon–Fri (Jul & Aug also Sat & Sun). 📷

THE FORMER canon's house at 5 Kanonicza Street has retained much of its Gothic form. In 1980 it became the home of the renowned avant-garde theatre Cricot 2. This theatre was founded in 1956 on the initiative of Tadeusz Kantor, the outstanding painter and stage designer. It became famous for performances which were permeated by a symbolic representation of man's existence. Performances relied on traditional theatrical forms while also borrowing from the "happenings" fashionable at the time. The most unusual sets added a surreal flavour. *The Dead Class, Wielopole, Wielopole* and *Let Artists Drop Dead* were among Cricot 2's most successful productions. After the death of Kantor in 1990 his actors continued his work.

The house in Kanonicza Street is too small to have a stage, so performances take place in other venues. The Cricothéque housed here is a small museum and archive documenting the work of the theatre. Costumes, stage designs and props, photographs of the performances, as well as drawings and paintings by Kantor, are all kept here.

Archaeological Museum ⑭

Muzeum Archeologiczne

Senacka 3. **Map** 1 C5 (6 D4). ☎ 422 71 00. 🚌 103, 124, 502. ⛴ 6, 8, 10, 18. ◷ 9am–2pm Mon–Wed, 2–5pm Thu, 10am–2pm Sun. 📷 free on Thu.

THE MUSEUM is housed in the former Friary of the Discalced Carmelites, founded in 1606. At the end of the 18th century the Austrian authorities took the building over and converted it into a prison. Mostly political prisoners were held here. In 1945 a group of imprisoned soldiers was rescued following heroic action by the Home Army (AK). After the prison closed down a museum was established here.

The collection of Archeological Museum has its beginings in 1850. It was initially called the Museum of Antiquities.

The collection includes artefacts that tell the earliest history of the Lesser Poland region, but also Egyptian mummies. The statue of the idol Światowid, salvaged from the Zbrucz River, jewellery found in the tomb of a Scythian princess in Ryżanówka, gold objects from the tomb of a Hun from Jakuszowice and iron objects used as a form of payment (see p19) are the highlights of the collection.

Franciscan Church ⑮

Kościół Franciszkanów

See pp86–7.

Elaborate entrance to the Wielopolski Palace

Wielopolski Palace ⑯

Pałac Wielopolskich

Plac Wszystkich Świętych. **Map** 1 C5 (6 D3). ☎ 616 12 07. ⛴ 1, 2, 6, 8, 18. ◷ by prior telephone arrangement only.

THE WIELOPOLSKI Palace was sold in the second half of the 19th century and transformed into a seat of municipal administration. Following remodelling work carried out from 1907–12 by architect Jan Rzymkowski, the building acquired a simplified modern form. A porch supported by pseudo-Romanesque columns covered by a timber roof was added to the wall facing Poselska Street. An Art Nouveau frieze featuring coats of arms of a number of cities can also be seen here. Inside the palace, the Debate Room and Portrait Hall are both worth visiting.

Archaeological Museum and garden

Statue of Józef Dietl ⓱
Pomnik Józefa Dietla

Pl. Wszystkich Świętych. **Map** 1 C5 (6 D3). 🚃 1, 2, 6, 8, 18.

JÓZEF DIETL (1804–78) was a medical professor who advocated treating the sick in spas. He was Rector of the Jagiellonian University, and became the first President (Mayor) of Cracow to be elected, in 1866, in the autonomous Galicia. He reformed the education system in Cracow, set up a project for the renovation of the city's heritage and was responsible for the restoration of the Cloth Hall.

The statue of Dietl was made between 1936 and 1938 by Xawery Dunikowski. The artist not only created the monumental figure but also took much trouble to find it a prominent location. Using a model he travelled all over Cracow and tried it out in various places before deciding upon the present location in All Saints Square. The result is stunning. The Statue of Dietl is regarded as one of the grandest and best located monuments in Poland.

Church of the Bernardine Nuns ⓲
Kościół Bernardynek

Poselska 21. **Map** 1 C5 (6 D4). 🕿 422 22 46. 🚃 1, 2, 6, 8, 18. ◷ 9am–6:30pm daily and during services.

A SMALL convent of the Bernardine Nuns was established in Poselska Street in 1646. The Church of St Joseph was built here between 1694 and 1703 for the nuns. Though small and modest the church interior displays splendid furnishings which include altars and a pulpit from the workshop of Jerzy Hankis. The miraculous image of St Joseph and Child in the high altar was a gift from Jakub Zadzik, Bishop of Cracow, who possibly received it from Pope Urban VIII.

A small 17th-century statue of the child Jesus in the side altar is much venerated. It

Interior of the small Church of the Bernardine Nuns

originally came from the Church of the Nuns of St Colette in Stradom and is therefore called the Koletański Christ.

Bernardine Church ⓳
Kościół Bernardynów

Bernardyńska 2. **Map** 3 C1 (6 D5). 🕿 422 16 50. 🚃 6, 8, 10. ◷ during services only.

GIOVANNI da Capistrano, the reformer of the Franciscan Order, later canonized, arrived in Cracow in 1453. For the next year he preached repentance and the renouncement of wealth and the immoral way of life. He also incited the people against the Jews. Influenced by his sermons, a few Cracovians took up the habit of the Reformed Franciscans, then called the Observants but known as the Bernardines in Poland. In 1453 Cardinal Zbigniew Oleśnicki built in Stradom a small timber church for this new monastic community, and soon after began building a large brick church. It was completed by Jan Długosz after Oleśnicki's death.

In 1655, while preparing to defend Cracow against the Swedes, Stefan Czarniecki gave orders to set fire to the Bernardine Church, which was located at the foot of Wawel Hill, so that the invaders could not use the church for their own protection. The beautiful statue of the Virgin and Child with St Anne, from Veit Stoss's workshop, and remnants of Mannerist tombs (now on the porch wall) are the only furnishings to have survived.

The new Baroque Church of the Bernardines was built between 1659 and 1680. Krzysztof Mieroszewski is believed to have been the architect. The marble shrine of Blessed Simon of Lipnica was erected in 1662 and the high altar between 1758 and 1766.

The 17th-century Baroque Bernardine Church

Częstochowa Seminary ❷⓿
Seminarium Częstochowskie

Bernardyńska 3. **Map** 3 C1 (6 D5).
[422 47 03. **[** 6, 8, 10, 18.
Chapel ☐ *by prior telephone arrangement only.*

In 1925 the Bishop of Częstochowa, Teodor Kubina, founded a seminary affiliated with the Faculty of Theology at the Jagiellonian University, for seminarists from his diocese. The monumental Modernist building was constructed between 1928 and 1930 to the designs of Zygmunt Gawlik and Franciszek Mączyński.

The façade is decorated with sculptures which were carved under the supervision of Xawery Dunikowski, one of the foremost Polish sculptors of the 20th century. The bas-relief at the top is particularly interesting. It shows Christ blessing the allegorical figure of Poland and the representatives of all social ranks, as well as the Virgin Mary accompanied by clergymen. The scene depicting a seminarist tempted by the devil, also on the façade, is worth noting.

Relief of a seminarist tempted by the devil, Częstochowa Seminary

Church of the Missionaries ❷❶
Kościół Misjonarzy

Stradomska 4. **Map** 3 C1 (6 E5).
[422 88 77. **[** 103, 124 **[** 6, 8, 10, 18. ☐ *2–7pm daily and during services.*

The missionaries were brought to Stradom in 1682 but built the Church of the Conversion of St Paul only in the years 1719 to 1728. The architect, Kacper Bażanka, was influenced in his design by two outstanding examples of Roman Baroque architecture. The interior of the Cracow church resembles that of Francesco Borromini's Church of the Magi at the Collegio di Propaganda Fide, and the

Baroque façade of the Church of the Missionaries

exterior is close to Sant' Andrea al Quirinale designed by Gianlorenzo Bernini. Some of the methods applied by Bażanka, such as the use of mirrors in the nave to direct reflected light onto the chapels, are characteristic of High Baroque. The church is regarded as one of the finest examples of 18th-century Baroque Polish architecture.

The same applies to the interior. Most altarpieces were painted by Tadeusz Kuntze and decorated with sculptures by Antoni Frączkiewicz.

Natural History Museum ❷❷
Muzeum Przyrodnicze

Św. Sebastiana 9/11. **Map** 3 D1 (6 E5). **[** 422 59 59. **[** 6, 8, 10. ☐ *10am–2pm Tue–Fri, 9am–1pm Sat–Sun.* 🖼

The core of the Natural History Museum was the collection of the Physiographic Commission of Cracow's Learned Society, established in 1865. It consisted mainly of stuffed birds and invertebrates. Today, the museum keeps numerous entomological specimens (insects) and pressed plants which can be found in Poland. A rhinoceros dating from the Pleistocene era, found in 1920 in Starunia, is a highlight of the collection.

Dietl Plantations ❷❸
Planty Dietlowskie

Map 3 D1 (6 E5, F4). **[** 128.
[19, 22.

The old river bed of the Vistula, from Stradom to Kazimierz, was filled in during the years 1878 to 1880 and transformed into a modern thoroughfare designed by Bolesław Malecki. It was a dual carriageway 1 km (0.6 mile) in length and 100 m (328 ft) wide, with a garden in the middle. The new scheme was named Planty Dietlowskie after Józef Dietl. This President of Cracow was first to advocate the filling in of the old Vistula bed which hindered the integration of Cracow with Kazimierz. Both sides of the avenue are lined with high tenement blocks and elegant public buildings, one of which is the PKO Bank built from 1922 to 1924.

Tree-lined avenue separating Dietl's dual carriageway

Franciscan Church ⓯

THE FRANCISCANS arrived in Cracow in 1237. The construction of the church was undertaken in 1255 as a foundation of Duke Bolesław the Chaste and his wife the Blessed Salomea. After the Swedish invasion, which caused much damage, the church was rebuilt in the Baroque style. The great fire of Cracow of 1850 damaged the church again. It was rebuilt partly in the Neo-Romanesque and partly in the Neo-Gothic style. The work of Stanisław Wyspiański on the interior decoration is of prime importance. Around 1900 this artist executed the Art Nouveau murals and designed a series of unusual stained-glass windows in expressive colours.

A 13th-century wall of the first church

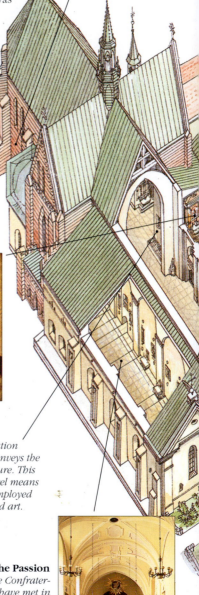

Blessed Salomea
Stanisław Wyspiański's stained glass in the north window of the choir shows the foundress of the church who rejected the ducal coronet before taking the habit of a Poor Clare nun.

★ Mater Dolorosa
This late Gothic image by Master Jerzy, of Mary surrounded by angels holding instruments of Christ's Passion, is much venerated.

★ Murals
The polychrome decoration features flowers and conveys the Franciscan love of nature. This work illustrates the novel means of artistic expression employed by Wyspiański in sacred art.

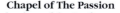

Chapel of The Passion
The brothers of the Confraternity of The Passion have met in this chapel since the end of the 16th century to conduct their rituals (see p52). Their liturgy is theatrical and evokes the spirit of Baroque devotion.

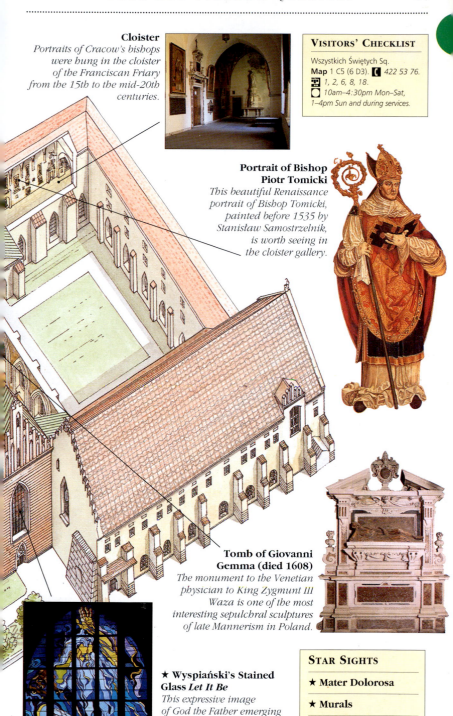

Cloister
Portraits of Cracow's bishops were hung in the cloister of the Franciscan Friary from the 15th to the mid-20th centuries.

VISITORS' CHECKLIST

Wszystkich Świętych Sq.
Map 1 C5 (6 D3). ☎ 422 53 76.
🚋 1, 2, 6, 8, 18.
◯ 10am–4:30pm Mon–Sat,
1–4pm Sun and during services.

Portrait of Bishop Piotr Tomicki
This beautiful Renaissance portrait of Bishop Tomicki, painted before 1535 by Stanisław Samostrzelnik, is worth seeing in the cloister gallery.

Tomb of Giovanni Gemma (died 1608)
The monument to the Venetian physician to King Zygmunt III Waza is one of the most interesting sepulchral sculptures of late Mannerism in Poland.

★ Wyspiański's Stained Glass *Let It Be*
This expressive image of God the Father emerging from the cosmic chaos was rendered using bold colours and sinuous, flowing Art Nouveau forms.

STAR SIGHTS

★ **Mater Dolorosa**

★ **Murals**

★ **Wyspiański's Stained Glass *Let It Be***

OLD QUARTER

In 1257 Duke Bolesław the Chaste gave Cracow her charter. This law was of key importance to the city as it determined local government and trade privileges, thus stimulating the city's future development. The charter stipulated strict rules for this development: a large, centrally located square, surrounded by a regular grid of streets, was to become the city centre. The

Coat of arms of Cracow in St Mary's Church

size of each plot determined the size of the houses. Although the architecture became ever more opulent, this urban scheme has survived almost intact. To this day the Old Quarter remains the heart of modern, fast developing Cracow. It is an area with a great concentration of important historic sights and other places for visitors to enjoy, including the restful Planty gardens.

SIGHTS AT A GLANCE

Churches
Church of St Anne pp108-9 **15**
Church of St John **23**
Church of St Mark **20**
Church of St Mary pp94-7 **1**
Church of the Holy Cross **32**
Church of the Dominican Nuns **33**
Church of the Reformed Franciscans **19**
Dominican Church pp116-7 **34**
Piarist Church **25**
St Adalbert's Church **9**
St Barbara's Church **3**

Historic Streets and Squares
Floriańska Street **30**
Market Square pp98-101 **4**
St John Street **22**
St Mary's Square **2**

Historic Monuments and Buildings
Barbican **27**
Collegium Nowodvorianum **14**
Collegium Novum **11**

Christopher Palace **5**
Episcopal Palace **10**
Jama Michalika Café **28**
Old Theatre **16**
Polish Academy of Skills **21**
Słowacki Theatre **31**
Statue of Copernicus **12**
Statue of Adam Mickiewicz **8**
St Florian's Gate and the City Wall Remnants **26**
Town Hall Tower **6**

KEY

▦	Street-by-Street map *pp90-91*
🅿	Parking

Museums and Galleries
"Bunker of Art" **18**
Cloth Hall pp102-3 **7**
Collegium Maius pp106-7 **13**
Czartoryski Museum pp112-3 **24**
Matejko House **29**
Palace of Art **17**

GETTING THERE
Tram and bus routes serve Podwale, Franciszkańska, Dominikańska, Westerplatte, Basztowa and Dunajewskiego streets, which all run along the Planty green belt.

0 metres   200
0 yards   200

◁ **Allegory of Poetry, a figure at the base of the Mickiewicz Statue**

Street-by-Street: Market Square

THE MARKET SQUARE (Rynek Główny) is located in the centre of Cracow's Old Quarter. Public, cultural and commercial activities have always concentrated around the Market Square. Museums and galleries of both old and modern art can be found here. Antiquarian shops selling works of art, bookshops and the best restaurants, cafés and bars are located in the houses around the square. Each summer nearly 30 street cafés open until the early hours. Flower stalls, street musicians, artists selling their works by the Cloth Hall and the general hustle and bustle made by the vendors of souvenirs and their clients all contribute to the lively atmospere of this place.

Market Square
This is the largest town square anywhere in Europe. The life of medieval Cracow was centred around the square **4**

★ Christopher Palace
The Museum of Cracow is housed in this palace **5**

★ Cloth Hall (Sukiennice)
Originally a market hall, the Sukiennice houses shops, cafés and the renowned Picture Gallery **7**

Town Hall Tower
The only remaining fragment of the Old Town Hall, the tower was remodelled after World War II **6**

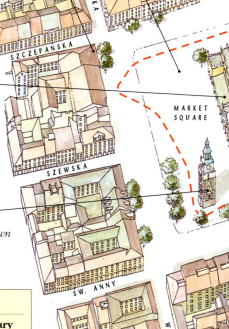

STAR SIGHTS

★ **Church of St Mary**

★ **Cloth Hall**

★ **Christopher Palace**

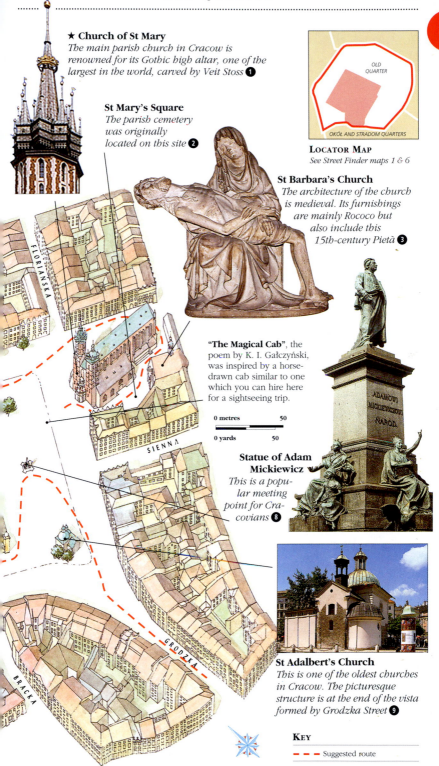

★ Church of St Mary
The main parish church in Cracow is renowned for its Gothic high altar, one of the largest in the world, carved by Veit Stoss ❶

St Mary's Square
The parish cemetery was originally located on this site ❷

LOCATOR MAP
See Street Finder maps 1 & 6

OLD QUARTER

OKÓŁ AND STRADOM QUARTERS

St Barbara's Church
The architecture of the church is medieval. Its furnishings are mainly Rococo but also include this 15th-century Pietà ❸

"The Magical Cab", the poem by K. I. Gałczyński, was inspired by a horse-drawn cab similar to one which you can hire here for a sightseeing trip.

| 0 metres | 50 |
| 0 yards | 50 |

Statue of Adam Mickiewicz
This is a popular meeting point for Cracovians ❽

ADAMOWI
MICKIEWICZOWI
NARÓD.

St Adalbert's Church
This is one of the oldest churches in Cracow. The picturesque structure is at the end of the vista formed by Grodzka Street ❾

KEY

– – – Suggested route

Church of St Mary ❶
Kościół Mariacki

See pp94–5.

St Mary's Square ❷
Plac Mariacki

Map 1 C4 (6 D2).

ST MARY'S SQUARE was once a parish grave-yard. It was relocated between 1796 and 1804. The statue of the Virgin Mary which was here originally is now in the Planty by Jagielloń-ska Street. The bas-relief attributed to Veit Stoss, which once decorated the Calvary Porch, has survived and is now in the National Museum. A copy can be seen on the wall at No.8 on the square. The prelate House and a Vicarage are among the houses in which original beamed ceilings and plasterwork have survived. St Barbara's Church is on the east side of the square, which also features a small water pump decorated with a figure of a student of medieval Cracow. It is a copy of a figure from the high altar in St Mary's *(see pp96–7)*.

A student of medieval Cracow, St Mary's Square

St Barbara's Church ❸
Kościół św. Barbary

Mały Rynek 8. **Map** 1 C4 (6 D2).
428 15 00. ☐ *during services only.*

ACCORDING to a legend St Barbara's Church was built using the bricks

that were left over from the construction of the Church of St Mary. St Barbara's actually dates from 1394 to 1399, which coincides with one of the stages in the construction of St Mary's. Between 1415 and 1536 sermons were delivered in Polish in the former church, and in German in the latter. During this period the patricians of Cracow were mostly German and it was only much later that they became a minority among the Polish population. In 1586 the church was taken over by the Jesuits. Piotr Skarga preached here and Jakub Wujek, the translator of the Bible, is buried here. Added on the outside in 1488 to 1518 is late Gothic chapel with a porch decorated with sculptures made by Veit Stoss' workshop. Furnishings date mostly from the 18th century but there is also an interesting early 15th-century Pietà in stone and a 15th-century crucifix on the high altar.

A Porch with Christ in Gethsemane at St Barbara's

Market Square ❹
Rynek Główny

See pp98–101.

Christopher Palace ❺
Pałac Krzysztofory

Rynek Główny 35. **Map** 1 C4 (6 D2).
Museum of Cracow 422 99 22.
☐ *9am–3:30pm Wed–Sun, 11am–6pm Thu. Closed 2nd Sat & Sun every month.* ☒ Ⓦ *www.krakow.pl*

THIS IS ONE of the oldest and most beautiful palaces in Cracow, with a magnificent arcaded courtyard. It was remodelled in 1682 to 1685 by Jacopo Solari for Kazimierz Wodzicki, one of the richest noblemen in Lesser Poland.

The Palace is named after St Christopher, whose 14th-century statue decorates the building. It houses the Museum of Cracow, which is dedicated to the history and culture of the city. Old documents, maces, gold artefacts from local workshops, memorabilia and paintings are all displayed in rooms decorated with stuccowork by Baldassare Fontana. In the cellars there is a café and the art gallery of the Cracow Group (Grupa Krakowska), first established in 1930 and revived in 1957.

THE KHAN OF CRACOW

Every year, on the Thursday ending the Corpus Christi octave, a parade led by the Khan proceeds from the Convent of the Premonstratensian Nuns in Zwierzyniec to the Market Square. The event commemorates the victory over the Tatars in 1287. On his way, the Khan strikes some spectators with his mace, a sign which is thought to bring good luck, especially to girls. At the Market Square the Khan receives a symbolic tribute. The original costume of the Khan, designed in 1904 by Stanisław Wyspiański, is now in the Museum of Cracow.

The Khan of Cracow

Town Hall Tower ❻
Wieża Ratuszowa

Rynek Główny 1. **Map** 1 C4 (6 D2).
Museum [📞] *422 99 22 ext. 218.*
[🕐] *May–Oct: 9am–6pm Wed,
9am–4pm Sat & Sun.* [♿]

UNTIL the early 19th century there were several public buildings on Market Square: the Town Hall, the Small Weigh-House, the Large Weigh-House and a pillory. The 70-m (230-ft) high Town Hall Tower is, unfortunately, the only structure to have survived. The Gothic Town Hall itself was remodelled many times and finally demolished in 1846. The present dome is Baroque. The tower houses a branch of the Museum of Cracow dedicated to the history of local government, as well as the Ludowy Theatre and café.

Cloth Hall ❼
Sukiennice

See pp102–3.

Statue of Adam Mickiewicz ❽
Pomnik Adama Mickiewicza

Rynek Główny. **Map** 1 C4 (6 D2).

THE STATUE of the poet Adam Mickiewicz has occasioned, as often happens in Cracow, many scandals. Although the famous artist Jan Matejko had submitted a project, the competition was won by Teodor Rygier. After the statue was unveiled in 1895 it raised such criticism that the artist was forced to replace some of the figures.

The allegorical figures accompanying the poet represent the Mother-

Church of St Adalbert on Market Square

land (a maiden facing Sienna Street), Education (an old man lecturing a boy), Poetry (a female figure playing a lute) and Patriotism or Courage (the soldier facing the Cloth Hall).

St Adalbert's Church ❾
Kościół św. Wojciecha

Rynek Główny 3. **Map** 1 C4 (6 D2).
Museum of the History of the Market Square (Muzeum Dziejów Rynku). [🕐] *May–Sep: 9am–4pm Mon–Tue & Thu–Fri, 9am–1pm Wed, 1–5pm Sun.* [♿]

THE SMALL church of St Adalbert is one of the oldest in Cracow. A legend tells that St Adalbert preached here before leaving on his missionary journey to try to convert the Prussians in 997.

The architecture of the church amalgamates several styles, from Romanesque and Gothic, through Renaissance and Baroque, to the modern interior design. This mixture reflects various stages in the development of the Market Square, whose museum is located in the basement. The display includes a cross-section of the ground beneath the square, as well as medieval water pipes and other objects found during the excavations carried out after World War II, which have also revealed the remnants of the building dating from the time of St Adalbert.

Statue of Adam Mickiewicz in Market Square

Church of St Mary ❶
Kościół Mariacki

ST MARY'S, or the Church of the Assumption of the Virgin, was the main parish church of Cracow's burghers. It is a Gothic basilica composed of nave, aisles and side chapels. There are two towers. The north tower was extended in the early 15th century and in 1478 topped with a spire by Matthias Heringk. It was the city's watch-tower. Inside the church there are many outstanding works of art, among which the magnificent high altar by Veit Stoss *(see pp96–7)* should be mentioned. Other furnishings include the Baroque pulpit, marble altars decorated with paintings by the Italian artist Giovanni Battista Pittoni, and Renaissance tombs in the chapels.

South Bell Tower

Bugle-call Tower
The spire is decorated with turrets and topped by a gilt crown. The famous bugle-call (hejnał) is played here at hourly intervals and broadcast at noon by the Polish radio.

The tracery of the Great West Window
was designed by Jan Matejko and the stained glass is by Józef Mehoffer and Stanisław Wyspiański.

The Porch (1750–2)
The late-Baroque porch was designed by Francesco Placidi. Carved busts of the Apostles and saints by Karol Hukan were added to the door panels in 1929.

Main entrance

TIMELINE

1221–2 Building of the Romanesque church		**1477–89** High altar completed		**1585** Choir stalls completed
	1392–7 Nave and aisles built			
1200	**1300**	**1400**	**1500**	**1600**
End of the 13th century Construction of the Gothic church begins	**1355–65** New choir built	**1478** North tower receives a spire	*Detail of the main door*	

Choir Stalls
The stalls were made in 1585 but the biblical scenes in low relief which decorate the backs of the seats date from 1635.

High Altar
(see pp96–7)

VISITORS' CHECKLIST

Mariacki Sq 5. **Map** 1 C4 (6 D2).
📞 422 05 21. 🕐 11:30am–
6pm Mon–Fri, 2–6pm Sun and
during services. 📷 ♿

The Montelupi Tomb
This Mannerist tomb of one of the richest Cracow families was made around 1600 in the workshop of Santi Gucci.

Visitors entrance

The murals on the walls and vault were designed and executed by Jan Matejko between 1890 and 1892.

★ The Slacker Crucifix (1496)
The figure of the suffering Christ, carved in stone by Veit Stoss, is the most expressive sculpture ever made by the artist.

★ The Ciborium
This Renaissance ciborium (receptacle for containing the Eucharist) at the entrance to the choir was made around 1552 to the design by Giovanni Maria Mosca.

STAR SIGHTS

★ The Ciborium

★ The Slacker Crucifix

Exploring St Mary's: The High Altar

THE HIGH ALTAR by Veit Stoss was made between 1477 and 1489. It is dedicated, like the church itself, to the Assumption of the Virgin Mary. The altar is a polyptych, some 11 m (36 ft) long and 12 m (39 ft) high. It was even higher originally. The iconography determined its composition. The shutters were closed throughout the liturgical year but opened during important church feasts. The treatment of the human figure is naturalistic, dynamic and dramatically expressive. The low reliefs and figures of saints are masterpieces of late Gothic art.

The Lamentation
The design of this particular panel was influenced by Netherlandish painting.

The Meeting of St Anne and St Joachim

The middle shutters are opened every day at noon.

The Capture of Christ

The Birth of the Virgin

The Crucifixion

The Three Maries at the Sepulchre

The Descent into Hell

The Presentation of the Virgin in the Temple

The Risen Christ appearing to Mary Magdalene

The Entombment

The Presentation of Christ in the Temple
In this scene the artist tries to recreate the interior of the temple.

Christ Among the Doctors
This scene testifies to Stoss' masterly depiction of the diverse physiognomies.

VEIT STOSS (WIT STWOSZ)

Veit Stoss (1447–1533), one of the greatest wood-carvers of the late Gothic age, was born in Horb am Neckar in Germany. He lived in Cracow from 1477 to 1496, where he was exempted from paying taxes by the City Council. He contributed here a number sculptural works.

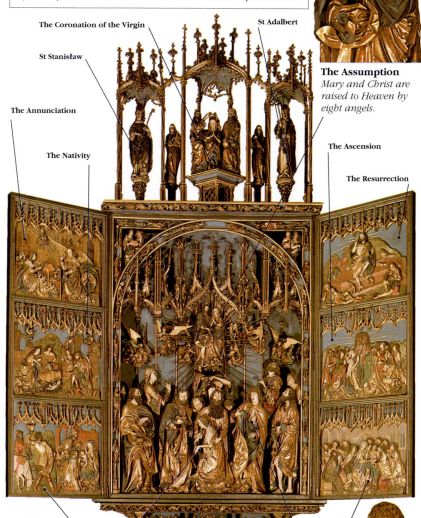

The Coronation of the Virgin

St Stanisław

St Adalbert

The Annunciation

The Nativity

The Assumption
Mary and Christ are raised to Heaven by eight angels.

The Ascension

The Resurrection

The Adoration of the Magi

Pentecost

Predella with the Tree of Jesse

The Death of the Virgin
The figure of the youthful Mary is one of the greatest sculptures ever made in Poland.

St John
Slightly hesitant, the saint is about to put a cape on the fainting Mary.

Market Square: North and West Sides ❹

THE CHARTER given to Cracow in 1257 determined the plan of the city. The square located in the middle of the medieval city has remained the centre of Cracow ever since. This square, some 200 m (656 ft) by 200 m (656 ft), is surrounded by a regular grid of streets, with three streets on each side. Only the off-the-grid location of the Church of St Mary, which pre-dates the charter, and Grodzka Street, with its funnel-like shape, vary the rigidity of the urban planning in this area. There were formerly many buildings in the square, but of those the Cloth Hall and the Town Hall Tower are the only ones to have survived. The square was a venue for many important events, including coronation ceremonies.

Deer House
This was once an inn. Johann Wolfgang von Goethe and Tsar Nicholas I both stayed here.

Horse House

Phoenix House

Kenc House

NORTH SIDE

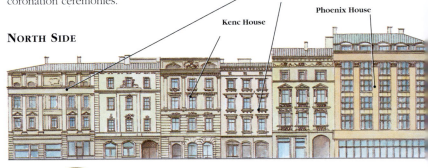

Palace of the Rams (Pałac Pod Baranami)
One of the most magnificent palaces owned by the Potocki family now houses a famous cabaret.

"PIWNICA POD BARANAMI" CABARET

The cabaret which is housed in the Palace of the Rams was established in 1956. Although it was originally intended to exist no longer than "five years, possibly even less", the cabaret has been active for more than 40 years and is one of Cracow's top attractions. Piotr Skrzynecki (1930–97) was the founder and heart and soul of the cabaret. Wiesław Dymny,

Ewa Demarczyk, Marek Grechuta, Krystyna Zachwatowicz, Zygmunt Konieczny, Leszek Wójtowicz, Anna Szałapak, Grzegorz Turnau and Zbigniew Preisner were among the best-known contributors and performers. The cabaret is a lively place full of poetry and music, joy and laughter.

Piotr Skrzynecki

WEST SIDE

Lamb House

House with a Tin Roof

Małachowski Palace

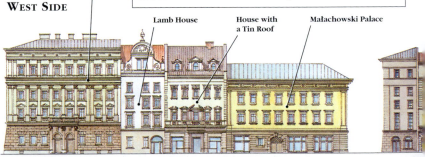

Betman House
This is also known as "Under the Beheaded" after a bas-relief which depicts the martyrdom of St John the Baptist.

LOCATOR MAP

Market Square: North and West sides

42 Market Square
belonged to the Boner family and in the 19th century to the renowned collector Feliks Manggha Jasieński.

Margrave's House
A former mint and presently a bank, the façade of this house features a splendid Rococo portal.

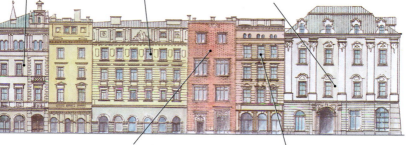

Red House

Eagle House (Dom Pod Orłem)
The basement of this fine Renaissance house formerly housed the Starmach Gallery of contemporary art.

House under Three Stars

Christopher Palace (Pałac Krzysztofory)
This palace houses the Museum of Cracow, among whose highlights is a gilded plaque, made in 1609, depicting St Eligius.

Spiš Palace (Pałac Spiski)
is home to the exclusive Hawełka Restaurant.

Market Square: South and East Sides ❹

THERE are many stories about the Market Square. According to one of the legends Cracow's pigeons are the enchanted knights of Duke Henryk Probus, who agreed to their metamorphosis in exchange for gold that he needed to secure papal acceptance for his coronation. The knights were supposed to regain their human form after the coronation. But the duke lost the gold and his knights are still awaiting the promised transformation. The legend about the two brothers who built the St Mary's towers is more popular. When the older mason completed the taller tower he stabbed his younger brother to death in order to prevent him from surpassing his work but then, remorseful, killed himself.

Madonna House (Dom Pod Obrazem)
Formerly the palace of a wealthy burgher family called Cellari, its façade is decorated with the Madonna painted in 1718.

SOUTH SIDE

Wierzynek Restaurant

Hetman's House (Kamienica Hetmańska)
The Baroque portal leads to shops on the ground floor, in which Gothic vaults with carved keystones have survived.

Potocki Palace (Pałac Potockich)
Behind the Neo-Classical façade the original interiors and a small arcaded courtyard have survived.

4 Market Square
This is one of a few houses with Art Nouveau decoration. It was added during the remodelling carried out in 1907–8 by Ludwik Wojtyczka.

Grey House (Kamienica Szara)

EAST SIDE

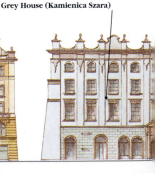

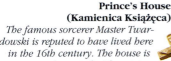

Prince's House (Kamienica Książęca)

The famous sorcerer Master Twardowski is reputed to have lived here in the 16th century. The house is decorated with a statue of St Giovanni da Capistrano.

Lanckoroński House, also known as 'Under the Evangelists', features the remnants of an 18th-century chapel on the first floor.

The pharmacy 'Under the Gold Crown' was once housed here. Its emblem has survived above the entrance.

Kromer House (Kamienica Kromerowska)

Canary House (Kamienica Pod Kanarkiem)

LOCATOR MAP

■ *Market Square: South and East sides*

The Raven House (Kamienica Pod Krukiem) is a seat of the International Centre of Culture and Cracow's Cultural Club.

Lizards House (Kamienica Pod Jaszczurami)
Gothic vaults have survived in this house, in which a student club is located.

Italian House (Dom Włoski)
The first Polish post office was housed here and coaches passed through this arch.

Boner House (Kamienica Bonerowska)
This is topped by a beautiful Mannerist parapet decorated with herms.

The Cloth Hall (Sukiennice) ❼

A mask from the parapet

THE CLOTH hall originated from a covered market. A stone structure protecting the stalls, with an internal passage, was probably here at the time of Kazimierz the Great. It was rebuilt to the design of Giovanni Maria Mosca following a fire in 1555, and remodelled entirely in 1875 by Tomasz Pryliński. The Gallery of 19th-century Polish Painting is housed here. The stalls sell a variety of souvenirs. The Noworolski Café, one of the best in Cracow, is a good place to relax after seeing the paintings.

Folly **(1894) by Władysław Podkowiński**
This Modernist painting aroused much controversy. It began a Symbolist phase in Podkowiński's career.

Four-in-hand **(1881) by Józef Chełmoński**
Paintings by Symbolists as well as Realists are exhibited alongside the Four-in-hand.

Roof with sunken rafters

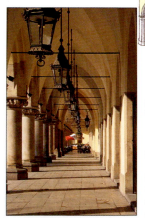

Entrance to stalls

Arcades
The side arcades and oriels were added during the rebuilding in 1875. The arcades echo the medieval architecture of Venice.

The Renaissance parapet is not only decorative but also offers protection from fire.

★ *Blue Hussars* by
Piotr Michałowski
*A separate room
is dedicated to the
work of Michałowski,
the foremost Polish
Romantic artist
who lived between
1800 and 1855.*

**Renaissance
parapet**

★ *Wernyhora*
by Jan Matejko
*Jan Matejko and
Henryk Siemiradzki
were both exponents
of 19th-century
history painting
which is displayed in
the room dominated
by Matejko's* Prussian
Homage.

**Entrance to Gallery
of Polish Painting**

The Death of Ellenai by Jacek Malczewski
*Characteristic of the artist's early work, which
was permeated by the memories of people who
had been imprisoned in Siberia, this painting
was inspired by a poem by Juliusz Słowacki.*

The Chocim Treaty by
Marcello Bacciarelli
*Late 18th- and early
19th-century Neo-
Classical paintings
are displayed in
the same room.*

John Paul II

Karol Wojtyła was born in 1920 in Wadowice *(see p156)*, but lived in Cracow for many years. He arrived here in 1938 to read Polish philology at the Jagiellonian University. The outbreak of World War II put a stop to his studies. During the war he worked for the Solvay Chemical Plant and was active in the underground Rhapsody Theatre. In 1942 he entered the underground theological Seminary. As a devout priest and artists' friend, he became very popular. Despite his election to the Apostolic See in 1978 his links with Cracow have remained as close as ever. He has returned here with his apostolic missions on many occasions, and is always received with a warm welcome.

Statue of John Paul II in the courtyard of the Episcopal Palace

Episcopal Palace ⑩

Pałac Biskupi

Franciszkańska 3. **Map** 1 C5 (5 C3). 429 74 14. 1,2, 6, 8, 14, 18. to the public.

First recorded in the 13th century, this is one of the oldest buildings in Cracow. It was damaged by fire and remodelled several times. Giovanni Maria Mosca contributed to the decoration. The present palace dates from the times of Bishop Piotr Tomicki (16th century) and Bishop Piotr Gembicki (17th century). A fire in 1850 caused extensive damage but the splendid furnishings have partly survived.

John Paul II lived here between 1964 and 1978. He was then the Archbishop of Cracow. A statue of him, made in 1980 by Ione Sensi Croci, is in the courtyard.

Collegium Novum ⑪

Gołębia 24. **Map** 1 B4 (5 C3). 422 10 33. 1, 2, 6, 8, 14, 15, 18.

The Collegium Novum replaced the Jerusalem College after it was destroyed by fire in the 19th century. The ruins were demolished between 1883 and 1887 and the new building constructed. Its official opening turned into a patriotic demonstration attended symbolically by delegations from all three parts of the partitioned Poland. According to the contemporary records the architect of the new building, Feliks Księżarski, intended to emulate the vernacular architecture, especially the crystal vaults and decoration of the Collegium Maius, but in fact he imitated German and Austrian models. The magnificent staircase is similar to the one in the Town Hall in Vienna. The College is the seat of the Rector of the Jagiellonian University. It also houses departmental offices, the bursary and the Great Hall where inauguration and graduation ceremonies take place. The Hall has a beamed and coffered ceiling and is decorated with portraits by Jan Matejko and other paintings.

Statue of Copernicus ⑫

Pomnik Mikołaja Kopernika

Gołębia. **Map** 1 B4 (5 C3). 1, 2, 6, 8, 14, 15, 18.

The statue of Nicolaus Copernicus was made in 1900 by Cyprian Godebski. The astronomer is represented as a young scholar holding an astrolabe. The statue was originally in the courtyard of the Collegium Maius, where it had replaced the well, but was moved to the present location in front of the Witkowski College in 1953. You may notice that the statue was intended to function as a fountain.

Collegium Maius ⑬

See pp106–7.

Collegium Nowodvorianum ⑭

Św. Anny 12. **Map** 1 B4 (5 C2). 422 0411. 4, 8, 14, 15. 103, 124, 502.

The Collegium Novodvorianum was founded by Bartłomiej Nowodworski, a Knight Hospitaller of St John, Secretary to the King and a warrior in the Battle of Lepanto. This foundation was a result of his bequest of 1617 to the Classes, one of the university colleges and the first secular secondary school in Cracow, established in 1586. The Collegium was built between

The Neo-Gothic building of the Collegium Novum

Arcaded courtyard of the Collegium Nowodvorianum

1636 and 1643 by Jan Leitner. A beautiful courtyard with arcades and a grand stairway is one of the best preserved Baroque buildings in Cracow. Departmental offices of the Collegium Medicum are housed here.

Church of St Anne ⑮
Kościół św. Anny

See pp108–9.

Old Theatre ⑯
Teatr Stary

Jagiellońska 1. **Map** 1 C4 (5 C2). 422 40 40. 4, 13, 15. 124, 502. **Museum** 11am–1pm Tue–Sat and one hour prior to performances.

THE OLD, or Modrzejewska Theatre is named after the great actress Helena Modrzejewska. The oldest theatre building in Poland, it has been in use continuously since 1798. It was remodelled in the Neo-Renaissance style between 1830 and 1843 by Tomasz Majewski and Karol Kremer. The next major rebuilding was undertaken in 1903 to 1905 by Franciszek Mączyński and Tadeusz Stryjeński. The reinforced concrete construction applied to the interior, and the exterior Art Nouveau decoration, both date from this time. The stucco frieze was made in 1906 by Józef Gardecki. The plaques on the Jagielloń-ska Street side commemorate the composer Władysław Żeleń-ski, the director Konrad Swinar-ski and the actor Wiktor Sadecki.

The Old Theatre is regarded as one of the best in Poland. Many outstanding directors worked here, including Zygmunt Hübner, Konrad Swinarski, Andrzej Wajda and Jerzy Jarocki.

A small museum dedicated to the history of the Theatre is on the ground floor, and in the basement there is the Mask café run by the actors.

Palace of Art ⑰
Pałac Sztuki

Plac Szczepański 4. **Map** 1 C4 (5 C2). 422 66 16. 4, 13, 15. 124, 502. Nov–Apr: 8am–6pm daily; May–Oct: 8am–8pm daily.

IN 1854 the Friends of the Fine Arts Society was established in Cracow for the encouragement of Polish art.

The Society embarked upon the organization of exhibitions by living artists, the acquisition of paintings and sculptures and the setting up of a comprehensive records office gathering documents of the history of Polish art in the 19th and early 20th centuries. The Art Nouveau building was designed by Franciszek Mączyński and modelled on the famous Secession Pavilion in Vienna. The finest Cracow artists worked on the decoration. Jacek Malczewski designed the frieze depicting the vicissitudes of fortune and the struggle of artistic genius. The sculptors Antoni Madeyski, Konstanty Laszczka and Teodor Rygier contributed busts of great Polish artists. A portico attached to the façade is topped with a statue of Apollo crowned with a sun halo. Exhibitions of 19th-century and contemporary art are held here.

"Bunker of Art" ⑱
„Bunkier Sztuki"

Plac Szczepański 3a. **Map** 1 C4 (5 C2). 423 12 43. 4, 13, 15. 124, 502. 11am–6pm Tue–Sun.

THIS GLOOMY building in the Socialist Realist style of the 1960s, constructed on the site of an Art Nouveau coffee house, is regarded as one of the ugliest in the city centre. However, in recent years it has become a venue for some of the most interesting exhibitions of contemporary art, including one-man shows of Polish and foreign artists.

Sculptural decoration on the Palace of Art

Collegium Maius 🕙

THE COLLEGIUM MAIUS is the oldest building within the Academy of Cracow (now the Jagiellonian University). It was constructed in the 15th century by amalgamating a number of townhouses. Lecture rooms and accommodation for professors were originally located here. In the 19th century the building housed the Jagiellonian Library. Between 1840 and 1870 the architects Karol Kremer, Feliks Księżarski and Hermann Bergman rebuilt the college in the Neo-Gothic style. After World War II the University Museum, established in 1867, was moved here.

★ Libraria
The Libraria was built in the 16th century as the College Library. Today it is a meeting place of the Senate and is decorated with portraits of rectors and professors of the University.

Oriel
This oriel window projecting from the Stuba Communis enlivens the austere exterior wall.

Porta Aurea (Golden Gate)

★ Stuba Communis
The Stuba Communis, or Common Room, served as the professors' refectory. The hall features a 14th-century statue of Kazimierz the Great and a 17th-century staircase made in Danzig.

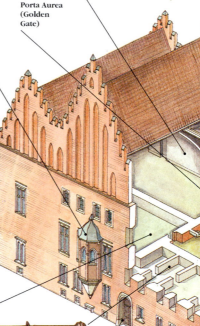

Entrance

University Treasury
The insignia of the rector, including a late 15th-century mace bequeathed by Bishop Zbigniew Oleśnicki and that of Queen Jadwiga from around 1405, are among the treasures.

Copernicus Room
The Room is dedicated to the great astronomer, who studied here between 1491 and 1495, thus rendering the Academy famous. The display features the so-called Jagiellonian armillary sphere made in 1510.

Cloister
The Gothic cloister, whose columns have a cut crystal-like decoration, is reminiscent of those in medieval Italian universities.

A lavishly inlaid door was originally in the Senior Room of the old Town Hall.

Green Hall
A collection of national memorabilia, including the piano that Frédéric Chopin played, can be visited by prior arrangement.

Rector's Stairs

★ Great Hall
The Great Hall features stalls used by the Senate during the ceremonies at which honorary degrees are conferred.

Chapel
The former apartment of John of Kęty, the Professor of Theology who became the patron saint of the Jagiellonian University, has been converted into a chapel, which is on the ground floor.

STAR SIGHT

★ Great Hall

★ Libraria

★ Stuba Communis

Church of St Anne ⑮

St Anne

A PROFESSOR of the Cracow Academy, John of Kęty (Jan Kanty) was already considered a saint at the time of his death in 1473, when he was buried in the Gothic Church of St Anne. Following his beatification, the Senate of the Academy commissioned Tylman van Gameren to build a new church. The construction began in 1689 under the supervision of Father Sebastian Piskorski. The Italian architect and sculptor Baldassare Fontana contributed the decoration and most of the furnishings, including the altars, between 1695 and 1703. He was assisted by the painters Carlo and Innocente Monti and Karl Dankwart. St Anne's, with its sumptuous interior, is considered to be a leading example of Baroque ecclesiastical architecture in Poland.

Nave
The architecture, sculpture and painting all contribute to the decoration of the nave and vault, and exemplify particularly well the wholeness of the Baroque design.

Procession Commemorating St John of Kęty, 1767
To mark the canonization of John of Kęty, a procession with his holy relics was held in Cracow. The saint's relics were carried into the Church of St Anne with great pomp and ceremony.

West Portal
The "scenographic" effect of the main entrance to the Church is a result of the superimposition of three portals, one within another.

STAR FEATURES

★ **High Altar**

★ **Shrine of St John of Kęty**

Main entrance

Gloria Domini
The dome fresco by Carlo and Innocente Monti is an allegory of triumphant Catholicism, represented as the true Christian faith.

★ High Altar
The high altar is decorated with sculptures by Baldassare Fontana and the altarpiece, depicting the Virgin and Child with Anne, is by the painter to Jan III Sobieski, Jerzy Eleuter Siemiginowski.

Pulpit
The angel supporting the pulpit was carved in 1727 by the Cracow artist Antoni Frączkiewicz, who was influenced by the art of Baldassare Fontana.

★ Shrine of St John of Kęty
The relics of the saint rest in a sarcophagus supported by four figures personifying the faculties of the Academy of Cracow: Theology, Philosophy, Law and Medicine.

Choir Stalls
The stalls are decorated with paintings by Szymon Czechowicz, a leading Polish painter of the 18th century.

Church of the Reformed Franciscans ⓳

Kościół Reformatów

Reformacka 4. **Map** 1 C4 (4 D1).
📞 422 06 23. 🚌 124, 152, 192.
🚊 4, 13, 15. ⏱ during services only.

THE CHURCH of the Reformed Franciscans was built between 1666 and 1672. The architecture and modest furnishings conform to the strict rule of the order. The altarpiece on the left, depicting St Kazimierz (Casimir), is an outstanding 17th-century work.

The specific microclimate within the crypt beneath the church causes the reposing corpses to undergo mummification. Those visitors seeking a shocking experience may request access.

Crucifix on the altar in the Church of St Mark

Church of St Mark ⓴

Kościół św. Marka

Św. Marka 10. **Map** 1 C4 (6 D1).
📞 422 21 78. 🚌 124, 152, 192.
🚊 3, 4, 5, 7, 13, 15, 19. ⏱ during services only.

THE EARLY GOTHIC church of the Monks of St Mark was founded in 1263 by Duke Bolesław the Chaste. It was remodelled a number of times and the interior acquired an early Baroque appearance in the first half of the 17th century. The high altar, with its lavish Mannerist ornamentation, was made in 1618 in the

workshop of Baltazar Kuncz. On the left is the 17th-century tomb of Blessed Michał Giedroyć (died 1485).

Polish Academy of Skills ㉑

Gmach Polskiej Akademii Umiejętności

Sławkowska 17. **Map** 1 C4 (6 D1).
📞 422 54 22. 🚌 124, 152, 192.
🚊 3, 4, 5, 7, 15, 19. ⏱ 9am–4pm Mon–Fri. 🖥 www.pau.krakow.pl.

THE BUILDING was constructed between 1857 and 1866 as the seat of the Academic Society of Cracow, which in 1872 became the Academy of Skills (from 1919 the Polish Academy of Skills), the first academic body to bring together scholars from all three parts of partitioned Poland. It was designed by Filip Pokutyński in the Neo-Renaissance style. The exterior is decorated with portrait medallions in low relief of people who made important contributions to Polish academic and cultural life. In the great hall, on the first floor, there are more portraits of eminent Academicians. A small meeting room

Entrance to the Neo-Classical Polish Academy of Skills

features an impressive coffered ceiling. The rich print collection includes works by Albrecht Dürer and Rembrandt.

St John Street ㉒

Ulica św. Jana

Map 1 C4 (6 D2). 🚌 124, 152, 192.
🚊 3, 4, 5, 7, 13, 15, 19.

THIS QUIET street leading away from the Market Square, and closed off at

Portal to the House of the Cistercian Abbots of Jędrzejów, 20 St John Street

its north end by the façade of the Piarist Church, is lined with some fine secular and ecclesiastic Baroque and Neo-Classical buildings.

The House of the Cistercian Abbots of Jędrzejów at No.20 is of particular interest. Remodelled in 1744 by Francesco Placidi, the house is decorated with a magnificent late Baroque portal featuring atlantes.

The Wodzicki Palace at No.11 was given a Neo-Classical façade by Ferdinand Nax after 1781. Around 1818 the Bernardine Friary was converted after a great deal of rebuilding.

Church of St John ㉓

Kościół św. Jana

Św. Jana 7. **Map** 1 C4 (6 D2). 𝄢 422 65 00. 🚌 124, 152, 192. 🚋 3, 4, 5, 7, 15, 19. ⭘ during services only.

T HE CHRONICLER Jan Długosz records that this church was founded in the 12th century. The Romanesque architecture has been lost through much remodelling. The Gothic buttresses still project from the exterior side walls, but the façade and the interior are Baroque. The high altar of 1730 is decorated with sculptures by Antoni Frączkiewicz and the 16th-century miraculous Madonna, the Refuge of Prisoners.

Czartoryski Museum ㉔

Muzeum Czartoryskich

See pp112–3.

Piarist Church ㉕

Kościół Pijarów

Pijarska 2. **Map** 1 C4 (6 D1). 𝄢 422 22 55. 🚌 124, 152, 192. 🚋 3, 4, 5, 7, 13, 15, 19. ⭘ during services only.

T HIS BAROQUE church was built between 1718 and 1728 probably to designs by Kacper Bażanka. The Rococo façade designed by Francesco Placidi was added in 1759 to

St Florian's Gate at the end of Floriańska Street

1761. Inside, the church is decorated with frescoes by a master of illusion, Franz Eckstein. The high altar painted on the wall is by the same artist, as is the fresco in the nave vault that glorifies the name of the Virgin Mary. The altars in the aisles feature 18th-century paintings by Szymon Czechowicz.

The crypt under the church is renowned for the decoration of Christ's Tomb, which usually alludes symbolically to patriotic themes, and is set up here every year during Holy Week. The crypt is also a venue for theatre performances and various exhibitions.

The Rococo façade of the 18th-century Piarist Church

St Florian's Gate and the City Wall Remnants ㉖

Brama Floriańska i Resztki Murów Miejskich

Map 2 D4 (6 E1). 🚌 124, 152, 192. 🚋 3, 4, 5, 7, 13, 15.

I N 1285 Duke Leszek the Black gave Cracow the right to have the city surrounded by walls. These fortifications developed during the following centuries, finally consisting of inner and outer moated walls and 47 towers. Eight fortified gates lead into the city. With the introduction of artillery, the defence system became redundant. Disused, it fell into disrepair by the end of the 18th century. The walls were dismantled early in the 19th century and later replaced by the Planty gardens *(see pp160–1)*. St Florian's Gate, dating possibly from the turn of the 13th century, and a small stretch of the adjoining walls have been saved, largely through the efforts of Professor Feliks Radwański. East of St Florian's Gate is the Haberdashers' Tower, and the towers of the Joiners and Carpenters are to the west.

Czartoryski Museum ㉔

A T THE CORE of the Czartoryski Museum is the collection assembled late in the 18th century by Princess Izabella Czartoryska. It was initially at Puławy, but partly moved to Paris following the 1830 November Uprising. In 1876 the collection was brought to Cracow, thanks to the efforts of Prince Władysław Czartoryski. It is located in three houses and the adjoining City Arsenal at St John Street. Works of art are displayed in period interiors which contribute to the museum's homely, intimate atmosphere.

Madonna and Child
By the Venetian Vincenzo Catena, this painting is a highlight of the Czartoryski's Italian collection.

Jesuit Saints
This fine bas-relief by the 17th-century Roman sculptor, Alessandro Algardi, depicts the Polish Jesuit, Stanisław Kostka, being admitted to the congregation of Jesuit saints.

GALLERY GUIDE
There is no gallery space on the ground floor. The first-floor display is dedicated to Polish history of the 14th-18th centuries as well as Western European decorative arts. The picture gallery is on the second floor.

Porcelain Figures
These two figures of a Polish nobleman and noblewoman were made in Meissen.

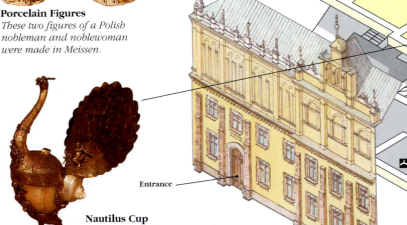

Entrance

Nautilus Cup
The museum collection is rich in decorative arts and includes this 17th-century drinking vessel made in Danzig (now Gdańsk) from a large shell.

★ **Lady with an Ermine**
by Leonardo da Vinci
This late 15th-century work
probably portrays Cecilia
Gallerani.

Portrait of a Boy by
Caspar Netscher
This sweet little portrait is one
of several paintings in the
collection by lesser Dutch
artists of the 17th century.

Second
floor

First
floor

★ **Landscape with the Good Samaritan**
by Rembrandt
One of the masterpieces in the collection of
Western painting, Rembrandt's treatment
of the natural world is breathtaking.

Landscape by **Alessandro**
Magnasco
This dramatic landscape is
characteristic of Italian
painting of the 18th century.

Ground
floor

STAR PAINTINGS

★ *Lady with an Ermine*

★ *Landscape with*
the Good Samaritan

KEY

Non-exhibition space

History of Poland
1300–1900

Decorative Arts of Western Europe

Picture Gallery

The impressive exterior of the Barbican

Barbican ㉗
Barbakan

Basztowa. **Map** 2 D3 (6 E1). 🚋 *3, 4, 5, 7, 13, 15.* 🚌 *124.*

THE BARBICAN, a round bastion, was constructed in 1498–1499 after King Jan Olbracht was defeated by the Turks in Bukowina, and further Turkish incursions were feared. It shows the changes that had been introduced to military architecture as a result of the rapid development of artillery. This relatively low structure projecting from the city walls with a considerable overhang enabled the defenders to fire with precision at the enemy from the loop-holes, positioned at different levels. The Barbican was originally surrounded by a moat and linked to St Florian's Gate by a corridor. It is the best preserved barbican in Europe.

Jama Michalika Café ㉘
Jama Michalika

Floriańska 45. **Map** 2 D4 (6 E1). 📞 *422 15 61.* 🚋 *3, 4, 5, 7, 13, 15.* 🚌 *124.* ⏰ *noon–midnight daily.* 🈲

IN 1895 Jan Michalik opened a patisserie near the Market Square. It became very popular with students of the Fine Arts School who called the place *jama* (grotto) for its lack of windows. Poets, writers and artists soon joined in and in 1905 established here the cabaret Zielony Balonik (The Green Balloon). The performances, based on texts by Tadeusz Boy-Żeleński, soon attracted a large audience. Satirical Christmas puppet shows, with marionettes by Ludwik Puget and Jan Szczepkowski, became particularly popular.
  In 1910 Michalik extended and redecorated the premises

to designs by Franciszek Mączyński. The main room received a glass ceiling. Karol Frycz designed the interior decoration, furniture and most of the stained glass in the Art Nouveau style.
  The café is still an inviting place where customers can go back in time and enjoy the atmosphere of the fin de siècle, as well as see the enduring puppet show.

Matejko House ㉙
Dom Matejki

Floriańska 41. **Map** 2 D4 (6 E1). 📞 *422 59 26.* 🚋 *3, 4, 5, 7, 13, 15.* 🚌 *124.* ⏰ *9am–3:30pm Tue & Thu, 11am–6pm Wed & Fri, 10am–3:30pm Sat & Sun.* 🈲

THE ARTIST Jan Matejko was born here in 1838, and in 1873 returned to live with his family. He rebuilt the house and added a new façade designed by Tomasz Pryliński in the Neo-Baroque style. After Matejko died in 1893 the house was transformed into a museum and opened to the public five years later. The statue of a hussar on horseback, on the ground floor, was part of Leon Wyczółkowski's design for the Matejko Monument. Private rooms on the first floor remained unchanged, and the second floor used for a display of the artist's works, which include cartoons for the murals in the Church of St Mary. His studio on the third floor is full of props and curiosities he collected. Pieces of old armour and instruments of torture excavated on the site of the old Town Hall are of particular interest.

Floriańska Street ㉚
Ulica Floriańska

Map 1 C4, 2 D4 (6 D2, 6 E1, 2). 🚋 *3, 5, 7, 13, 15, 19.* 🚌 *124.*

THIS STREET, leading from St Florian's Gate to the Market Square, formed part of the Royal Route which became fully established after the court moved from Cracow

The interior of the Jama Michalika Café

Visitors in front of St Florian's Gate at Floriańska Street

to Warsaw. The Royal Route was often used by a sovereign arriving for a coronation, and again when his body was taken in procession for the funeral at Wawel. In the 19th century Floriańska was the busiest street in Cracow, with trams introduced in 1881. Medieval walls have survived in most houses, but the original architecture has been lost through later remodelling. More storeys and new eclectic façades were added to most buildings early in the 20th century, when Floriańska gained its present appearance.

Słowacki Theatre ③

Teatr im. Juliusza Słowackiego

Pl. Świętego Ducha 1. **Map** 2 D4 (6 E2). 422 45 47. 2, 4, 5, 7, 8, 13, 15. 124.

THE PROPOSAL for a new theatre in Cracow, one which would replace the small and dilapidated Old Theatre, was put forward in 1872. Jan Zawiejski submitted the design and was put in charge of the works which were to be financed entirely through donations. The foundation stone was laid in 1891, and the theatre opened in 1893. Zawiejski designed an opulent building in which vernacular elements, such as the parapet inspired by the Cloth Hall, and foreign influences were blended into an eclectic whole. Allegorical sculptures decorate the exterior of the theatre.

The opulent interior features a grand staircase decorated with stuccowork by Alfred Putz. The four-tiered auditorium can seat up to 900 people. The stage curtain, one of the major attractions, was painted by Henryk Siemiradzki. It depicts Apollo striking an accord between Beauty and Love, surrounded by muses as well as other allegorical figures which represent Art drawing inspiration from man's fate.

Church of the Holy Cross ③

Kościół św. Krzyża

Świętego Krzyża 23. **Map** 2 D4 (6 E3). 422 62 47. 2, 4, 5, 7, 8, 15. 124. during services only.

THE GOTHIC church of the Order of the Holy Cross was built in two stages. The construction of the choir began immediately after 1300. The main nave and tower date from the first half of the 14th century. The interior is extremely well preserved and the nave impresses with its intricate pattern of vaulting ribs, supported on a single, round pillar. Among its furnishings, the Gothic font made in 1423 by Jan Freudenthal and the late Renaissance triptych in the Węgrzyn Chapel (next to the porch) are of particular interest. There are also Baroque altars and stalls. A number of memorial plaques of famous sculptors, active at the turn of the 19th century, are also noteworthy.

The Church of the Holy Cross

Church of the Dominican Nuns ③

Kościół Dominikanek

Mikołajska 21. **Map** 2 D4 (6 E3). 422 79 25. 2, 3, 7, 8, 10. during services only.

THE CHURCH, dedicated to the Virgin Mary, Queen of Snow, was founded in 1632–1634 by Anna Lubomirska. Prior to the church, a fortified manor of Albert, Cracow's *wójt* (chief officer) was on this site in the 14th century. As a result of Albert's revolt against King Władysław the Short, a new building for the local government was erected. The latter was converted in the 1620s into a convent for the Dominican nuns. The church contains a miraculous 17th-century icon of the Virgin.

Dominican Church ③

Kościół Dominikanów

See pp116–7.

The eclectic façade of the Słowacki Theatre

Dominican Church 34

THE DOMINICANS began the construction of a new church in 1250. It contained the shrine of St Jacek, a place of mass pilgrimage. Opulent mausolea, modelled on the Zygmunt Chapel at Wawel, were added in the 17th century by noble families, and in the 18th century the church was furnished with late

Angel in the Chapel of the Virgin Mary of the Rosary

Baroque altars. The fire of Cracow in 1850 destroyed the church almost completely. It was rebuilt by 1872 and today is an important evangelical centre which attracts masses of the faithful.

Cloister
The Gothic cloister was a burial place of burghers whose memorial plaques and tombs can still be seen here.

★ Zbaraski Chapel
The fine decoration of the chapel, built in 1627 to 1633 by the Castelli artists, is in sharp contrast with the monumental forms of the altar and tombs in black marble.

Crowstep gable

The Lubomirski Chapel displays lovely paintings and sculptures.

Tomb of General Jan Skrzynecki (died 1860)
This beautiful monument carved by Władysław Oleszczyński commemorates the hero of the November Uprising of 1830.

★ Shrine of St Jacek
The Renaissance Chapel of St Jacek was rebuilt around 1700 by Baldassare Fontana, who also designed the magnificent monument. The chapel is decorated with paintings by Tommaso Dolabella.

The memorial plaque of Filippo Buonacorsi (Callimachus) (died 1496) honours the great humanist at the Polish royal court *(see p43)*.

Chapel of the Virgin Mary of the Rosary
In 1621 the icon of the Virgin of the Rosary was carried in the procession in order to secure, through prayers, victory over the Turks at Chocim.

The Myszkowski Chapel
This was built between 1603 and 1614 by masters from Santi Gucci's circle, using marble from the Świętokrzyskie (Holy Cross) Mountains. Portrait busts of the Myszkowskis form part of the splendid decoration of the dome.

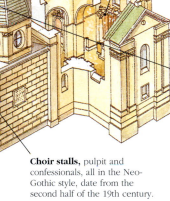

Choir stalls, pulpit and confessionals, all in the Neo-Gothic style, date from the second half of the 19th century.

Tomb of Prospero Provano
The monument of this salt magnate (died 1584) is one of the finest Polish sculptural works of circa 1600. It is located next to the Myszkowski Chapel.

KAZIMIERZ QUARTER

A sepulchral matzeva

THE TOWN of Kazimierz near Cracow was founded in 1335 by Kazimierz (Casimir) the Great. With its own Town Hall and a defence wall, Kazimierz competed with the capital in position and wealth. The king built two large churches, St Catherine's and Corpus Christi, and planned to establish a university here. After King Jan Olbracht had moved the Jewish population here from Cracow in the late 15th century, the separate nature of Kazimierz became more pronounced. The town was soon to become a leading centre of Jewish culture. Although Kazimierz was integrated administratively into Cracow in 1791, the distinctive character of this quarter is still evident. With narow streets lined with low buildings, it seems to belong to a different world. It bears witness to centuries of peaceful coexistence of two nations, Jewish and Polish. Magnificent sacred architecture of both religions can be seen as further confirmation of this symbiosis.

SIGHTS AT A GLANCE

Churches
Church of the Order
  of St John of God **11**
Church of St Catherine **12**
Corpus Christi Church **8**
Paulite Church
  "On the Rock" **13**

Historic Buildings
Hospital of the Order
  of St John of God **10**
Kazimierz Town Hall **9**

Historic Cemeteries
New Jewish Cemetery **7**
Remu'h Cemetery **6**

Synagogues
Isaac's Synagogue **2**
High Synagogue **3**
Old Synagogue **4**
Remu'h Synagogue **5**
Tempel Synagogue **1**

GETTING THERE
Trams 3, 9, 11 and 13 stop at Starowiślna Street in the Jewish Quarter. Trams 6, 8 and 10, which stop at Krakowska Street, are best for the major churches.

KEY

(red)	Street-by-Street map *pp120–1*
P	Parking
(police)	Police station

◁ **Bimah in the Old Synagogue**

Street-by-Street: Szeroka Street Area

THE JEWISH QUARTER was located in the east part of Kazimierz and concentrated first around Szeroka Street, then Libusza Square, which was later known as New Square. As well as the Jews displaced here in the late 15th century from Cracow, Czech and German refugees also came to live in Kazimierz. The Jewish community had its own jurisdiction and culture, and was never totally assimilated with the Poles. Many synagogues, baths, schools and cemeteries were established in Kazimierz, which became an active centre of Judaic culture and learning. The Nazis annihilated this unique world. Recently, however, a number of art galleries and restaurants have been opened here, which evoke the past.

Tempel Synagogue
The decoration of this synagogue, built in the Neo-Renaissance style, was influenced by Moorish art ①

JEWISH TOMBS

The signs carved on tombs convey symbolic meanings. The grave of a rabbi is indicated by hands joined in prayer. Basins and jugs for the ritual ablution of hands can be found on graves of the Levites. Three interlaced snakes feature on the grave of a physician, and a crown of knowledge on that of a learned man. A lion or a six-pointed star of David identify a descendant of Judah.

0 metres	50
0 yards	50

KEY

– – – Suggested route

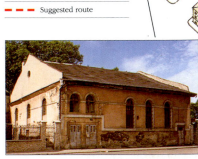

The Kupa Synagogue was built in the 17th century, financed by the Kahal of Kazimierz. It was remodelled many times and was also used for non-religious purposes. It is now disused and neglected.

★ Remu'h Cemetery
The Wailing Wall commemorates the tragic fate of the Jews from Cracow during World War II ❻

LOCATOR MAP
See Street Finder map 4

Bath (mikvah)   **Poper Synagogue**

DAJWÓR

Remu'h Synagogue
This synagogue is dedicated to the rabbi Remu'h, who was reputed to be a miracle worker. His grave is still venerated by pious Jewish pilgrims ❺

SZEROKA

Synagogue on the Hill

Isaak's Synagogue
The stuccowork in this Baroque synagogue is of great interest ❷

High Synagogue
With its late Gothic architecture and Renaissance decoration, this is one of Cracow's most picturesque synagogues ❸

★ Old Synagogue
This menorah is among the treasures in Poland's oldest synagogue. The building was destroyed by the Nazis, and later painstakingly restored ❹

STAR SIGHTS

★ **Old Synagogue**

★ **Remu'h Cemetery**

Tempel Synagogue ❶
Synagoga Tempel

Miodowa 24. **Map** 4 D1 (6 F5). 🚋 *3, 9, 11, 13.* 🚌 *103.* ⭕ *by appointment only, phone* 📞 *429 57 35.*

THE MOST recent of all the synagogues in Kazimierz, the Tempel, also known as the Progressive Synagogue, was built in the Neo-Renaissance style between 1860 and 1862. It is used by non-orthodox Jews. Inside note the stained glass and period decoration.

Façade of Isaak's Synagogue

Isaak's Synagogue ❷
Bożnica Izaaka

Kupa 18. **Map** 4 D1. 📞 *430 55 77.* 🚋 *3, 8, 9, 11, 13.* 🚌 *103.* ⭕ *9am–7pm Mon–Sat.* ⭕ *public hols.*

THIS SYNAGOGUE was built between 1638 and 1644 as a foundation of Izaak Jakubowicz, an elder of the Jewish community. Inside, the plaster work by Giovanni Battista Falconi has survived in a large nave with a barrel vault. The Jewish Education Centre is housed here.

High Synagogue ❸
Bożnica Wysoka

Józefa 38. **Map** 4 D1. 🚋 *3, 6, 8, 9, 10, 11, 13.*

THIS SYNAGOGUE dates from 1556 to 1563. It is a picturesque structure supported by buttresses. A Renaissance portal is worth noting. Only a few furnishings have survived, including a money box and the remains of an altar. The Studio for the Restoration of Monuments is located here.

Old Synagogue ❹
Synagoga Stara

Szeroka 24. **Map** 4 D1. 🚋 *3, 6, 9, 13.* **Jewish Museum (a branch of the Museum of Cracow).** 📞 *422 09 62.* ⭕ *9am–3:30pm Wed–Thu, 11am–6pm Fri–Sun.* ⭕ *first Sat & Sun of each month.* 📷

THE OLD SYNAGOGUE was used in the past as a temple and was also a seat of the Kahal and other offices of the Jewish community. Religious and social life was concentrated here. The synagogue houses the Jewish Museum, which is dedicated to the history and culture of Cracow's Jews.

The brick building goes back to the mid-15th or beginning of the 16th century. Its present appearance is the result of a remodelling carried out by Matteo Gucci in 1557–70. The parapet, and two-aisled Gothic interior with ribbed vaulting supported by slender columns, all date from this period.

The hall used for prayer is almost bare, in accordance with the rule of the Jewish religion. The bimah, an elevated platform with an iron balustrade used for readings from the Torah, is the only piece of furnishing.

The east wall features the aron hakodesh, an ornamental shrine for the Torah Scrolls.

Entrance to the Remu'h Synagogue and Cemetery

Remu'h Synagogue ❺
Bożnica Remuh

Szeroka 40. **Map** 4 D1. 📞 *422 12 74.* 🚋 *3, 9, 11, 13.* ⭕ *by appointment only.* 🚫

ONE of the two still active synagogues, the Remu'h temple is used by orthodox Jews. It was founded by Israel Isserles Auerbach around 1553 and named after his son, the great author, philosopher and reputed miracle worker, Rabbi Moses Remu'h.

Inside, the bimah and an ornamental aron hakodesh are worth noting.

Remu'h Cemetery ❻
Cmentarz Remuh

Szeroka 40. **Map** 4 D1. 📞 *422 12 74.* 🚋 *3, 9, 11, 13.* ⭕ *9am–4pm Mon–Fri.*

THE REMU'H CEMETERY, established in 1533, is one

Hall of Prayers in the Old Synagogue

of the very few Jewish cemeteries in Europe with so many tombs, both gravestones (matzeva) and sarcophagi. Their rich floral and animal decoration is of particular interest.

The cemetery was almost entirely destroyed during World War II. However, the tomb of Remu'h, which still attracts pilgrims from all over the world, was spared from Nazi destruction. Over 700 tombs have been excavated since World War II. They were probably buried during the Swedish invasion in the early 18th century. The Wailing Wall by the entrance was made using fragments of tombstones destroyed during the war.

New Jewish Cemetery **7**
Nowy Cmentarz Żydowski

Miodowa 55. **Map** 4 E1. 🚋 *3, 9, 11, 13.*

E STABLISHED in the early 19th century, this cemetery is a burial place of the great Jews of Cracow of the 19th and 20th centuries. All Kazimierz's rabbis and many of the great benefactors of Cracow rest here. They include Józef Oettinger and Józef Rosenblatt (professors of the Jagiellonian University), Józef Sare (the city President), and Maurycy Gotlieb (one of the foremost Polish artists of the 19th century).

Corpus Christi Church **8**
Kościół Bożego Ciała

Bożego Ciała 25. **Map** 4 D2. 🚋 *6, 8, 10.* ⬤ *9am–noon and 1:30–7pm Mon–Sat and during services.*

T HE CORPUS CHRISTI church was built on marshland where, according to legend, a monstrance with the Eucharist stolen from the Collegiate Church of All Saints had been found. A mysterious light shining in the darkness indicated the site where the profaned monstrance had been abandoned. The

Town Hall in Kazimierz, housing the Ethnographical Museum

construction of the church, founded by King Kazimierz the Great, began in 1340 and was completed in the early 15th century. As a parish church it was bestowed by local burghers with sumptuous furnishings, most of which have survived.

In 1634 to 1637 the high altar was decorated with a painting of *The Nativity* by Tommaso Dolabella, court artist to Zygmunt III Waza. The large stalls for monks, matching the altar, were made in 1632. An opulent 17th-century stone altarpiece with the relics of Blessed Stanisław Kazimierczyk is located in the north aisle.

The altar of Christ the Redeemer, decorated with sculptures by Anton Gegenbaur, is also worth noting. A slab in the north aisle indicates the burial place of the architect Bartolomeo Berecci, who was assassinated in 1537.

Image of the Madonna in the Church of Corpus Christi

Kazimierz Town Hall **9**
Ratusz kazimierski

Pl. Wolnica 1. **Map** 4 D2. 📞 *430 60 23.* 🚌 *502.* 🚋 *3, 6, 8, 10.* **Ethno-graphical Museum** ⬤ *10am–6pm Mon, 10am–3pm Wed–Sun.* 🎟

T HE TOWN HALL was the seat of local government until 1791. The oldest parts of the building date back to 1414, the year of its foundation. After much remodelling, the north section of the Town Hall was completed in 1620. The crenellated parapet is the most interesting feature. The south section of the Town Hall was added in 1875 to 1877 by Filip Pokutyński.

The Ethnographic Museum was established here in 1947. Its rich collection includes costumes from Lesser Poland and Silesia, traditional Cracovian Christmas cribs, folk art and musical instruments.

Hospital of the Order of St John of God **10**
Szpital Bonifratrów

Trynitarska 11. **Map** 4 D6. 📞 *430 55 10.* 🚌 *C.* 🚋 *6, 8, 10.*

T HIS MONUMENTAL building was constructed between 1897 and 1906 to commemorate the 50th anniversary of the reign of the Emperor Franz Joseph. It was designed by Teodor Talowski in the late Modernist style. The façade, with its central bay projection decorated with the Crucifix and bust of St John of God, is of particular interest.

Church of the Order of St John of God, detail of the façade

Church of the Order of St John of God ⓫

Kościół Bonifratrów

Krakowska 48. **Map** 4 D2.
📞 430 61 22. 🚌 502. 🚊 6, 8, 10.
◯ during services only.

THIS INTERESTING Baroque church was built between 1741 and 1758 to designs by Francesco Placidi. A rather small structure is hidden behind a monumental, wavy façade inspired by the best designs of the leading Roman Baroque architect, Francesco Borromini. The façade, intended to be viewed at an angle, closes the vista formed by Krakowska Street. Inside, the excellent trompe l'oeil painting of the vault was made by Josef Piltz of Moravia in 1757–1758. It depicts St John of Matha buying slaves from the heathens. The side altars, with their architectural forms painted directly on the walls, are unusual. They are decorated with Rococo paintings, among which the effigy of St Cajetan is worth noting.

Church of St Catherine ⓬

Kościół św. Katarzyny

Augustiańska 7. **Map** 4 D2.
📞 430 62 42. 🚌 124, 128. 🚊 6, 8, 10, 18, 19, 22. ◯ during services only.

ACCORDING to the chronicler Jan Długosz, the Church of St Catherine was built by King Kazimierz the Great as a penance for murdering Father Marcin Baryczka in 1349. Baryczka delivered a document issued by bishops excommunicating the king. The king repaid the messenger with the order to have Baryczka drowned in the Vistula. However, the construction of the church possibly began in 1343 and continued until the early 16th century. Regarded as one of the most beautiful Gothic churches in Cracow, its furnishings were lost in the 19th century when it was briefly transformed into a warehouse. The Baroque high altar, decorated

Fresco in the cloister in the Church of St Catherine

with the *Mystical Marriage of St Catherine* by Andrea Venesta, 1634, has survived. Worth visiting is the Gothic cloister which dates from the time of Kazimierz the Great. It features late Gothic murals and large 17th-century paintings. Two chapels adjoin the cloister: one houses the miraculous *Madonna of Consolation* and the other the relics of Blessed Isaiah Boner.

Paulite Church "On the Rock" ⓭

Kościół Paulinów Na Skałce

Skałeczna 15. **Map** 3 C2.
📞 421 74 18. 🚌 124, 128. 🚊 6, 8, 10, 18, 19, 22. ◯ 9am–4pm Mon–Sat and during services. **The Crypt** ◯ 9am–noon and 1:30pm–3pm Mon–Sat. 📷

A SMALL church of St Michael "On the Rock" was recorded already in the 11th century. This was the site where Bishop Stanisław of Szczepanów, later canonized, was murdered (*see pp20–21*). In the 14th century this small Romanesque church was replaced by a large Gothic church founded by Kazimierz the Great. Four hundred years later it was in danger of collapsing. It was, therefore, rebuilt in the late Baroque style, between 1733 and 1742. The design by Anton Gerhard Müntzer was modified by Antonio Solari. The uniform furnishings all date from the 1740s. A small font by the church is decorated with a statue of St Stanisław, made in 1731. The tormentors of the saint, who are said to have quartered his body, threw his cut-off finger into the font. The water is reputed to have healing properties ever since.

Paulite Church and Monastery "On the Rock"

The Crypt in the Church "On the Rock"

Jan długosz, the great Polish historian of the Middle Ages, was buried in the crypt beneath the Church "On the Rock" in 1480. In 1876 it was decided to transform the crypt into a national pantheon for the burial of those who had made important contributions to Polish culture. The architect Teofil Żebrawski remodelled the crypt, transform-

Pantheon in the Church "On the Rock"

ing it into a gallery with a separate chapel housing the altar. Side recesses, three on each side, were designed to house the sarcophagi. The stained-glass window above the altar depicts the Madonna of Częstochowa, the Queen of Poland. Coats of arms of provinces of the Polish-Lithuanian Commonwealth were painted on the vault.

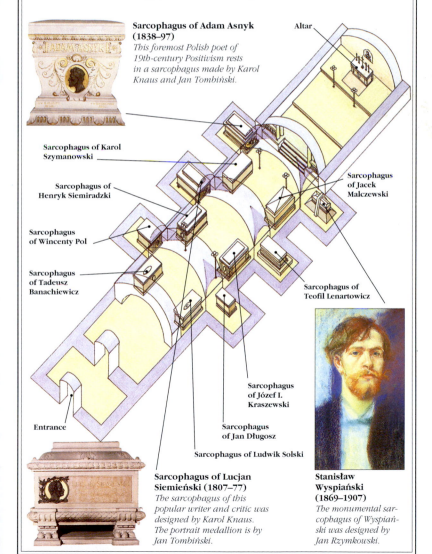

Sarcophagus of Adam Asnyk (1838–97)
This foremost Polish poet of 19th-century Positivism rests in a sarcophagus made by Karol Knaus and Jan Tombiński.

Altar

Sarcophagus of Karol Szymanowski

Sarcophagus of Henryk Siemiradzki

Sarcophagus of Wincenty Pol

Sarcophagus of Tadeusz Banachiewicz

Sarcophagus of Jacek Malczewski

Sarcophagus of Teofil Lenartowicz

Sarcophagus of Józef I. Kraszewski

Entrance

Sarcophagus of Jan Długosz

Sarcophagus of Ludwik Solski

Sarcophagus of Lucjan Siemieński (1807–77)
The sarcophagus of this popular writer and critic was designed by Karol Knaus. The portrait medallion is by Jan Tombiński.

Stanisław Wyspiański (1869–1907)
The monumental sarcophagus of Wyspiański was designed by Jan Rzymkowski.

WESOŁA, KLEPARZ AND BISKUPIE

A NUMBER of settlements developed around Cracow over the centuries. They were linked culturally and economically with Cracow but were independently administered. As there were no specific boundaries between them and land ownership often changed, the settlements north and east of the city walls developed to constitute a complex urban mosaic, and included: Przedmieście Mikołajskie, the royal town of Kleparz, and the privately owned Wesoła, Lubicz and Biskupie. They all

Statue of St Florian, St Florian's Church

looked like small towns. Imposing churches and a few palaces were surrounded by irregularly scattered residential timber buildings. Merchants and craftsmen who were active here avoided paying taxes to the Town Hall, thus contributing to the economic decline of Cracow. As a result, in 1791 the City Council decided to incorporate these quarters into Cracow. This part of the city saw the greatest surge in building activity during the great development of Cracow in the second half of the 19th century.

SIGHTS AT A GLANCE

Historic Monuments and Buildings
Academy of Fine Arts ⑫
Astronomical
 Observatory ⑥
Cracow Main Railway
 Station ⑧
Globe House ⑮
Grunwald Monument ⑩
National Bank
 of Poland ⑪
Polish State Railways
 Headquarters ⑬
Society of Physicians ②

Churches and Monasteries
Church of the Discalced
 Carmelite Nuns ⑤
Church of the Immaculate
 Conception of the Virgin
 Mary ④

Church of the Nuns
 of the Visitation ⑯
Church of St Nicholas ①
Church of St Vincent
 de Paul ⑭

Jesuit Church pp132–3 ③
St Florian's Church ⑨

Historic Parks
Jagiellonian University
 Botanical Gardens ⑦

GETTING THERE
Tram routes 3, 4, 5, 7, 10, 15, 19 and bus routes 124 and 502 all serve Basztowa Street. Tram routes 2, 3, 7, 10 and 19 serve Westerplatte Street.

KEY

▮	Street-by-Street map *pp128–9*
▮	Street-by-Street map *pp134–5*
P	Parking
🚏	Coach station
🚌	Bus depot
⊠	Post office
i	Tourist information

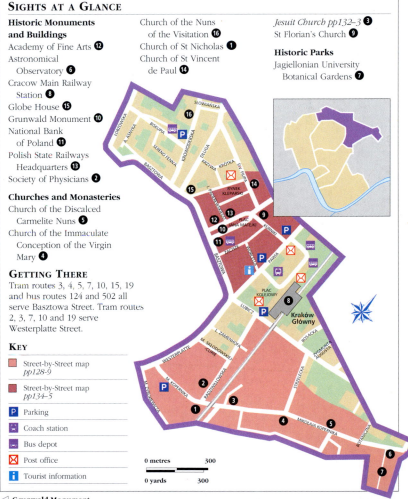

◁ **Grunwald Monument**

Street-by-Street: Along Kopernika Street

Wᴇsᴏᴌᴀ Quarter, originally a small settlement by the Romanesque Church of St Nicholas, developed along the old route to Mogiła, which is today Kopernika Street (ulica Mikołaja Kopernika). Its skyline was dominated by churches, monasteries and suburban residences of the nobility, set in well kept gardens. In the 19th century a number of university buildings, mostly hospitals belonging to the Medical School, were built here. Some of these buildings display interesting architectural forms.

★ **Jesuit Church**
This is one of the most interesting examples of modern ecclesiastical architecture ❸

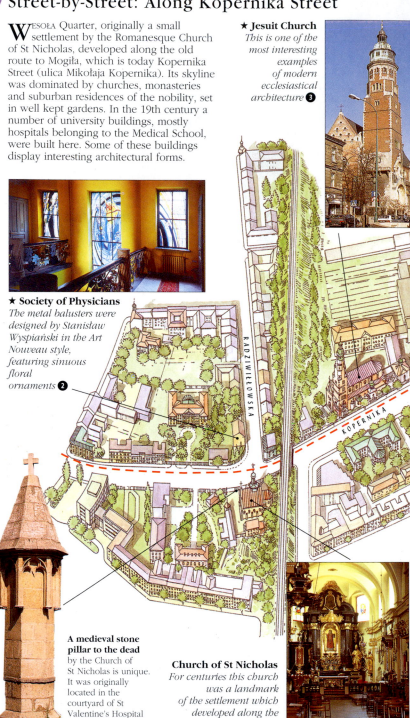

★ **Society of Physicians**
The metal balusters were designed by Stanisław Wyspiański in the Art Nouveau style, featuring sinuous floral ornaments ❷

A medieval stone pillar to the dead
by the Church of St Nicholas is unique. It was originally located in the courtyard of St Valentine's Hospital in Kleparz.

Church of St Nicholas
For centuries this church was a landmark of the settlement which developed along the Cracow-Mogiła route ❶

RADZIWIŁŁOWSKA

KOPERNIKA

Kopernika Street, lined densely with trees, is one of the most beautiful streets in Cracow.

LOCATOR MAP
See Street Finder maps 1 and 3

Church of the Discalced Carmelite Nuns
The Baroque façade, one of the most beautiful in Cracow, is worth seeing ❺

Astronomical Observatory
Belonging to the Jagiellonian University, with its elegant architecture and location next to the Botanical Gardens, this observatory looks more like a Neo-Classical villa than a university building ❻

Jagiellonian University Botanical Gardens
Exotic and local flora make the gardens a favourite place for days out ❼

Church of the Immaculate Conception of the Virgin Mary
The entrance to the Baroque interior is through this monumental portal ❹

KEY

- - - Suggested route

STAR SIGHTS

★ **Society of Physicians**

★ **Jesuit Church**

0 metres   50
0 yards   50

**Madonna and Child with Saints
Adalbert and Stanisław**

Church of St Nicholas ❶
Kościół św. Mikołaja

Kopernika 9. **Map** 2 D4 (6 F3).
🚋 431 22 77. 🚊 2, 3, 6, 7, 10, 13, 19, 24. ◯ during services only.

RECORDED in the first half of the 13th century, this is one of the oldest churches in Cracow. The remnants of the Romanesque church and a Gothic portal have survived in the chancel. The present church is the result of a Baroque remodelling undertaken between 1677 and 1682. Furnishings were commissioned by the Academy of Cracow, whose patronage over this collegiate foundation goes back to 1465. A coat of arms of the Academy (a shield with crossed maces) decorates the backs of the stalls. The high altar was probably designed by Francesco Placidi. It features an effigy of St Nicholas and architectural decoration forming coulisses. The church also houses a late Gothic triptych, depicting the Coronation of the Virgin, and a Renaissance Madonna and Child with Saints Adalbert and Stanisław, patron saints of Poland. A bronze font dating from 1536, used for christenings, is worth noting.

It is also of interest that Feliks Dzierżyński, who was to become the founder of the *Cheka* (Bolshevik secret police) and a Bolshevik revolutionary, was married in this church in 1910.

Society of Physicians ❷
Gmach Towarzystwa Lekarskiego

Radziwiłłowska 4. **Map** 2 D4 (6 F2).
No phone. 🚊 2, 3, 6, 7, 10, 13, 19. ◯ 10am–3pm daily.

THIS BUILDING was constructed in 1904 to designs by the architects Władysław Kaczmarski and Józef Sowiński. A rather modest Neo-Classical exterior is in contrast to the sumptuous interior decoration designed by Stanisław Wyspiański. This multi-talented artist created here complex decoration in which, typically for the Art Nouveau movement, the arts and crafts complement each other. Wyspiański chose colour schemes for the walls and designed the exquisite stained glass showing *Apollo, The Solar System,* as well as the metal balusters and furniture which were inspired by folk art.

***Apollo, The Solar System,* a stained glass window by S. Wyspiański in the Society of Physicians building**

Jesuit Church ❸
Kościół Jezuitów

See pp132–3.

The Baroque Church of the Immaculate Conception

Church of the Immaculate Conception of the Virgin Mary ❹
Kościół Niepokalanego Poczęcia NMP

Kopernika 19. **Map** 2 E4. 🚋 618 86 99. 🚊 2, 3, 6, 7, 10, 13, 19, 24. ◯ 8am–4pm daily and during services.

THIS CHURCH, also known as the Church of St Lazarus, was used in the past by novices of the order of the Discalced Carmelites. The rigidity of the Baroque architecture of this church, built between 1634 and 1680, reflects the strict building regulations of the Carmelite order. Large and complex, the high altar dominates the small interior. Modelled on the high altar in the Carmelite Church of Santa Maria della Scala in Rome, it was made in 1681 of black marble from the Dębnik quarry, which was owned by the Carmelites.

Church of the Discalced Carmelite Nuns ❺
Kościół Karmelitanek Bosych

Kopernika 44. **Map** 2 E4. 🚋 421 41 18. 🚌 124, 128. 🚊 4, 5, 9, 10, 15. ◯ during services only.

A LARGE convent was built in the neighbourhood of the friary of the same order between 1720 and 1732. The church is small and has a Greek cross groundplan. The interior with its many columns is impressive. The sumptuous façade has elegant decoration in the late Baroque style.

The architect of the church is unknown. Karol Antoni Bay of Warsaw and Kacper Bażanka are considered likely to have designed it. Due to the strict rule of the order, the church is open to the public only during services. The painting on the high altar depicts Saint Theresa of Avila, to whom the church is dedicated.

Portal in the Church of the Discalced Carmelite Nuns

Astronomical Observatory [6]

Obserwatorium Astronomiczne UJ

Kopernika 27. **Map** 2 F4. *421 02 77. 124, 128, 184, 501, 502. 4, 5, 9, 10, 15. to the public.*

THE ESTABLISHMENT of the Observatory in Wesoła was directly linked to the reform of the Academy of Cracow carried out in the 1770s by Hugo Kołłątaj, a task he was given by the Commission for National Education. As a result, experimental sciences gained

a more prominent role in the curriculum. The suburban Jesuit residence, taken over by the Commission after the abolition of the order, was rebuilt to house the Observatory. Stanisław Zawadzki, the architect to King Stanisław Augustus, redesigned the building in an austere Neo-Classical style. He decorated the façade with astronomical signs.

The building is now occupied by the Jagiellonian Botanical Institute. A modern astronomical observatory is located in the former Skała fortress in Bielany.

Jagiellonian University Botanical Gardens [7]

Ogród botaniczny UJ

Kopernika 27a. **Map** 2 F4. *421 02 77. 124, 128, 184, 501, 502. 4, 5, 9, 10, 15. May–Oct: 9am–7pm daily.* **Greenhouses** *10am–1pm Sat–Thu.* **Museum of Botanical Gardens** *10am–2pm Wed & Fri, noon–4pm Sat. 10am–2pm Mon–Fri.*

NEXT to the Observatory, the Botanical Gardens of the Jagiellonian University are located on the former grounds and lodge of the Czartoryski family. The gardens were established in 1780 by Jan Jaśkiewicz and designed by the Viennese gardener Franz Kaiser. A 500-year-old oak tree in the depths of the garden, as well as exotic and native plants, are particularly worth seeing. Also of interest are late-Gothic pillars, originally from the Collegium Maius, used here as plinths supporting plant pots.

Two of the gardens' palm houses are interesting

Flowers in the Botanical Gardens

examples of 19th-century architectural structures. They are complemented by a third palm house designed by Stanisław Juszczyk and built in 1964 to mark the 6th centenary of the Jagiellonian University. Busts of celebrated botanists decorate the gardens.

Cracow Main Railway Station [8]

Dworzec Główny PKP

Pl. Kolejowy 1. **Map** 2 D3 (6 F1). *Served by most bus and tram routes.*

A RAILWAY link was established in 1847 between Cracow and Silesia. It was known as the Northern, or Franz Joseph Railway. Between 1844 and 1847 a new station was built north of the city. It was designed by Piotr Rosenbaum, an architect from Breslau, and was considered to be one of the most elegant stations in Europe. It was later rebuilt. In 1898 Teodor Talowski constructed a viaduct next to the station, in the Romanesque Revival style. Work is currently being carried out on the platforms.

Cracow's Main Railway Station

Jesuit Church ❸

THIS MONUMENTAL CHURCH was built between 1909 and 1921 to designs by the architect Franciszek Mączyński. He applied a number of historic styles which he modified and combined in new ways. What he created is one of the most interesting ecclesiastical buildings of the first quarter of the 20th century in Poland. Leading artists worked on the interior. Karol Hukan carved sculptures for the altars, while Jan Bukowski painted murals of striking beauty and designed unusual confessionals. The mosaic above the high altar is by Piotr Stachiewicz, and the south portal facing Kopernika Street was designed by Xawery Dunikowski. A small statue of Mączyński on the exterior of the east wall is also by Dunikowski.

★ **South Portal**
The main entrance to the church is through this monumental portal. Note the exquisite ornaments and figures which are both regarded as outstanding examples of Polish sculpture of the early 20th century.

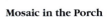

Mosaic in the Porch
Made of mosaic pieces in vivid colours and set against a shiny background, the figures of Mary and the Child have an almost unreal, mystical appearance.

Entrance

Murals Decorating the Nave Vaulting
These murals contribute to the rich and monumental character of the interior. They were painted by Jan Bukowski, who also executed decoration in other churches in Cracow, including St Mary's and the Bernardine Nuns' church, as well as the Loretto Chapel by the Capuchin Church.

★ Altar of St Joseph
Altars in the aisles were made by the sculptor Karol Hukan. Of particular interest is the altar of St Joseph, made in 1922 to 1923. It features this figurative group, which is rich in dynamic and wavy forms.

VISITORS CHECKLIST

Kopernika 26. **Map** 2E4.
☎ 429 44 16. **🚌** 2, 3, 6, 7, 10, 13, 19. **◻** 9:30am–noon daily and during services.

Confessional
The confessionals were designed by Jan Bukowski Professor of the Industrial School of Art, in the style of the Baroque Revival and are freely decorated with ornaments.

Mosaic above the high altar

High Altar
The design of the high altar, featuring a half-dome supported by a free-standing colonnade, was influenced by Italian Renaissance architecture. The statues above the altar portray Christ and Jesuit saints.

Side porch and tower

Statue of Franciszek Mączyński
The Jesuit Church was Mączyński's most important design. His statue, outside the east wall, is by Xawery Dunikowski.

STAR FEATURES

★ **South Portal**

★ **Altar of St Joseph**

Street-by-Street: Matejko Square

KLEPARZ, an independent settlement north of Cracow, was granted a municipal charter in 1366. It was incorporated into Cracow in 1791. After the introduction of the railway, Kleparz developed rapidly around the railway station. In the heart of the quarter, the empty space in front ot the Barbican was transformed into an elegant square welcoming visitors to Cracow, arriving here by rail or approaching the city from the north, via Warszawska Street.

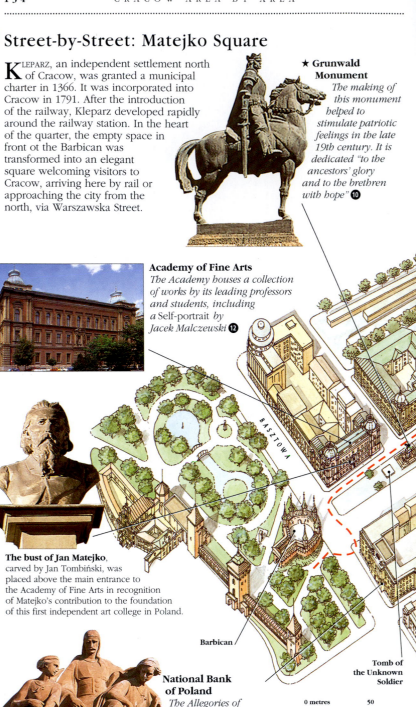

★ Grunwald Monument
The making of this monument helped to stimulate patriotic feelings in the late 19th century. It is dedicated "to the ancestors' glory and to the brethren with hope" ⑩

Academy of Fine Arts
The Academy houses a collection of works by its leading professors and students, including a Self-portrait *by Jacek Malczewski* ⑫

The bust of Jan Matejko, carved by Jan Tombiński, was placed above the main entrance to the Academy of Fine Arts in recognition of Matejko's contribution to the foundation of this first independent art college in Poland.

BASZTOWA

Barbican

National Bank of Poland
The Allegories of Industry and Agriculture, carved by Karol Hukan, decorate the façade of this bank ⑪

Tomb of the Unknown Soldier

0 metres   50
0 yards   50

KEY

– – – – –   Suggested route

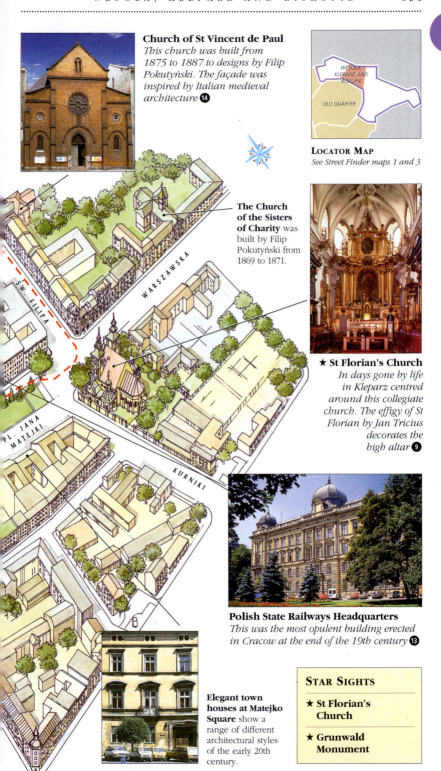

Church of St Vincent de Paul
This church was built from 1875 to 1887 to designs by Filip Pokutyński. The façade was inspired by Italian medieval architecture **14**

LOCATOR MAP
See Street Finder maps 1 and 3

The Church of the Sisters of Charity was built by Filip Pokutyński from 1869 to 1871.

★ St Florian's Church
In days gone by life in Kleparz centred around this collegiate church. The effigy of St Florian by Jan Tricius decorates the high altar **9**

Polish State Railways Headquarters
This was the most opulent building erected in Cracow at the end of the 19th century **13**

Elegant town houses at Matejko Square show a range of different architectural styles of the early 20th century.

STAR SIGHTS

★ **St Florian's Church**

★ **Grunwald Monument**

The Baroque altar of St John of Kęty in St Florian's Church

St Florian's Church ❾

Kościół św. Floriana

Warszawska 1. **Map** 2 D3.
📞 422 48 42. 🚌 105, 129, 130, 154, 179. ⭘ during services only.

IN 1184 Duke Kazimierz the Just received the relics of St Florian from Pope Lucius III and decided to deposit them in Cracow. The horses which drew the carriage carrying the relics of the martyr stopped suddenly in Kleparz, before reaching the city's gate, and refused to move forward. This was interpreted as a miraculous sign indicating where the relics should be placed. The church was, therefore, built on this spot between 1185 and 1212. After the capital was transferred to Warsaw, the church came to prominence as it was used to receive the deceased royalty brought from Warsaw for burial at Wawel. The funeral processions started here.

The church was damaged by frequent invasions and no trace of the medieval architecture has remained. The present interior and its decoration date from 1677 to 1684. The high altar with an effigy of St Florian, painted by Jan Tricius in the late 17th century, as well as an incomplete late-Gothic altar of St John the Baptist are of interest. The exterior was entirely remodelled by Franciszek Mączyński in the early 20th century.

Grunwald Monument ❿

Pomnik Grunwaldzki

Pl. Matejki. **Map** 2 D3 (6 E1).
🎞 124, 152, 502. 🚋 3, 4, 5, 7, 12, 13, 15, 19.

THE MONUMENT, featuring King Władysław Jagiełło on horseback, was raised to mark the 500th anniversary of the 1410 victory at Grunwald (Tannenberg in German) over the Teutonic Knights. It was commissioned by the statesman, composer and pianist, Ignacy Jan Paderewski, from the sculptor Antoni Wiwulski.

The monument was inspired by grandiose German monuments of the second half of the 19th century. It was generally well received but some critics mocked the theatrical treatment of the figures. Some even suggested that the only lifelike figure was that of the dead Grand Master Ulrich von Jungingen. The monument was destroyed by the Nazis in 1939 and only reconstructed in 1975 by the sculptor Marian Konieczny.

National Bank of Poland ⓫

Basztowa 20. **Map** 2 D3 (6 E1).
📞 618 58 00. 🚌 124, 152, 502. 🚋 3, 4, 5, 7, 13, 15, 19. ⭘ 7am–5pm Mon–Fri.

THE BANK, built between 1921 and 1925 by the architects Teodor Hoffman and Kazimierz Wyczyński, exemplifies the Neo-Classical style which became popular during the interwar years.

Neo-Classicism was then applied to important public buildings housing administrative and financial institutions, and was in sharp contrast to the Functionalism favoured in left-wing circles. The exterior sculptural decoration is by Karol Hukan and Stanisław Popławski. Inside, the domed counters hall is worth a visit.

The Academy of Fine Arts in Renaissance Revival style

Academy of Fine Arts ⓬

Pl. Matejki 13. **Map** 2 D3 (6 E1).
📞 422 11 31. 🚌 124, 152, 502. 🚋 3, 4, 5, 7, 13, 15, 19. **Museum** by appointment only.

THE SCHOOL of Fine Arts in Cracow gained independent status in 1873 through the efforts of the artist Jan Matejko. Three years later the school was allocated a plot in Kleparz by the city's authorities. The building was constructed in 1879 to 1880 to designs by Maciej Moraczewski. The

The imposing building of the National Bank of Poland

architect adopted the Renaissance Revival style for this building, in accordance with the spirit of 19th-century Historicism which favoured such forms for school architecture. On the first floor is a studio where Matejko painted his *Kościuszko at Racławice* and *The Vows of King Jan Kazimierz*.

In 1900 the school gained university status, becoming the Academy of Fine Arts. Some of the best Polish artists were among its students. The building in Kleparz is currently the seat of the Academy's governing body and houses the faculties of painting, printmaking and sculpture.

Polish State Railways Headquarters ⑬

Pl. Matejki 12. **Map** 2 D3 (6 E1).
🚌 124, 502. 🚊 3, 4, 7, 13, 15, 19.
⚫ to the public.

THIS IMPOSING building was constructed in 1888 by an unknown Viennese architect who combined the forms of both Romanesque and Baroque Revival into an eclectic whole. It is possibly the only building in Cracow to have been directly influenced by the 19th-century monumental architecture of its Austrian neighbour, Vienna.

Church of St Vincent de Paul ⑭

Kościół św. Wincentego de Paul

Św. Filipa 19. **Map** 2 D3.
📞 422 56 40. 🚌 124.
🚊 3, 4, 5, 7, 13, 15, 19. ⚪ during services only.

THE PRESENT church was built between 1875 and 1877 and replaced the medieval Church of Saints Philip and James which had been dismantled by the Austrian authorities in 1801. The architect, Filip Pokutyński, was inspired by Italian late-Romanesque architecture. Although modest in design, the church differs from other

The interior of St Vincent de Paul

19th-century ecclesiastical architecture in Cracow because of its clear, compact and monumental forms.

The side altar features a miraculous icon depicting Christ Crucified. This much venerated image was brought after World War II from Milatyn near L'viv.

Globe House ⑮

Dom pod Globusem

Długa 1. **Map** 1 C3. 📞 422 54 23.
🚌 124. 🚊 3, 4, 5, 7, 12, 13, 15, 19. **Mehoffer Hall** by appointment only.

THIS HOUSE was built in 1904 to 1906 for the Chamber of Commerce and Industry. It was designed by the architects Franciszek Mączyński and Tadeusz Stryjeński. The building is considered to be one of the best examples of the Art Nouveau style in Polish architecture. It is an interesting asymmetrical structure dominated by a pyramidal tower topped by a globe. The interior decoration, including murals in the great hall on the

The Globe House, a prime example of Art Nouveau architecture, topped by a pyramidal tower and globe

first floor, is mainly the work of Józef Mehoffer. Stained-glass windows above the stairs depict allegorical subjects such as the progress of mankind through industry and commerce, thus reflecting the function of the building. Cast-iron decorations in many parts of the building are also of interest. The publishers 'Wydawnictwo Literackie' are housed here today.

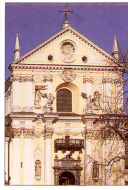

The façade of the Church of the Nuns of the Visitation

Church of the Nuns of the Visitation ⑯

Kościół Wizytek

Krowoderska 16. **Map** 1 C3.
📞 422 16 28. 🚊 3, 5, 7, 21.
⚪ during services only.

THE CONVENT was founded by Bishop Jan Małachowski as a votive offering after he was miraculously saved from drowning in the Vistula. The church is an interesting example of Cracow's Baroque ecclesiastical architecture. It was built from 1686 to 1695 by Giovanni Solari. The façade is richly decorated with sculptures and ornaments. Some lavish decoration is also characteristic of the interior which, although small, is very elegant. The unusual high altar was made in 1695 by the sculptor Jerzy Golonka. The plasterwork is by Jan Liskowicz. The 18th-century murals decorating the vault have been much altered.

PIASEK AND NOWY ŚWIAT

PIASEK, KNOWN AS GARBARY until the 19th century, is located west of the Old Quarter. Its development was hindered in the past by frequent invasions and lack of fortifications. A number of settlements with independent jurisdictions were located between Garbary and Wawel. They included Groble, Smoleńsko, Wielkorządowa, Wygoda, Retoryka and Rybaki, as well as Nowy Świat which remained under Cracow's juris-

A singing frog

diction. All these settlements were integrated by the Austrian authorities. By the end of the 19th century Piasek (Sand) and Nowy Świat (New World) began to flourish; wealthy residents moved in, drawn by the pleasant and quiet atmosphere away from the noisy town centre. As a result, some of the best residential architecture can be found here. It is mostly eclectic in style, dating from the turn of the 20th century.

SIGHTS AT A GLANCE

Historic Monuments and Buildings
Academy of Mines and Metallurgy, Main Building **18**
Ekielski House **7**
Former Museum of Industry and Technology **2**
House of the Singing Frog **6**
Jagiellonian Library **17**

Philharmonic Hall **1**
School of Industry **16**
"Sokół" Gymnastics Society **8**
Spider House **21**
Wyspiański Monument **14**

Museums and Galleries
Hutten-Czapski Palace **10**
Mehoffer Museum **12**
National Museum, Main Building pp146–7 **15**

Churches
Capuchin Church **11**
Carmelite Church **22**
Church of the Felician Nuns **3**
Church of the Merciful God **4**
Church of the Sisters of the Sacred Heart of Jesus **9**

Historic Streets
Avenue of Three Poets **19**
Karmelicka Street **20**
Retoryka Street Fields **5**

Open Fields
Błonia **13**

0 metres   200
0 yards   200

KEY

	Street-by-Street map *See pp140–1*
P	Parking
⊠	Post office

GETTING THERE
Tram routes 4, 8, 13, 14, 15 and 18 and bus routes 124 and 152 all serve Dunajewskiego Street. Tram route 15 and bus routes 124, 152 and 192 serve Piłsudskiego Street.

Street-by-Street: Piłsudski Street

Piłsudski (FORMERLY WOLSKA) Street formed part of the route connecting Cracow with Wola Justowska. This route was first recorded in the 16th century. After Nowy Świat and the neighbouring jurisdictions were incorporated into Cracow, it became one of the main avenues in this part of town. The vista formed by the street is closed by the vast Błonia Fields with Kościuszko's Mound in the distance, from behind which Piłsudski's Mound can also be seen. Elegant residential and public architecture developed here by the end of the 19th century. Some of the buildings show Polish architecture at its best.

Church of the Sisters of the Sacred Heart of Jesus
The square in front of this church was once a flood plain of the Rudawa river which was filled in prior to the construction of the convent buildings **9**

"Sokół" Gymnastics Society
Looking at this beautiful mosaic frieze, one does not expect a building that houses an ordinary sports hall **8**

★ **Ekielski House**
This unusual house was built by the architect Władysław Ekielski as his own home **7**

House of the Singing Frog
This house was designed by Teodor Talowski and is decorated with some exquisite, though somewhat overdone, sculptures of fantastic creatures **6**

★ **Retoryka Street**
The houses designed by Teodor Talowski have a unique "antiquarian" look and contribute to the picturesque character of the street **5**

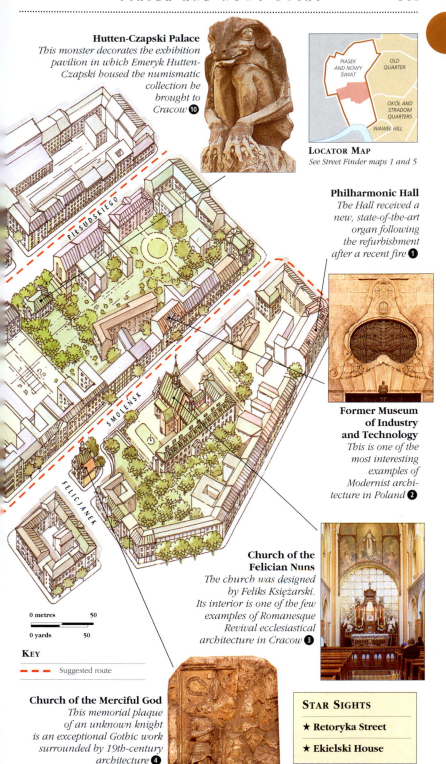

Hutten-Czapski Palace
This monster decorates the exhibition pavilion in which Emeryk Hutten-Czapski housed the numismatic collection he brought to Cracow ❿

LOCATOR MAP
See Street Finder maps 1 and 5

PIASEK AND NOWY ŚWIAT

OLD QUARTER

OKÓŁ AND STRADOM QUARTERS

WAWEL HILL

Philharmonic Hall
The Hall received a new, state-of-the-art organ following the refurbishment after a recent fire ❶

Former Museum of Industry and Technology
This is one of the most interesting examples of Modernist architecture in Poland ❷

Church of the Felician Nuns
The church was designed by Feliks Księżarski. Its interior is one of the few examples of Romanesque Revival ecclesiastical architecture in Cracow ❸

0 metres   50
0 yards   50

KEY

– – – Suggested route

Church of the Merciful God
This memorial plaque of an unknown knight is an exceptional Gothic work surrounded by 19th-century architecture ❹

STAR SIGHTS

★ **Retoryka Street**

★ **Ekielski House**

The exterior of the Neo-Classical Philharmonic Hall

Philharmonic Hall ❶
Filharmonia

Zwierzyniecka 1. **Map** 1 B5 (5 C3).
C 422 94 77. 🚋 124. 🚌 1, 2, 6, 8, 13, 14, 18.

THE SOCIETY of Friends of Music which was active in Cracow between 1817 and 1884 was regarded as the first philharmonic organization in occupied Poland. The Szymanowski State Philharmonia was established in Cracow in 1945. Walery Bierdiajew, Andrzej Panufnik and Krzysztof Penderecki were among the principal conductors. The orchestra and choir are complemented by the renowned chamber orchestra, *Capella Cracoviensis*. The Hall is housed in the former Catholic Cultural Institution. It was built between 1928 and 1930 by Pokutyński and Filipkiewicz in the Neo-Classical style which was popular with Polish architects around 1930.

Former Museum of Industry and Technology ❷
Gmach dawnego Muzeum Techniczno-Przemysłowego

Smoleńsk 9. **Map** 1 B5 (5 B3).
C 422 15 46. 🚋 124. 🚌 1, 2, 6, 8, 18.

THIS MUSEUM was established in 1868 by Andrzej Baraniecki who presented the city with his library and large collection of decorative arts. The museum ran courses in fine art, as well as a school of painting for women, and workshops on crafts. Collaboration with other institutions at the forefront of modern design was established. The museum published a number of titles, including journals such as *Przegląd Techniczny* (Technical Revue) and *Architekt* (The Architect). It also played an important role in the development of Polish applied art.

The museum was initially housed in the west wing of the Franciscan friary. The new building was constructed in 1908–1914 to designs by Tadeusz Stryjeński. Józef Czajkowski designed the elegant façade, which is rich in geometrical forms. The structure of the building, which uses reinforced concrete, was novel at the time and the layout of the rooms was unusual. It is a leading example of Modernist architecture in Poland. The Museum of Industry and Technology was closed down in 1952. Today the Faculty of Industrial Design of the Academy of Fine Arts is housed here.

Façade detail, the former Museum of Industry and Technology

Church of the Felician Nuns ❸
Kościół Felicjanek

Smoleńsk 4/6. **Map** 1 B5 (5 B3).
C 422 00 39. 🚋 124. 🚌 1, 2, 6, 8, 18. ⏰ 8:30am–6pm daily and during services.

THE CHURCH of the Felician Nuns is one of the largest churches built in Cracow in the 19th century. This basilica in the Romanesque Revival style was built between 1882 and 1884 to designs by Feliks Księżarski, but modified by Sebastian Jaworzyński. The monumental and austere forms are striking, but softened inside through lavish decoration of the altars. The church houses relics of Blessed Maria Angela Truszkowska, the foundress of the Order, who died in 1899.

Altar of blessed Maria Angela, Church of the Felician Nuns

Church of the Merciful God ❹
Kościół Miłosierdzia Bożego

Bożego Miłosierdzia 1. **Map** 1 B5 (5 B3). 🚌 1, 2, 6, 15, 18. ⏰ during services only.

IN 1555 Jan Żukowski established in Nowy Świat a home for the destitute and a small church. The church was consecrated in 1665. Located outside the city wall, both buildings were badly damaged during a number of invasions. The church has survived. On the outside wall facing Smoleńsk Street, remnants of a Gothic sepulchre, with a kneeling figure of a knight, can be seen.

Among the rather modest Baroque furnishings, the one of most interest is the image of the *Misericordia Domini* (The Suffering Christ and Sorrowful Mary) of 1650, hanging in the chancel.

Adjacent to the church is a presbytery, built in the eclectic style in 1905 to 1906 by Jan Zubrzycki.

Retoryka Street 5
Ulica Retoryka

Map 1 B5 (5 B3, 4). 15, 18.

THE NAME of this street comes from the Retoryka jurisdiction, which was established in this area by the Ossolińskis in the first half of the 18th century. In the late 19th century the construction of boulevards began along the Rudawa river, which ran here. They were lined with houses whose architecture was marked by imaginative forms and unusual decoration. In 1910 the river was enclosed in a tunnel beneath street level. The houses designed by Teodor Talowski are most interesting. He used pseudo-antiquarian, intentionally damaged motifs such as mosaics and plaques bearing popular Latin inscriptions for the external decoration. The plaque on his own house reads *festina lente* (hasten slowly) and that on the Ass House, *faber est suae quisque fortunae* (one works one's own destiny).

The houses in Retoryka Street, designed by Talowski and other leading architects active in Cracow around 1900, are interesting examples of Polish architecture at the dawn of the modern age.

House of the Singing Frog 6
Dom Pod Śpiewającą Żabą

Retoryka 1. **Map** 1 B5 (5 B3). 15, 18.

THE CORNER house at No. 1 Retoryka Street is considered to be the most interesting of Talowski's

House of the Singing Frog

designs. It was built in 1889 to 1890. The unusual structure consists of a number of segments varying in height and decoration. It was intended to be viewed at an angle from the adjacent street corner. The name of the house is a joke which refers to both the function and location of the building: it used to house a music school whose singing students were often accompanied by croaking frogs in the nearby Rudawa river.

Ekielski House 7
Dom W. Ekielskiego

Piłsudskiego 40. **Map** 1 A5 (5 A3). 103, 114, 124, 152, 173, 179, 192. 15, 18.

THIS WAS the house of Władysław Ekielski, one of the foremost architects active in Cracow around 1900. He built this eclectic house for himself in 1899, borrowing from medieval and Renaissance architecture. The historic forms received a novel treatment. Fanciful

and asymmetrical, the finished building is closer to an imaginary castle than a tenement house. Some features, such as the open loggia and the towers enclosing stairs, are characteristic of a suburban villa.

"Sokół" Gymnastics Society 8
Gmach Towarzystwa Gimnastycznego „Sokół"

Piłsudskiego 27. **Map** 1 B5 (5 A3). 421 73 97. 15, 18. *to the public.*

THE "SOKÓŁ" Gymnastics Society was established in Lwów (L'viv) in 1867. The Society promoted physical fitness and ran a programme of lectures and self-educational courses. It also organized celebrations commemorating important events throughout Polish history.

The Society's sports hall is a simple brick building. It was constructed in 1889 to designs by Karol Knaus. In 1894 Teodor Talowski extended the eastern part of the building and embellished the whole exterior with decoration inspired by Romanesque and Gothic art. The original building was also decorated with a *sgraffito* frieze in which its designer, Antoni Tuch, depicted the Society's goals: physical fitness, spiritual self-development and the virtues of good citizenship. Important sporting events continue to take place in this hall.

The "Sokół" Gymnastics Society

Church of the Sisters of the Sacred Heart of Jesus **9**

Kościół Sercanek

Garncarska 26. **Map** 1 B5 (5 B3).
📞 421 86 68. 🚃 15. 🕐 during services only.

THE CONVENT of the Sisters of the Sacred Heart of Jesus was built between 1895 and 1900 to designs by Władysław Kaczmarski and Sławomir Odrzywolski. The architects designed the building along Garncarska Street so as to close one side of a square located here. They adjusted the façade of the church and the adjoining buildings of the convent to fit the slight bend in the street. This explains the irregularity of the plan.

The church is eclectic in style. The exterior walls show bare brickwork, ornamented in the Romanesque Revival style, as well as with pseudo-Renaissance *sgraffiti* and Neo-Classical sculptures by Jan Tombiński. Furnishings display Neo-Romanesque forms.

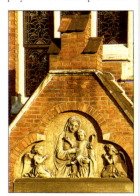

Detail from Church of the Sisters of the Sacred Heart of Jesus

Hutten-Czapski Palace **10**

Pałac Hutten-Czapskich

Piłsudskiego 12. **Map** 1 B5 (5 B3).
📞 422 27 33. 🚃 15, 18. 🕐 Access to the collection to professional researchers only.

THIS small palace in the Renaissance Revival style was built in 1884 by the

The Hutten-Czapski Palace in the Renaissance Revival style

architect Antoni Siedek for Hubert Krasiński. A few years later the property was purchased by Emeryk Hutten-Czapski who moved from the Vilnius area, bringing with him an exquisite numismatic collection. A pavilion, purpose-built to house this collection, was added in 1896. It was designed by Tadeusz Stryjeński and Zygmunt Hendel. The inscription decorating the pavilion reads *Monumentis Patriae naufragio ereptis* (To the national heritage salvaged from destruction). In 1903 the Czapskis bequeathed the palace and collection to the city of Cracow.

Today the palace is the seat of the directors of the National Museum and houses the Museum's special holdings. A collection of salvaged architectural fragments can be found outside.

Capuchin Church **11**

Kościół Kapucynów

Loretańska 11. **Map** 1 B4 (5 B2).
📞 422 48 03. 🚌 124. 🚃 4, 8, 13, 14, 15, 18. 🕐 9:30am–4:30pm and 5–7pm daily as well as during services.

THE CAPUCHIN friars arrived in Cracow in 1695. They began constructing the church and friary a year later. The work was supervised at first by Carlo Ceroni, who was later succeeded by Martino Pellegrini. The architecture and furnishings, the latter dating from 1775, reflect the strict rule of the Order which espouses extreme poverty. Hence the simplicity and

functionalism of the architecture and the modest composition of the altars made of painted timber and lacking decoration. The altars, however, feature good paintings. They include *The Annunciation* by Pietro Dandini, *St Erasmus and St Cajetan*, two 18th-century effigies by Łukasz Orłowski, and *St Francis of Assisi* by Szymon Czechowicz.
A number of sepulchres are of interest. A wooden crucifix in front of the church indicates the tomb of the Confederates of Bar who fell in a rebellion against the Russians in 1768.

Between 1712 and 1719 an external Loreto Chapel was built to the design by Kacper Bażanka; this is linked to the church through a cloister. The chapel houses a Neo-Classical altar with a miraculous statue of the Madonna of Loreto and a beautiful tabernacle. The latter was also designed by Bażanka. An animated Christmas crib is erected here every year. It features historic Polish characters.

The interior of the Loreto Chapel by the Capuchin Church

Mehoffer Museum **⓬**
Muzeum Józefa Mehoffera

Krupnicza 26. **Map** 1 B4 (5 B2).
C 421 11 43. 🚌 103, 114, 144, 164, 173, 179, 439, 444. 🚊 8, 13, 24. ◻ 9am–3:30pm Tue & Thu, 11am–6pm Wed & Fri, 10am–3:30pm Sat & Sun. 📷

Stanisław Wyspiański was born in this house in 1869. In 1930 it was bought by Józef Mehoffer (1869–1946), one of the foremost Modernist artists in Poland. He was a painter, stage and interior designer. In 1968 the house was acquired by the National Museum and the Mehoffer Museum was established. The interiors have been preserved in the tasteful way they were arranged by the artist himself. Many of his works, including paintings, stained glass, cartoons for stained glass and murals, are on display.

Portrait of Mrs Mehoffer by Józef Mehoffer

Błonia Fields **⓭**

Map 1 A5. 🚌 100, 103, 114, 164, 173, 179. 🚊 15, 18.

The Błonia Fields formed part of the grounds owned by the Convent of Premonstratensian (Norbertine) Nuns in Zwierzyniec and were originally used as pastures. In 1366 the nuns made a rather bad deal with the city's authorities and exchanged Błonia for a house in Floriańska Street. The house proved to be unprofitable and was eventually destroyed by fire. This gave rise to a joke about the nuns who had exchanged pastures for a bonfire. For centuries the nuns tried in vain to regain the fields. The Błonia Fields remain the property of the City of Cracow.

Błonia were used in the past as a venue for mass religious and national celebrations. The first football match in Cracow took place here in 1894. Pope John Paul II said a Holy Mass here on two occasions. Today it is a wildlife sanctuary in the centre of Cracow and a popular place for recreation. It should, however, be avoided on days when football matches between Wisła and Cracovia take place.

Wyspiański Monument **⓮**
Pomnik S. Wyspiańskiego

Map 1 A5 (5 A3). 🚌 103, 114, 164, 173, 179.

The monument was unveiled in 1982 to mark the 75th anniversary of the death of the great artist and playwright of the so-called Young Poland movement (Polish Modernism). The sculptor, Marian Konieczny, depicted Stanisław Wyspiański surrounded by the characters from two of his plays, *The Wedding* and *November Night*. The monument was badly received and prompted unfavourable interpretations. Its location, right behind the parking place in front of the National Museum, proved to be particularly unfortunate as the figures seem to emerge from behind parked cars. The agitated gestures of the figures have even been interpreted as an expression of their astonishment at the fast rate of motor development.

National Museum, Main Building **⓯**

See pp146–7.

School of Industry **⓰**
Szkoła Przemysłowa

Krupnicza 44. **Map** 1 A4 (5 A2).
C 422 32 20. 🚌 103, 114, 164, 173, 179, 439, 444. ◐ to the public.

In 1834 the Institute of Technology was established in Cracow, and funded by the bequest of the architect Szczepan Humbert. It was later transformed into the State School of Industry. In 1912 the school moved to a new building designed by Sławomir Odrzywolski. This irregular brick structure, decorated with Art Nouveau ornaments, resembles an imaginary castle.

Wyspiański Monument

National Museum, Main Building ⑮

Jacek Malczewski by W. Szymanowski

THE MODERN building of the National Museum was designed by Czesław Boratyński, Edward Kreisler and Bolesław Schmidt in 1934 but the building was not completed until 1989. Permanent galleries display Polish painting and sculpture of the 20th century, decorative arts and arms and other mementoes of the Polish Army. Temporary shows are also organized here. The painting collection is one of the largest in Poland and includes works by leading Modernist artists, as well as some outstanding works from the period between the two World Wars. Post-1945 art, however, predominates.

Execution *(1949)*
The art of Andrzej Wróblewski, who died prematurely, is a personal analysis of the tragic war years.

Emballage *(1975)*
This work by Tadeusz Kantor is an artistic interpretation of Jan Matejko's great history piece depicting The Prussian Homage.

The Uniform of Józef Piłsudski
"The uniform of the grey rifleman" reminds one of the tragic but nevertheless victorious history of the Polish Legions between 1914 and 1917.

First floor

Ground floor

Baton
This gilded "buzdygan" baton belonged to Grand Hetman Stanisław Jabłonowski, who fought in the Battle of Vienna in 1683.

Main entrance

KEY

- 🟪 Temporary exhibitions
- 🟩 Arms and Colours in Poland
- 🟨 Gallery of Polish Art of the 20th c.
- 🟦 Gallery of Decorative Arts
- ⬜ Non-exhibition space

Self-Portrait with Masks
This self-portrait by Wojciech Weiss (1875–1950) dates from the early years when the artist remained under the influence of Symbolism.

Second floor

★ A Design for Mickiewicz's Statue in Vilnius
This monumental statue by the Cubist artist Zbigniew Pronaszko (1885–1958) was never executed and exists only as a model.

GALLERY GUIDE
Temporary displays and the exhibition "Arms and Colours in Poland" are located on the ground floor. The display on the first floor is dedicated to decorative arts and temporary exhibitions. The Gallery of Polish Art of the 20th Century is housed on the second floor.

★ Polonia, a Cartoon for Stained Glass
Stanisław Wyspiański's cartoons for stained-glass windows in the Cathedral symbolically depict visions of the past but also relate to modern issues.

Nike of the Legions
This is one of Jacek Malczewski's symbolic tours de force. Nike, the goddess of victory, is sitting by the body of a legionary whose face resembles Józef Piłsudski.

STAR EXHIBITS

★ **Polonia, a Cartoon for Stained Glass**

★ **A Design for Mickiewicz's Statue**

Jagiellonian Library ⑰
Biblioteka Jagiellońska

Al. Mickiewicza 22. **Map** 1 A4 (5 A2). 📞 633 63 77. 🚋 15, 18. 🚌 103, 114, 144, 164, 173, 179. ◯ 8am–8pm Mon–Fri, 8am–3pm Sat.

FOR MANY centuries the Library of the Jagiellonian University was housed in the Collegium Maius (see pp106–7). The new building was constructed between 1931 and 1939 to designs by Wacław Krzyżanowski. It has impressive modern forms and a spacious and functional interior. It is not only the success of the design but also the high quality of craftsmanship and the use of luxurious materials that make this building an outstanding example of Cracow's architecture in the interwar years.

During the 1990s work was undertaken on a new wing of the Library, designed by Romuald Loegler. Completion is scheduled for 2001, when the University will celebrate the 6th centenary of its re-establishment. The new wing matches the forms of the old building and is one of the most interesting examples of architecture of the 1990s.

The Library's holdings include 25,000 priceless manuscripts and 100,000 rare books and prints. It has national library status.

Academy of Mines and Metallurgy, Main Building ⑱

Al. Mickiewicza 30. **Map** 1 A3, 4 (5 A1). 📞 617 33 33. 🚌 103, 114, 129, 139, 144, 159, 164, 173, 179, 238. ◯ 7:30am–8pm daily.

THE ACADEMY of Mines was established in Cracow in 1919. In 1922 the Faculty of Metallurgy was added. After 1945 the Academy was transformed into a large and well equipped technological university. It has its own nuclear reactor and modern acoustic laboratory. The enormous main building, with 110,000 sq m (1,183,600 sq ft)

Statues in front of the Academy of Mines and Metallurgy

of floor space, was built between 1923 and 1935. It was designed by Sławomir Odrzywolski and Wacław Krzyżanowski in a Neo-Classical style that is particularly prominent in the façade and portico. The statues of miners and steel workers in front of the building are by Jan Raszka.

In German-occupied Poland the building became the seat of the Governor General. A museum housed in Building C-1 is dedicated to the history of the Academy.

Avenue of Three Poets ⑲
Aleje Trzech Wieszczów

Map 1 A3, 1 A4, 1B2, 1 C2. 🚌 103 114, 129, 139, 144, 164, 173, 179, 511.

IN THE MID-19TH century an earthen embankment was constructed along what is today this avenue, and in 1887 to 1888 a railway line was laid for trains connecting Cracow to Płaszów. East of the embankment, new streets were laid out and new houses constructed in the eclectic and Art Nouveau styles. When in 1910 the borders of Cracow were extended, the railway and the embankment were dismantled. Their site was replaced by a wide avenue comprising a dual carriageway with a belt of greenery in the middle. Each of the sections of the avenue was named after a Romantic poet, namely Krasiński, Mickiewicz and Słowacki. The intention was to transform the avenue into Cracow's Champs Elysées.

An illuminated page in the Behem Codex, Jagiellonian Library

A view looking down Karmelicka Street

Karmelicka Street ⑳

Ulica Karmelicka

Map 1 B3, 4 (5B, C1). 🚌 100, 114, 124, 152, 159, 164, 179. 🚋 4, 8, 13, 14.

Karmelicka Street formed part of the old route connecting Cracow to Czarna Wieś and Łobzów. Formerly known as Czarna, Karmelicka was always the main street in the Garbary Quarter. The Carmelite Church and, at No. 12, the Town Hall of Garbary were built here. Initially the street was divided into two parts: the wider part stretched from the Cobblers' Gate to a small bridge, beyond which the street narrowed considerably. This explains why the Carmelite friary building projects into the present-day street.

By the end of the 19th century Karmelicka became one of the most elegant streets in Cracow. Splendid houses were built to designs by Maksymilian Nitsch, Teodor Talowski and Filip Pokutyński. The writers Stanisław Przybyszewski and Tadeusz Boy-Żeleński were among the celebrated residents.

Spider House ㉑

Dom pod Pająkiem

Karmelicka 35. Map 1 B3 (5 C1). 🚋 4, 8, 13, 14. ⬤ to the public.

This house was built in 1889 by Teodor Talowski, one of the leading architects in Cracow in the late 19th century. His intention was to give this irregular structure "an ancient appearance" by adding a "Gothic" round corner tower and a high gable in the style of Netherlandish Mannerism. By using different architectural styles of the past he wanted to pretend that the house had been rebuilt many times. He inserted, for example, a parapet modelled on the Renaissance Cloth Hall into the crenellated "Gothic" frieze. The decoration is rich in inventive detail.

Carmelite Church ㉒

Kościół Karmelitów

Karmelicka 19. Map 1 B3 (5 C1). 📞 632 67 52. 🚌 124, 144, 152, 192. 🚋 4, 8, 13, 14. ⬤ 9:30am–4:30pm and 5–7pm daily and during services.

According to a legend, Duke Władysław Herman cured his skin disease by rubbing sand on the infected areas. He took the sand from a site miraculously indicated by the Virgin Mary. This site was therefore named Piasek (sand), and a votive church founded by the duke was built in 1087. Thus was born the legend of the Madonna of the Sand.

The church was actually founded by Queen Jadwiga in 1395. The church was almost entirely destroyed during the Swedish invasion in the 17th century. Its remnants were incorporated into the new Baroque church which was consecrated in 1679. The magnificent high altar, made in 1698 to 1699, and lavishly decorated with acanthus leaves, is worth noting. The splendid stalls and the balcony with the organ, both by Jan Hankis, are also of interest. An icon of the Madonna of the Sand, painted directly on the wall, is much venerated.

The Calvary Chapel in the side wall of the Carmelite Church

QUEEN JADWIGA (HEDWIG)

Queen Jadwiga (c. 1374–99) was famous for her piety and charity. She contributed to the development of the Academy of Cracow. Venerated since the Middle Ages, she was finally canonized in 1997. A touching legend links Jadwiga to the Carmelite Church. It tells the story of a mason employed at the construction of the church who lamented to Jadwiga about his poverty and lack of money to buy medicine for his wife. The Queen removed a gold brooch from her shoe and offered it to the man. The imprint of her foot can still be seen today.

The imprint of Queen Jadwiga's foot

FURTHER AFIELD

LESSER POLAND is the most densely populated and richest region of the former Polish-Lithuanian Commonwealth. Until the 17th century the local nobility held the highest offices and played an important political role at the royal court of Cracow, influencing matters of state. The nobles spent their time carrying out official duties in the capital as well as staying in their country estates, where they built castles, churches and monasteries. They introduced the art and culture of Cracow to the rest of Lesser Poland. In the centuries that followed, Cracow continued to dictate

A font holding holy water in Kalwaria Zebrzydowicka

the local fashion and was a centre of artists for the whole province. Cracow's strong influence over neighbouring regions contributed to the their unique artistic climate, in which the elitist merged with the vernacular, often with surprising effects. To appreciate the long tradition of Cracow's links with the area, visitors should certainly consider excursions out of town. They are ideal for those who are interested in historic/traditional architecture and places of historical interest, as well as those who like to relax in beautiful natural surroundings.

SIGHTS AT A GLANCE

Branice ❸
Grodzisko ❽
Kalwaria Zebrzydowska ⓭
Mogiła ❷
Niepołomice ❹
Nowa Huta ❶
Ojców ❼
Oświęcim (Auschwitz) ⓬
Pieskowa Skała ❾
Staniątki ❺
Tyniec ❿
Wadowice ⓫
Wieliczka ❻

KEY

🟥	City Centre
🟨	Greater Cracow
🚉	Railway station
✈	Balice Airport
═	Motorway
═	Major road
═	Minor road

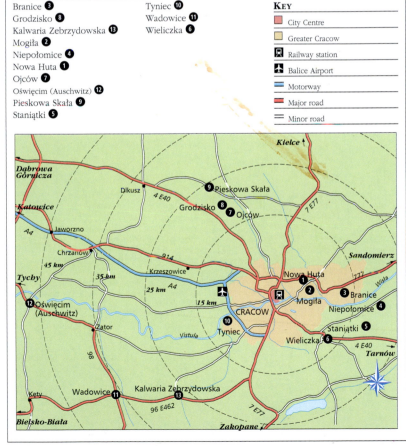

◁ **Pieskowa Skała Castle**

The Socialist Realist architecture of Nowa Huta

Nowa Huta ❶

🚌 125, 148, 163, 174.
🚊 4, 15, 22.

THE COMMUNIST authorities in Cracow suffered a humiliating and crushing defeat in the 1946 referendum. This they blamed upon an inappropriate social balance within the class-based society. In order to "rearrange" this balance, a programme of quick industrialization of Cracow's region was undertaken to increase the working class population. In 1948 a contract was signed between Poland and the Soviet Union for a new giant steelworks, named after Lenin. The construction of a new town named Nowa Huta (New Steelworks) began in 1949. It was designed by Tadeusz Ptaszycki in the Socialist Realist style. This Socialist Realism, a style imported directly from the Soviet Union, was influenced by classical and Renaissance architecture.

The housing estate, Centre, built between 1949 and 1955, is an interesting example of urban planning. Cheap concrete blocks predominated in the architecture that was developed after 1956. In this "model Communist town" there was no room for churches. But, despite official intentions, the people of Nowa Huta demanded, and from the 1950s even struggled for a church. The construction of churches on the estates of Nowa Huta began in the 1970s. Among these, the well-known Ark of God (*see p35*)

is an outstanding piece of modern sacred Polish architecture. During the period of Martial Law (1981–1983) the workers residing in Nowa Huta clearly demonstrated that they were not the best allies of the Communists. The town became notorious for riots, which were suppressed by the ZOMO stormtroopers.

The Lenin Steelworks have been renamed Sendzimir.

Mogiła ❷

7 km (4 miles) east of Cracow.
🚌 123, 153, 163. 🚊 15.
Cistercian Church Klasztorna 226.
📞 644 23 31. ⏰ 6am–7pm daily.

MOGIŁA village developed around the Cistercian Abbey, a religious centre of great importance in the past. The Cistercians were brought to Poland in 1222, or 1225, by Iwo Odrowąż, the Bishop of Cracow. They settled by the Dłubnia river, a tributary of the Vistula. The new monastery was named *Clara Tumba* (Bright Tomb, Jasna Mogiła, in Polish) because of the proximity of a prehistoric mound and the reputed burial place of the legendary princess Wanda. The church was consecrated in 1266.

This Romanesque church followed the strict building regulations of the Cistercian order. The chancel ended with a flat perpendicular wall; pairs of chapels which have a square ground-plan were added to the transept.

In 1447 the church was destroyed by fire. Gothic forms were introduced during its rebuilding. A wooden crucifix has miraculously survived. Stanisław Samostrzelnik decorated the interior with murals in the first half of the 16th century. These Renaissance paintings are complemented by 18th-century furnishings. The Baroque façade was added by Franz Moser as late as 1779 to 1780. Other wall paintings in the church were made by Jan Bukowski in the early 20th century.

The Gothic cloister built in the time of Kazimierz the Great is the most beautiful part of the Abbey. It leads to the Chapter House, which features murals painted in the 19th century by Michał Stachowicz. These illustrate scenes from the life of Wanda. Not far from the abbey is the Church of St Bartholomew. Built in 1466, it is one of the oldest timber churches in Poland.

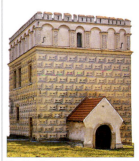

The Renaissance Old Manor in Branice

Branice ❸

12 km (7.5 miles) east from Cracow.
Manor Branice 131. ⬤ *Temporarily closed to the public.*

BRANICE is situated not far from Niepołomice and is worth visiting for its two manors which exemplify the small-scale residential architecture of the gentry of Lesser Poland. The Old Manor, later converted into a store, was built around 1603 for the Castellan of Żarnów, Jan Branicki, by an architect from the circle of Santi Gucci.

The exterior of the manor is decorated with *sgraffiti* and topped with a parapet. The doors and fireplace inside are lavishly decorated with imaginative Mannerist ornaments carved in stone.

The New Manor was built in the early 19th century. Its high hipped roof, and the entrance marked by a small portico supported by columns, make this building characteristic of Polish architecture of this type. Both manors are set in a picturesquely landscaped park, laid out in the 19th century.

Next to Branice is the village of Ruszcza with the Church of St George. The church was built around 1420 by the Royal Master of the Pantry, Wierzbięta of Branice. His Gothic memorial plaque and the Baroque high altar are both of interest.

Niepołomice ❹

24 km (15 miles) southeast of Cracow.
🚌 minibus from Cracow's Main Railway Station. 🚇 from Cracow's Main Railway Station. **Church**
📞 281 10 34. 🕐 7am–6pm daily.
Castle 📞 281 11 17. 🕐 8am–4pm Mon–Fri, 10am–2pm Sat & Sun.

THE ROYAL grounds in Niepołomice, situated on the outskirts of a vast woodland, were much favoured by Polish kings. They came here to rest and hunt, and developed magnificent buildings in the town they owned. The Gothic church in Niepołomice was founded by King Kazimierz the Great between 1350 and 1358. Like other sacred buildings founded by this sovereign, this church had two aisles separated by pillars.

It was later rebuilt in the Baroque style. Fragments of the rich stone decoration from the interior of the medieval church have survived and are displayed in the Old Sacristy. Outstanding Gothic paintings made

between 1370 and 1375 by an Italian master, commissioned by Princess Elżbieta (daughter of Władysław the Short), are also in the Old Sacristy.

Next to the church are two mausolea of noble families, both in the form of chapels covered by domes. Built in 1596, the Branicki Chapel is the earlier of the two. It features an ornamental tomb made by the Italian architect and sculptor Santi Gucci in the Mannerist style. In the Chapel of the Lubomirski family, built in 1640, wall paintings depicting scenes from the life of St Carlo Borromeo are of interest. Late-Baroque altars were added in the 18th century.

The hunting lodge in Niepołomice was originally built by Kazimierz the Great. It was transformed by Zygmunt August into a magnificent residence. The new castle was constructed between 1550 and 1571. Its regular plan and the central, square courtyard differ from other royal Renaissance houses in Poland. In 1637 the massive stone arcades were added to the courtyard. Part of the castle is used to house the Museum of Hunting.

The dense forest (Puszcza Niepołomicka), a favourite hunting ground of Polish kings, stretches right behind

Façade of the palace in Niepołomice, a residence of Polish kings

the town. Brown bears, bison, lynx, wildcat and deer are known to have inhabited it. The forest is not so magnificent as it used to be, though wild areas have been preserved, including the bison sanctuary in the Proszowo forest.

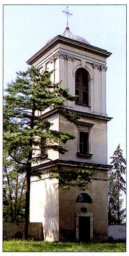

Belfry by the Church of the Benedictine Nuns in Staniątki

Staniątki ❺

24 km (15 miles) southeast of Cracow. 🚇 from Cracow's Main Railway Station and Cracow-Płaszów. **Church** 🕐 during services only.

THE CONVENT and Church of the Benedictine Nuns in Staniątki is not far from Niepołomice. The convent was founded in 1228 by Klemens of Ruszcza, Castellan of Cracow. The Church of St Mary and St Adalbert, dating from the same period, is Poland's oldest hall church (a type of church in which the aisles and nave are of the same height).

The church is a brick structure. Its rather modest decoration is carved in stone. The interior was refurbished completely in the 18th century. The lavishly decorated organ gallery, added in 1705, and wall paintings executed in 1760 by the Rococo artist Andrzej Radwański of Cracow, are of great interest.

Wieliczka ❻

12 km (7.5 miles) southeast of Cracow.
🚌 *Luxbus coaches from Cracow's Main Railway Station.* 🚉 *from Cracow's Main Railway Station and Cracow-Płaszów.* **Salt Mines** Daniłowicza 10. 📞 278 73 02. ✉ 🕐 16 Apr–15 Oct: 7:30am–7:30pm daily; 16 Oct–15 Apr: 8am–4pm daily.

Wieliczka developed and was granted a municipal charter in 1290 due to her rich deposits of salt. Salt was probably excavated here as early as the 11th century. The Latin name for Wieliczka was *Magnum Sal* (Great Salt) and indicated the importance of this mine in comparison to a smaller one in nearby Bochnia. According to a legend, the salt in Wieliczka constituted the dowry of the St Kinga (Cunegunda) when she married Duke Bolesław the Chaste. The salt dowry was supposedly transposed magically from Hungary to Cracow.

The salt in Wieliczka was regarded for centuries as a major natural asset of the Kingdom of Poland. An enormous network of underground galleries and chambers was created here over the years. Salt was also used as a building material in the carving of underground chapels and altars in front of which the miners prayed for God's providence and protection against accidents.

The Wieliczka Salt Mine Museum is housed inside the mine. The exhibits on display illustrate the old mining methods and tools. A unique underground sanatorium is also housed here.

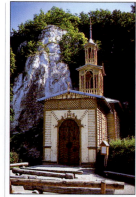

The small chapel overhanging the mountain river in Ojców

Ojców ❼

24 km (15 miles) northwest of Cracow. 🚌 *from Cracow's Main Coach Station.* **Ojców National Park Museum** 📞 389 20 40. 🕐 Apr–Oct: 9am–4:30pm daily; Nov–Mar: 8am–3pm Tue–Fri. **Castle Tower** 🕐 May–Sep: 9am–4pm Mon–Sat; Oct–Apr: 10am–3pm Mon–Sat.

The valley of the Prądnik river is the most beautiful part of the local uplands. The river eroded a deep gorge through the limestone cliffs. The steep cliffs are overgrown with trees through which rock formations can be seen. Some of these rocks have most unusual forms resembling pulpits, organs and needles.

Kazimierz the Great had a number of hill-top castles built in the area to guard the western border of his Kingdom. These castles were called eagles' nests. In 1956 part of the Prądnik valley was transformed into the Ojców National Park.

Among the natural formations of particular interest is a cave, which is said to have provided protection to King Władysław the Short while he was in hiding from the Czech King Venceslaus. Kazimierz the Great, the son of Władysław the Short, built in Ojców one of the most important fortresses in Poland, of which only remnants have survived.

Following the discovery of the healing propperties of the local springs in the mid-19th century, the village at the foot of the castle was transformed into a spa, and therapy clinics were set up. Newly built hotels imitated the architecture of luxurious foreign resorts. The Łokietek Hotel was regarded as the most sumptuous of all the buildings. It now houses the Museum of the Ojców National Park. During the Partition era, the Tsarist authorities refused to give planning permission for a church. So only a small timber chapel was built in 1901 to 1902 overhanging the Prądnik river.

Grodzisko ❽

28 km (17 miles) northwest of Cracow. 🚉 *from Cracow's Main Railway Station.* **Church** 🕐 9–10am Sun.

Grodzisko is situated not far from Ojców, on the opposite bank of the Prądnik river. The Convent of the Poor Clares was established here in 1262. Blessed Salomea, the sister of Duke Bolesław the Chaste, was the first Mother Superior. The nuns moved to Cracow in 1320 and the convent buildings fell into ruin. The cult of the Blessed Salomea developed over time, and in 1677 Canon Sebastian Piskorski transformed Grodzisko into a sanctuary devoted to this pious nun. He designed a complex hermitage consisting of a church and a number of chapels enclosed within a wall. This is a charming place with surprising Baroque ideas, some of which were borrowed from Bernini, the leading architect of Roman Baroque. The elephant bearing an obelisk, for example, was modelled on his art.

The Chapel of St Kinga in the Wieliczka salt mine

A room in the Pieskowa Skała Castle

Pieskowa Skała ❾

35 km (22 miles) northwest of Cracow. from Cracow's Main Coach Station. **Castle** 389 60 04. 10am–3:30pm Tue–Fri, 10am–5:30pm Sat, Sun (3:30pm Nov–May).

THE CASTLE in Pieskowa Skała was built by King Kazimierz the Great in the 14th century as an important part of the defence system on the Cracow-Częstochowa Uplands. It became private property in 1377.

Between 1542 and 1544, extensive enlargement of the castle was undertaken by Stanisław Szafraniec and his wife, Anna Dębińska. The commission was probably given to Italian architect, Nicolo da Castiglione. The rock on which the castle was built determined the scale of its enlargement. Despite limited space, the architecture of the castle developed around a trapezium-shaped inner courtyard and included arcades, modelled on the Wawel Castle, as well as a suite of rooms on the second floor with decorative ceilings. An external open gallery offering a view over the Prądnik valley was an interesting addition. A Gothic tower, later remodelled and covered with a Baroque dome, is a picturesque feature of Pieskowa Skała Castle's irregular structure.

The castle houses a museum affiliated to the Royal Castle at Wawel, which is dedicated to the history of Polish interiors from medieval times to the 19th century. Some lavish pieces of furniture, tapestries and other decorative objects, as well as paintings and sculptures, are on display. Of particular interest are paintings by 19th-century English artists.

Tyniec ❿

10 km (6 miles) west of Cracow. 112. **Benedictine Abbey** Benedyktyńska 37. 267 59 77. 7:30am–6:30pm daily.

THE BENEDICTINE Abbey at Tyniec is situated on a high rocky escarpment by the Vistula, west of Wawel. The monks were brought to Cracow in 1044, probably by King Kazimierz the Restorer. A Romanesque basilica was built here soon after. Only parts of the walls and a few architectural fragments of this basilica have survived. The new church and monastery were built in the 15th century. The church was remodelled in the early 17th century in the Baroque style, and magnificent stalls were added to the chancel. Large altars in black marble were made in the 18th century, possibly to designs by Francesco Placidi.

In the 12th and 13th centuries, during the period when Poland was fragmented into principalities, Tyniec was transformed into a fortress and played an important role during the struggles for the crown of the suzerain province of Cracow. By the end of the 16th century the fortifications were extended. A number of gates linked through an angled corridor were introduced as part of a defence system modelled on Wawel. Tyniec was a strategic site and often under attack from the enemy.

Today, the Benedictine Abbey is a picturesque sight.

Benedictine Abbey in Tyniec on the Vistula

The Church of the Presentation of the Virgin Mary in Wadowice

Wadowice ⓫

58 km (36 miles) southwest of Cracow. *from Cracow's Main Coach Station.* **Family House of John Paul II** *326 62.* *May–Sep: 9am–1pm and 2–6pm daily; Oct–Apr: 9am–noon and 2–6pm daily.*

WADOWICE was first recorded in 1327, but the town came to prominence in 1978 when Karol Wojtyła, born here on 18 May 1920, was elected Pope. The town became a place of mass pilgrimage and the sites associated with the Pope include the Baroque Church of the Presentation of the Virgin Mary in Market Square, where he was baptised. A museum was established in his family house.

A monumental votive Church of St Peter the Arch-shepherd was built on the outskirts of Wadowice in thanksgiving for the Pope's survival of an assassination attempt on 13 May 1981. Designed by Ewa Węcławowicz-Gyurkovich

and Jacek Gyurkovich, the walls of its nave seem to give way under the power of light, symbolizing the triumph of good over evil.

Auschwitz (Oświęcim) ⓬

Road map D5. 🏛 *43,000.* 🚆 🚌

THE SITE OF the largest concentration and extermination camp set up by the Nazis during World War II, Auschwitz *(see p33)* is today a UNESCO World Heritage Site. The camp has been preserved as a memorial, and the prison blocks that survive have been turned into a **museum** charting the history of the camp and of persecution in wartime Poland.

🏛 Oświęcim-Brzezinka Museum
ul. Więźniów Oświęcimia 20. *(0 33) 843 20 22.* www.auschwitz.org.pl *Jan–Dec: daily.*

Kalwaria Zebrzydowska ⓭

38 km (23.5 miles) sw of Cracow. *from Main Coach Station or Cracow-Dębniki.* *from Cracow's Main Railway Station or Cracow-Płaszów.* **Bernardine Church** *6am–7pm daily.*

CALVARIES, or Ways of the Cross, were introduced in the 16th century and were built throughout Europe to commemorate the Passion and Death of Christ. The landscaping of Calvary grounds had to imitate the topography of Jerusalem. They consisted of structures commemorating the "tragedy of Salvation" and imitations of holy sites connected to the Virgin Mary.

Poland's first Calvary was built by Mikołaj Zebrzydowski from 1600 onwards. He located the chapels representing the Stations of the Cross along Christ's route to Golgotha on the Żary Hill near his residence in Zebrzydowice.

Mystery plays enacting Christ's Passion are staged in Kalwaria during Holy Week. The "funeral of the Virgin" takes place on the feast of the Assumption. Crowds of pilgrims arrive to venerate the miraculous icon of the Mother of God, whose cult in the Bernardine Church goes back to the 17th century. Kalwaria is one of the main religious centres in Lesser Poland. It is also a place where the architectural heritage of Cracow's environs is seen at its best.

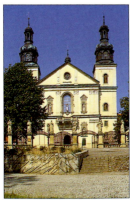

The Baroque façade of the early 17th-century Bernardine Church in Kalwaria Zebrzydowska

Kalwaria Zebrzydowska

T HE MOST interesting chapels in the Kalwaria Zebrzydowska are those designed by Paulus Baudarth, a Flemish architect and goldsmith. He was commissioned to design many chapels, and avoiding repetition must have been a difficult task. He applied many different ground-plans, including a Greek cross, a circle and even a triangle. In some chapels he resorted to truly Baroque ideas, and based the plans on the shape of a heart or rose.

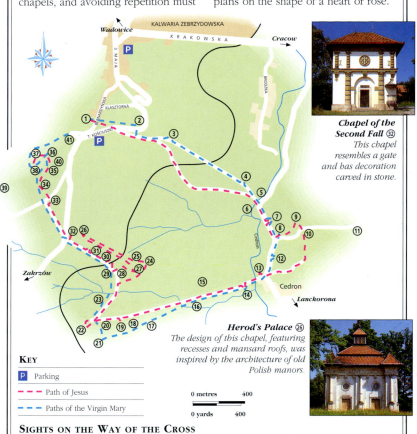

Chapel of the Second Fall ㉜
This chapel resembles a gate and has decoration carved in stone.

Herod's Palace ㉖
The design of this chapel, featuring recesses and mansard roofs, was inspired by the architecture of old Polish manors.

KEY

🅿	Parking
– – –	Path of Jesus
– – –	Paths of the Virgin Mary

0 metres   400
0 yards   400

SIGHTS ON THE WAY OF THE CROSS

St Raphael's Chapel ①
Chapel of the Throne ②
Chapel of the Joyful Patriarchs ③
Chapel of the Triumphant Apostles ④
Chapel of St John Nepomuk ⑤
Bridge of Angels ⑥
Chapel of Farewell ⑦
Church of the Sepulchre of the Virgin Mary ⑧
Gethsemane ⑨

Chapel of the Arrest of Christ ⑩
Church of the Ascension ⑪
Jewish Chapel ⑫
Bridge over the Cedron ⑬
East Gate ⑭
Bethsaida ⑮
Apostles' Chapel ⑯
Chapel of the Veneration of the Soul of the Virgin ⑰
Angels' Chapel ⑱
House of Annas ⑲
The Cenacle ⑳
House of Mary ㉑

House of Caiaphas ㉒
Chapel of the Fainting Virgin ㉓
Pilate's Town Hall ㉔
The Holy Steps ㉕
Herod's Palace ㉖
Chapel of the Taking up of the Cross ㉗
Chapel of the First Fall ㉘
Chapel of the Heart of Mary ㉙
Chapel of Simon of Cyrene ㉚
St Veronica's Chapel ㉛
Chapel of the Second Fall ㉜

Chapel of the Sorrowful Women ㉝
Chapel of the Third Fall ㉞
Chapel of the Stripping of Christ ㉟
Church of the Crucifixion ㊱
Chapel of the Anointment ㊲
Chapel of the Holy Sepulchre ㊳
Hermitage of St Mary Magdalene ㊴
Hermitage of St Helen ㊵
Chapel of the Madonna of Sorrows ㊶

THREE GUIDED WALKS

CRACOW is an ideal place for walks. The Old Quarter has become a pedestrian precinct with a large concentration of historic monuments, all within a short walking distance of each other. Suggestions for three walks, each with its own unique character, are included here. The first walk is along the Planty park which was laid out on the site of the medieval wall that surrounded the Old Quarter and Okół. It will give you an idea of the extent of the medieval city and provide an opportunity to enjoy this quiet park in the middle of a densely built city. Many statues decorate this park, commemorating those who had links with Cracow.

Cast-iron fixture, Camaldolese Monastery

The two other walks will lead you away from the noisy city centre to suburban Cracow, which has retained much of an idyllic countryside character. Zwierzyniec is rich in heritage and offers beautiful views over Cracow owing to its high location on hills. The Las Wolski (Wolski Wood) is an extensive woodland where you can enjoy nature at its best or visit first-class historic buildings situated on its peripheries. Among the finest buildings are the Villa of Decius, famous for its arcaded loggia and today a seat of the European Academy, and the complex of the Camaldolese Monastery. One must not forget that women are only allowed into the monastery on a few festive days. Children will certainly enjoy a visit to the Zoo in the middle of Wolski Wood.

Greater Cracow is quite large but every district is well served by buses and trams which run from early morning till late at night. An average journey by bus or tram lasts no more than a quarter of an hour. In recent years new restaurants, bars and cafés have opened around Cracow. Tourists can visit historic buildings, relax in the open, and enjoy nature and a good meal at the same time.

GREATER CRACOW

Olkusz
Skała
Kielce
914
Lublin
777
4E40
7E77
Planty
(see pp160–161)
Zwierzyniec
(see pp162–3)
Las Wolski
(see pp164–5)
4E40
7E77
Tarnów
Zakopane

KEY

- ··· Walking route
- — Major road
- — Railway line

0 kilometres 2
0 miles 1

◁ **The park by the Villa of Decius**

A Walk around Planty

THE PLANTY green belt in Cracow has replaced the city's medieval fortifications, built between the late 13th and 15th centuries. They were demolished early in the 19th century and the small stretch of wall by Floriańska Street is the only fragment to have survived. The gardens of Planty were landscaped to include a network of radiating lanes and beautiful vistas. In the second half of the 19th century the well-kept Planty became a popular venue for socializing. In 1988 a programme of regeneration began: the original appearance of Planty is being recreated through such additions as period fencing, benches and lamps.

One of many fountains in the Planty gardens

Wawel to the University

The walk begins by the Coat of Arms Gate at Wawel. Walk downhill and cross the street to enter the so-called Wawel gardens. The Gothic Revival Seminary building will be on your right, and a sculpture depicting *Owls* can be seen on your left ①.

Continue down the park some 40 m (130 ft) towards a little square decorated with a statue of the renowned translator of French literature into Polish, Tadeusz Boy-Żeleński, carved by Edward Krzak ②. Turn right and after some 50 m (165 ft) you will reach the wall enclosing the gardens of the Archaeological Museum *(see p83)*. Mounted in the wall are small plaques, overrun with greenery, commemorating the contributions made by the honorary Committee for the Renovation of Cracow's Monuments.

Carry straight on and cross Poselska Street. Those interested in archaeology may turn right to visit the museum. On the other side of the street is a plinth indicating the site of one of many medieval towers which formed part of the defence wall. The outline of the wall is marked by sandstones which you can see positioned along the lanes. Take a sharp left turn and walk

Owls (1964) by Bronisław Chromy ①

down 20 m (65 ft) to a little square where, hidden behind trees, is a statue made in 1884 of Grażyna and Litawor ③, two characters from a poem by Adam Mickiewicz.

From this statue, take a right turn to return to the main lane. You will notice the buildings of the Franciscan Friary *(see pp86–7)* and the Episcopal Palace *(see p104)*. Go straight ahead and cross Franciszkańska Street to enter the University Gardens. Walk down the main lane along the wall of the Episcopal Palace, passing by the end of Wiślna Street. Some 150 m (492 ft) further down, by Jagiellońska Street, is an 18th-century statue of the Virgin Mary of Grace ④, which originally was in the graveyard of Church of the St Mary.

After another 40 m (130 ft), you may choose to rest, looking at the Kościuszko Mound which can be seen through Piłsudski Street in the distance. Then carry on, passing by the façade of the Collegium Novum, the main university building. An oak planted in 1918, known as the Oak of Liberty, can be seen in front of the college. A red brick paved pattern in the square imitates the curves of Copernicus's astrolabe. The statue of the astronomer ⑤ *(see p105)*, surrounded by trees, is to the left of Collegium Novum and in front of the Witkowski College. Further down, you will pass by the Collegium Novovdorianum *(see pp104–5)* and after some 50 m (165 ft) cross St Anne's Street. The university Collegiate Church of St Anne *(see pp108–9)* will be on your right.

Planty in autumn, with visitors strolling along a path

while on your left will be a most beautiful statue of Artur Grottger ⑥ made in 1901 by Wacław Szymanowski. Cross St Thomas's Street (ulica św. Tomasza) and after some 300 m (985 ft) turn left. In this "corner" of the Planty is the statue of Lilla Veneda ⑦, the leading character in a play by Juliusz Słowacki. Walk some 200 m (655 ft) down one of the lanes which run along Basztowa Street. The next monument you will notice is that of Queen Jadwiga and King Władysław Jagiełło ⑧. It was raised to comme-morate the 5th centenary of the union between Poland and Lithuania in 1386. After crossing Sławkowska Street, you will find on your left a large pond where in summer swans can be seen. You can cross a little bridge over the pond and this will lead you to a statue of the Harpist ⑨. Continue down the main lane. Pass by the remains of the defence wall with St Florian's Gate *(see p111)* to finally reach the Barbican *(see p114).*

Cracow's Main Railway Station to Stradom
Walk some 300 m (985 ft) through the so-called Station Gardens. The major attractions here are the Słowacki Theatre *(see p115)* and the Church of the Holy

Cross *(see p115).* Continue to the subway entrance by which the Straszewski Obelisk ⑩ is located. Florian Straszewski was the man who laid out Planty. Behind the Church of the Holy Cross is a statue of the playwright Michał Bałucki ⑪. Walk another 300 m (985 ft) cross Mikołajska Street to enter the "Na gródku" Gardens. The Convent of the Dominican Nuns *(see p115)* will be on your right. Continue down the lane and cross Sienna Street. The Dominican Friary *(see pp116–7)* will be on your right. You will pass by an unusual statue of Colonel Narcyz Wiatr-Zawojny ⑫, who was shot dead in 1946 by the secret police (UB). The statue was made in 1992 by Bronisław Chromy. Stroll another 500 m (0.3 mile) down to enter the so-called Stradom Gardens and the Jesuit Monastery.

Statue of Lilla Veneda by Alfred Daun ⑦

KEY

••• Suggested route

Straszewski Obelisk

Palace of Art to the Barbican
Continue some 100 m (330 ft) and cross Szewska Street. The "Bunker of Art" *(see p106)* will be on your right. A little further down, some 20 m (65 ft) after crossing Szczepań-ska Street, continue to walk down the Planty's main lane. You will pass a little square where you will see the Palace of Art *(see p106)* on the right,

TIPS FOR WALKERS

Starting point: *At the foot of Wawel, by Kanonicza Street.*
Length: *approx. 5 km (3 miles).*
Getting there: *Bus Nos. 124, 144 and 444; the nearest stop is by Straszewskiego Street.*
Stopping-off points: *Café at the "Bunker of Art" near the Collegium Novum. There are benches near the Barbican and throughout the park.*

A Walk around Zwierzyniec

IN THE 12TH century Zwierzyniec was a small village, founded as the endowment to the Premonstratensian nuns, whose convent was located by the Rudawa river, a tributary of the Vistula. Polish sovereigns used to take a rest in the royal gardens located in this village. Henri de Valois is reputed to have organized orgies here to the outrage of his subjects. The richest Cracovians followed in the kings' footsteps by establishing their country residences in Zwierzyniec. Despite being incorporated into Cracow in the early 20th century, Zwierzyniec has managed to retain its original village character.

Zwierzyniecki Cemetery (5)

Altar in St Margaret's Chapel (2)

Salwator

After arriving at the tram depot, walk to the Church of the Premonstratensian Nuns (1). The church was founded in the second half of the 12th century but its appearance today is a result of a remodelling undertaken between 1595 and 1638. The Neo-Classical decoration of the choir is most interesting. It was created between 1775 and 1779 to designs by Sebastian Sierakowski. The convent building next to the church is one of the largest in Poland. It is worth visiting for its courtyard. After leaving the church, go up the steep Św. Bronisławy Street. The Chapel of St Margaret (2), built in 1690, will be on your left. Those who died of the plague were buried by the chapel. The Church of the Holy Redeemer (3) is further up. According to Polish chroniclers, it was built

Kościuszko Mound

0 metres 300

0 yards 300

KEY

- ••••• Suggested route
- ⁂ Viewpoint
- 🚊 Tram stop
- 🚌 Bus stop
- ℹ Tourist information

The Kościuszko Mound and Zwierzyniec seen from Wawel

immediately after Poland had accepted Christianity in 966, by Duke Mieszko I. The duke presented the church with a miraculous crucifix. Evidence shows, however, that the church was actually constructed later and consecrated in 1148. Despite extensive remodelling, the church has retained much of its Romanesque character. An interesting painting of 1605 by Kasper Kurch depicts a most unusual scene of the crucified Christ shaking off his shoe in order to pass it to a poor fiddler playing under the Cross. A 17th-century pulpit has also survived by the church, as well as a number of interesting tombs from the first half of the 19th century.

A residential estate ④ established in the early 20th century is located near the church. Its Art Nouveau architecture is worth seeing.

Zwierzyniecki Cemetery

Walk down Anczyc Street and turn right into Aleja Jerzego Waszyngtona (Washington Avenue). The small Zwierzy-niecki Cemetery ⑤ consecrated in 1865 is located on the outskirts of the Salwator estate. A chapel, built in 1888 to 1889 in the Neo-Gothic style, can be seen in the middle of the cemetery. Sebastian Jaworzyński was the architect. A great number of tombs of those who made important contributions to Polish culture can be found here.

Kościuszko's Mound

The tree-lined Aleja Jerzego Waszyngtona will lead you to the Kościuszko Mound on the Sikornik Hill. At its foot, the Chapel of St Bronisława ⑥ marks the site of the hermitage of the eponymous nun. The chapel was built between 1856 and 1861 by Feliks Księżarski in the Neo-Gothic style. The Kościuszko Mound ⑦ was erected between 1820 and 1823 to

Chapel of the St Bronisława at the foot of the Kościuszko Mound ⑥

commemorate the leader of the insurrection of 1794. This monument to the hero in the struggle for Polish independence was inspired by the mounds of two mythical Polish rulers, Krak and Wanda, which are located in the environs of Cracow. The construction of the mound became a patriotic endeavour and the monument itself a destination for national pilgrimages arriving in Cracow. Fortifications ⑧ at the foot of the Kościuszko Mound were constructed after 1850 by the Austrians as part of a project which aimed to transform Cracow into a massive fortress. The fortress is currently used as a hotel and houses the popular RMF FM radio station. A bus stop, which serves the city centre, is situated by the entrance to the hotel.

Church and Convent of the Premonstratensian Nuns at Salwator ①

TIPS FOR WALKERS

Starting point: The Salwator tram depot.
Length: 2.5 km (1.6 miles).
Getting there: The walk starts from the tram depot in Salwator. You can get there by tram Nos. 1, 2 and 6. Return by bus No. 100 which stops at the foot of the Kościuszko Mound.
Stopping-off points: Benches to relax can be found in Aleja Jerzego Waszyngtona. There is a café and restaurant in the Hotel "Pod Kopcem".

A Walk in the Las Wolski

L AS WOLSKI (THE WOLSKI WOOD) is the largest green area in Cracow. It has partly retained its original character as a forest, while the remaining ground is maintained as a park. Paths and lanes wind up and down this hilly terrain, leading to many wild spots of surprising beauty created either artificially or naturally. The lovely architecture of the Camaldolese Monastery and Decius Villa, both on the outskirts of the park, are worth exploring. The walk route described below includes sights in the Wolski Wood and the surrounding neighbourhood.

The park by the Decius Villa

Entrance to the Camaldolese Monastery ①

Srebrna Góra (Silver Mount)

The walk begins at the bus stop at the intersection of Aleja Wędrowników (Wędrowników Avenue) and Księcia Józefa Street. Walk some 500 m (0.3 mile) down Aleja Wędrowników then turn right into Aleja Konarowa (Konarowa Avenue). Climb up the Silver Mount to visit the Camaldolese Monastery ①. The monastery of this strict Reformed Benedictine order was built between 1605 and 1642 by two outstanding architects, Valentin of Säbisch and Andrea Spezza, among others. The stone-clad façade of the church is particularly impressive. The austerity of the interior is in striking contrast with the lavishness of the decoration of the chapels, which feature stuccowork by Giovanni Falconi. The so-called Royal Chapel, dating from 1633 to 1636, is very beautiful. The stairs on either side of the high altar lead down to the crypt which houses a catacomb. This subterranean gallery has recesses excavated in the sides for tombs of the deceased monks. Next to the catacomb is the *ossuarium,* a common grave containing bones removed from the recesses in the catacomb. The hermitages are closed to visitors but can be seen from the ossuary chapel. Women are allowed into the church on a few festive days only.

Camaldolese Church

The Wolski Wood, a favourite place for walks ②

KEY

•••• Suggested route

🚌 Bus stop

0 metres 400
0 yards 400

Wolski Wood (Las Wolski)
Leave the monastery by Aleja Konarowa (Konarowa Avenue), the same route by which you arrived, then turn right into Wędrowników Avenue which is the main lane of Wolski Wood ②. This wood was transformed into a common park in 1917 through the efforts of Juliusz Leo, the President of the City of Cracow. Turn right again into a path which leads to Aleja Żubrowa (Bison Avenue). After a few minutes' walk the entrance to the Zoo ③ will be in front of you. The Zoo was established in 1929. It differs

constructed between 1934 and 1936 as a monument commemorating the Poles who fell during the long struggle for independence from the three powers which partitioned Poland between 1772 and 1918. The mound is called "a Tomb of Tombs" and contains ashes from many battlefields. Walk down the mound and continue along Aleja Panieńskich Skał (Virgin Rocks Avenue) toward the Sanctuary of the Virgin Rocks ⑤ where you will find picturesque limestone

A statue of the Virgin in Panieńskie Skały ⑤

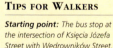
Komorowice Church
Decius Villa

from other zoological gardens owing to its location in the middle of a forest. Leave the Zoo via Al Do Kopca (Towards the Mound Avenue) which will take you to the Marshal Piłsudski Mound ④ on top of Sowiniec Mount. The mound was

formations. According to a legend, this was the place where the Premonstratensian nuns of Zwierzyniec took refuge and hid from the Tatars. A 16th-century timber church ⑥ at the end of the avenue was moved here from Komorowice.

Wola Justowska
Continue walking along Aleja Panieńskich Skał and turn right at the T-junction into

Aleja Kasztanowa (Chestnut Avenue). Wola Justowska, a fashionable district of Cracow, begins here. Carry on until you see the Decius Villa (Willa Decjusza) ⑦. Justus Decius was Secretary to King Zygmunt the Old. In 1530 he transformed a late-Gothic manor, dating from the 15th century, into a Renaissance residence. The villa was extended in the first half of the 17th century and a loggia added, offering a view over the area. The Villa houses the European Academy, which is dedicated to the study of European cultural heritage. A nearby bus stop serves the city centre.

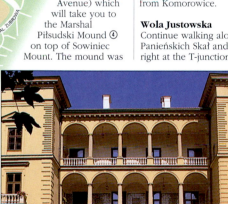
A suburban residence known as the Villa of Decius ⑦

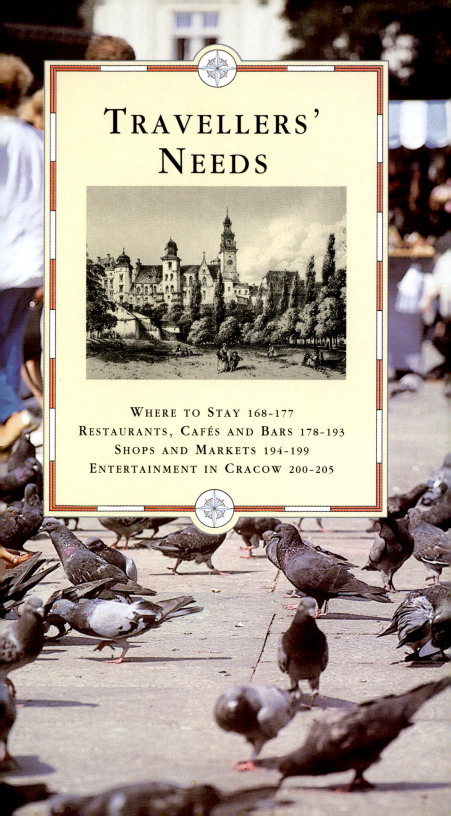

TRAVELLERS' NEEDS

WHERE TO STAY

THERE IS an absence of luxury hotels in Cracow that are part of international chains. Many hotels, however, are famous for their architecture, for traditions extending back to the 19th century, for their *fin de siècle* atmosphere and prime location. The best of these hotels are regaining the magnificence that was lost during the period of communist rule. Many require major repair but modernization is being systematically

undertaken. Hotel construction after 1989 has still not managed to keep up with the ever increasing number of tourists that arrive each year. Among those opened, there are hotels in former tenement houses that have been specially converted for use by tourists. From the hotels in Cracow, this section highlights some of the best; they have been categorized according to location and price on pages 174 to 177.

The Hotel Pollera *(see p175)*

WHERE TO LOOK

MOST OF CRACOW'S hotels can be found in the Old Quarter, which is surrounded by the Planty, or within close proximity. Cracow is not a sprawling metropolis so even the distant hotels should be no more than a 15–20 minutes' tram or bus ride from the centre of the town. It takes longer to come in from Nowa Huta whose hotels were built for workers. They now tend to accommodate traders from across the eastern borders who come to sell at the local markets. Tourists travelling by car may find overnight accommodation in hotels, motels, bed and breakfast in private homes and farms located in particularly attractive areas round Cracow. Myślenice is just such a place, located 27 km (17 miles) south of Cracow on the main route to Zakopane. It is

colourfully located on the hills of the middle Beskidy, within the Raba river valley. Some 30 km (19 miles) north of Cracow is Ojców, an old summer resort, lying at the heart of the Jurassic Ojców National Park. Close by lies the castle of Pieskowa Skała, a gem of Polish Renaissance architecture *(see p155)*.

Tourists with an exceptionally limited budget may care to take advantage of campsites and youth hostels *(see p170)*. Rooms and flats are available for rent from private landlords; many are for longer-term lets of several months, though some are available for short-term stays. On the other hand there are no problems in renting accommodation in private homes in the pleasantly located villages around Cracow. Local councils have lists of ecology-conscious farms, which offer accommodation and attractions such as horse-riding and local food.

MAKING A RESERVATION

EARLY BOOKING, preferably several weeks prior to your arrival, is advisable to make a successful reservation at a Cracow hotel. The tourist season lasts all year round, but in autumn and winter there may be fewer visitors. Nonetheless there are constant international conferences, meetings and festivals. Finding hotel accommodation at the time of arrival may prove to be difficult.

FACILITIES

IN MOST ROOMS there is a toilet and bathroom, a radio and frequently satellite television. In the better class of hotel, rooms may have videos, a mini bar, 24-hour room service and laundry service, while some have facilities such as computers, modems and fax machines for businessmen. You may obtain tourist information at the

A room in the Alef Hotel, formerly known as the Ariel *(see p176)*

reception desk and book tickets for various events.

Check-out time is generally noon but luggage may be left with reception. Some hotels accept pets. Hotel personnel frequently speak both English and German.

DISCOUNTS

THE BEST HOTELS are quite expensive. In the autumn-winter season some reduce their prices. Remember, it is always worth asking for a discount. You stand a good chance of negotiating a discount if you are planning a longer stay. The cheapest accommodation on offer is at the student halls of residence which become hotels in the summer months. Campsites and youth hostels (the latter open throughout the year) are also cheap.

The Royal Hotel *(see p175)*

HIDDEN EXTRAS

IN ALL HOTELS the prices quoted or displayed include tax and service. In most prices quoted breakfast is included, but it is best to check. Telephone calls from hotel rooms are more expensive than elsewhere, sometimes considerably so. In town there are numerous card-operated public telephones. Phonecards are available from newsagents and tobacco kiosks as well as post offices, where you will also find phones. Street telephone booths have their own

The reception area in the Novotel Hotel *(see p177)*

number and some are specially adapted for wheelchair users.

It is generally accepted that tips at hotel and other restaurants are customarily 10 per cent. You may, however, choose to give less. Tips are not offered to hotel staff except at the most exclusive of places. There are not many single-bed hotel rooms available for solo travellers, so negotiate a discount when offered a double room.

TRAVELLING WITH CHILDREN

CHILDREN are welcome everywhere. Most hotels offer additional beds for children and in some hotels no extra charge is made for this service. When making a reservation it is always advisable to ask about the extra cost, if any, for children. In hotel restaurants there should be no problem in ordering children's portions and some

places have high chairs. Hotels do not offer baby-sitting facilities. At an additional cost you can call upon this service from the Topolina Agency, 31 Fried-leina Street, tel. 633 06 62. It is open daily from 11am to 3pm. Outside these hours contact 0501 61 73 38. The agency works with British travel agents and their babysitters speak English.

ROOMS AND FLATS TO LET

IF YOU INTEND to rent a flat or room, approach an agent specializing in this type of letting. They have lists of private rooms and flats for rent. The majority deal with long-term lets in Cracow. However, it is quite a different matter out in the country resorts in season, as lettings are an additional source of income for the landlords. Lists are available from travel agents and local suburban councils.

Entrance to the Grand Hotel *(see pp175–6)*

KEY TO SYMBOLS

The hotels listed on pages 175–177 are grouped according to price category. To help you make your choice, the following symbols summarize the facilities offered at each hotel.

- ▥ Rooms with bath and/or shower
- ① Single-rate rooms available
- ⊞ Rooms for more than two people, or an extra bed can be put in a double room
- ㉔ 24-hour room service
- ▣ Television in all rooms
- ▨ Non-smoking rooms available
- ⚘ Good views from hotel
- ▤ Air-conditioning in all rooms
- ⛹ Gym/fitness facilities available
- ♒ Hotel swimming pool
- ⚐ Business facilities: information service, fax for guests, desk and telephone in each room, and conference room at hotel
- ⚐ Facilities for children including cots
- ♿ Access for wheelchairs
- ⬆ Lift
- ⓟ Hotel parking
- ⚑ Garden or terrace
- ⛾ Bar
- ⅱ Restaurant
- ⓘ Tourist information available
- ⬜ Credit cards accepted:
  - *AE* American Express
  - *DC* Diners Club
  - *MC* MasterCard/Acces
  - *V* Visa
  - *JCB* Japanese Credit Bureau

Price categories are for a double room with a bathroom or shower, including breakfast, service and 7% tax (in Polish Złotys).
- ⓩ less than 100
- ⓩⓩ 100-200
- ⓩⓩⓩ 200-300
- ⓩⓩⓩⓩ 300-400
- ⓩⓩⓩⓩⓩ over 400

YOUTH HOSTELS

Y OUTH HOSTELS offer cheap dormitory-style accommodation with communal washroom facilities. Hostels close their doors for the night at 10 or 11pm, and there is no access to the dormitories between mid-morning and early evening. Discounts are available to students or holders of the International Youth Hostel Federation card. The youth hostel at Kościuszki Street mainly caters for young student travellers.

CAMPING

I N SPITE of the fact that most campsites are located on the outskirts of Cracow, travelling into the centre does not take very long. Camp sites are usually open in the summer season from the beginning of May till the end of September.

On the **Krakowianka** camp site there is a cheap,

Entrance to the Polski Hotel
(White Eagle Hotel) *(see p175)*

single-storey hotel offering shared rooms for three people as well as public showers. During the summer months the open-air swimming pool is open for use by campers. The **Smok** camp site, which is open during the tourist season, is regarded as very clean and has a pleasant location.

Dom Polonii (Polonia House) in Market Square *(see p175)*

DIRECTORY

ACCOMMODATION INFORMATION

Tourist Information and Accommodation Centre (Centrum Informacji Turystycznej)
Pawia 8. **Map** 2 D4 (6 F1).
📞 422 60 91.
W www.jordan.pl
@ it@jordan.pl

Almatur
Grodzka 2.
Map 1 C4 (6 D3).
📞 422 46 68.

B & B Krakow
Szlak 14.
Map 1 C2.
📞 623 77 91.

Gromada
Pl. Szczepański 8.
Map 1 C4 (5 C1).
📞 422 72 13, 422 37 45.

Holiday Hotels
Rostafińskiego 2.
📞 637 24 16.

Juventur
Sławkowska 1.
Map 1 C4 (6 D2).
📞 422 24 37.

Malopolska Tourist Information
Rynek Główny 1/3.
Map 1 C4 (6 D2).
📞 421 77 06.

Orbis
Rynek Główny 41.
Map 1 C4 (6 D2).
📞 422 46 32, 422 26 76.

Point Travel Agency
Przy Rondzie 2.
Map 2 F3.
📞 421 84 33, 411 36 09.

Armii Krajowej 11.
📞 636 01 51, 638 68 94.
W www.point.travel.pl
@ point@point.travel.pl

Polish Tourist Promotion Agency (Polska Agencja Promocji Turystycznej)
Pl. Wszystkich Świętych 8.
Map 1 C5 (6 D3).
📞 422 71 27.

PTTK
Westerplatte 5.
Map 2 D4 (6 F2).
📞 422 26 76.

Waweltur
Pawia 8.
Map 1 D4 (6 F1).
📞 422 19 21.

TOURIST HOSTELS

Ekspres
Wrocławska 91.
📞 633 88 62.

Marina Hotel
Myślenice,
Stoneczna 13
📞 272 32 31.

Wagabunda
Oś. Złotej Jesieni 15c.
📞 643 02 22.

LETTING AND ESTATE AGENTS

Note: Leases are available from these agents for several months only.

Dom
Kazimierza Wielkiego 34.
📞 634 20 41.

Grodzkie Estate Agency (Grodzkie Biuro Nieruchomości)
Starowiślna 1/3.
Map 2 D5 (6 E3).
📞 422 32 21.

Nieruchomości
Szczepańska, pl., 7/3.
Map 1 C4 (5 C1).
📞 422 82 47.

GUEST ROOMS

Cicha 8.
📞 637 91 84.

Accommodation Hall (Dom Noclegowy)
Zielonki 573.
📞 633 70 49.

Modlniczka 129.
📞 285 12 61.

Ośrodek ZHP (Polish Scouts Centre)
Korzkiew.
📞 633 49 11 ext. 232.

Rekliniec
Myślenice, Leśna 2a.
📞 272 39 89.

YOUTH HOSTELS

Oleandry 4.
Map 1 A4.
📞 633 88 22.

Kościuszki 88.
📞 422 19 51.

Myślenice,Sobieskiego 1.
📞 472 66 74.

Szablowskiego 1.
📞 637 24 41.

Wrocławska 91.
📞 633 88 62.

STUDENT HALLS OF RESIDENCE

AWF
Al. Jana Pawła II 82.
📞 648 02 07.

Bydgoska
Bydgoska 19a.
📞 637 44 34.

Nawojka
Reymonta 11.
📞 633 58 77.

Olimp
Rostafińskiego 9.
📞 637 22 11.

Piast
Piastowska 47.
📞 637 21 76.

Strawberry Youth Hostel
Racławicka 9.
Map 1 A1.
📞 636 15 00.
⏱ Jul–Aug.

Żaczek
Al. 3 Maja 5.
Map 1 A5.
📞 633 54 77.

CAMPING

Cracow Automobile Club Camp Site (Automobilklub Krakowski Pole biwakowe)
Pcim Lipiny
📞 274 80 42.
⏱ 30 Apr–3 Sep.
Pcim Madoń
📞 274 81 19.
⏱ 30 Apr–3 Sep.

Clepardia
Mackiewicza 14.
📞 412 58 80.

Expans-Krak
Mackiewicza 14.
📞 415 16 74.

Kemping Ogrodowy
Al. Kasztanowa 49.
📞 425 23 12.

Korona
Gaj 51.
📞 270 13 18.

Krakowianka
Żywiecka Boczna 2.
📞 266 41 91.

Prima
Myślenice, Parkowa 1f.
📞 272 26 46.

Prima II
Myślenice, Zdrojowa 7a.
📞 272 23 41.

Smok
Kamedulska 18.
📞 421 02 55.

Cracow's Best: Hotels

THERE IS an insufficient number of hotels, as yet, to cater for the millions of tourists who come to Cracow each year. The selection in this guide includes some of the best hotels. They are often housed in historic buildings. New hotels tend to be located a short distance from the centre, some 15 minutes or so by car.

Demel
This modern hotel houses a beauty therapy clinic, as well as a pub serving Ottakringer beer from Vienna (see p177).

Piasek and Nowy Świat

Old Quarter

Novotel (formerly Continental)
Once part of the Holiday Inn chain, this is one of the largest hotels, offering the best facilities in Cracow (see p177).

Cracovia
Situated next to the Błonia Fields and only a ten-minute walk from the centre, the Cracovia has one of the best patisseries in town (see p176).

Wawel Hill

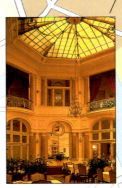

Grand
You will enjoy dining in the Art Nouveau dining room of this hotel, covered with a glass roof, which was a setting for Henryk Worcell's novel Enchanted Stations *(see pp175–6).*

VISTULA

Sofitel (formerly Forum)
This is the largest hotel in Cracow, with unforgettable views over the Vistula, Wawel and the Church "On the Rock" (see p177).

| 0 metres | 500 |
| 0 yards | 500 |

Francuski Hotel

This renowned hotel features in a number of literary works. It has retained much of the atmosphere and elegance of the fin de siècle *(see p175).*

Ibis

This international chain of modern hotels offers a uniform tourist standard (see p177).

Wesoła, Kleparz and Biskupie

Polski "Pod Białym Orłem" Hotel

This old hotel benefits from a prime location by the city wall and St Florian's Gate (see p175).

Okół and Stradom Quarters

Kazimierz Quarter

Alef (formerly Ariel)

A small but elegant hotel situated above a Jewish restaurant at the heart of Kazimierz offers smart rooms (see p176).

Elektor

An old town house has been converted into this luxurious hotel, whose famous guests included the Crown Prince of Japan and his wife (see p175).

Choosing a Hotel

THE CHOICE of hotels selected in this guide is based on quality of accommodation and service as well as location. The list of hotels covers all the areas with additional information to help you choose a hotel that best meets your needs. Hotels within the same price category are listed alphabetically. More details can be found on pages 175 to 177.

	Number of Rooms	Business Facilities	Children's Facilities	Recommended Restaurant	Close to Shops and Restaurants	Quiet Location	24-Hour Room Service
OKÓŁ AND STRADOM QUARTERS *(see p175)*							
Monopol zł zł	36		●		●		●
Wawel Tourist zł zł zł	35				●	■	●
Royal zł zł zł zł	180		●		●		●
OLD QUARTER *(see pp175–176)*							
Dom Polonii zł zł	3	■			●		
SARP zł zł	6				●		
Pollera zł zł zł	43		●		●		●
Saski zł zł zł	62		●		●		●
Polski "Pod Białym Orłem" zł zł zł	54		●		●	■	●
Elektor zł zł zł zł	21	■	●	■	●		●
Francuski zł zł zł zł	42	■	●		●	■	●
Grand zł zł zł zł	60	■	●		●		●
Pod Różą zł zł zł zł	53	■	●	■	●		●
KAZIMIERZ QUARTER *(see p176)*							
Mini zł zł zł	4				●		●
Alef zł zł zł	5	■		■	●	■	●
WESOŁA, KLEPARZ AND BISKUPIE *(see p176)*							
Europejski zł zł zł	53	■	●		●		
Hotel Wyspiański zł zł zł	160	■			●		
Polonia zł zł zł	70	■			●		
PIASEK AND NOWY ŚWIAT *(see p176)*							
Fortuna zł zł zł	30		●		●		●
Pensjonat Rycerski zł zł zł	16				●		●
Logos zł zł zł zł	49		●		●	■	●
Cracovia zł zł zł zł zł	314	■	●		●		●
FURTHER AFIELD *(see pp176–177)*							
Piast Student Hotel zł	50						
Korona zł zł	20				●		●
Perła zł zł	12	●				■	●
Wisła zł zł	25					■	●
Demel zł zł zł	62	■	●				●
Ibis zł zł zł	219	■	●		●		●
Novotel zł zł zł zł	304	■	●			■	●
Wanda zł zł zł zł	80	■	●			■	●
Piast zł zł zł zł	162	■	●				●
Pod Kopcem zł zł zł zł	11	■	●			■	●
Sofitel zł zł zł zł zł	279	■	●			■	●

Price range for a double room with bath or shower, inclusive of breakfast, service and tax
zł less than 150
zł zł 150–250
zł zł zł 250–350
zł zł zł zł 350–450
zł zł zł zł zł over 450

CLOSE TO SHOPS AND RESTAURANTS
Shops, bars, cafés and restaurants are within easy reach of the hotel.

BUSINESS FACILITIES
Telephones, fax machines and internet access are available, and the hotel has a conference or meeting room.

CHILDREN'S FACILITIES
Children are welcome, and cots can be provided.

OKÓŁ AND STRADOM QUARTERS

Monopol

Św. Gertrudy 6. **Map** 2 D5 (6 E3).
C 422 70 15. **Rooms:** 36. 1
24 P H AE, V, MC,
DC, JCB.

The advantages of staying at this old hotel, situated in a 19th-century town house, are its cheapness and its location opposite the Planty gardens. The Old Town is within easy reach.

Wawel Tourist

Poselska 22. **Map** 1 C5 (6 D4).
C 422 13 01. **Rooms:** 35. 1
24 AE, V, MC, DC.

Only a few years ago, this was a modest hostel for groups. Situated in an old town house, the place has been modernized and converted into a small hotel. It benefits from a prime location in one of the most charming spots in Cracow. The narrow Poselska Street leads towards Grodzka Street (which formed part of the old Royal Route) and Planty, and towards Franciszkańska Street at the other end. A number of excellent restaurants can be found close to the hotel in Poselska Street.

Royal

Św. Gertrudy 26–29. **Map** 3 C1 (6 D5).
C 421 49 79, 421 35 00. **Rooms:** 180.
1 24 TV P H
AE, V, MC, DC, JCB.
www.royal.com.pl

This hotel is situated by the Planty gardens, close to Wawel. Recently entirely redecorated, the hotel is housed in a building in the style of Viennese Art Nouveau. It was built under Austro-Hungarian rule as a garrison hotel, a function it still fulfils while also catering for other guests. For those familiar with the military hotels in Warsaw and their decor reminiscent of the Polish Army under the communist regime, you may find yourself pleasantly surprised here. The place has something of the spirit of Emperor Franz Joseph's era and Lehar's operettas. The staff are very kind and civil. Some rooms have retained elements of the Art Nouveau decoration.

OLD QUARTER

Dom Polonii

Rynek Główny 14. **Map** 1 C4 (6 D3).
C 422 63 41. **Rooms:** 3. 1 H
24 TV Y H

An old, entirely refurbished house situated in the heart of the city,

in the largest Gothic–Renaissance square in the world. Comfortable and cosy (only three rooms) and, bearing in mind its location, this is a moderately priced hotel. Early booking, months in advance, is necessary.

SARP

Floriańska 39. **Map** 1 C4 (6 E2).
C 429 17 78. **Rooms:** 6. 1 H
V, MC. www.hotel-sarp.com.pl

A small hotel with a fantastic location two minutes' walk from the Market Square, run by the Association of Polish Architects but open to non-members. It has self-catering facilities and one bathroom per two rooms.

Pollera

Szpitalna 30. **Map** 2 D4 (6 E1).
C 422 10 44. **Rooms:** 43. 1
H TV H AE, V, MC,
DC, JCB. www.pollera.com.pl

One of the best hotels in Austrian-occupied Cracow and in the Second Republic, this hotel was nationalized in communist Poland and became, typically, derelict. It was returned to its former owners some years ago and is currently undergoing modernization. All suites are air-conditioned. There is a good restaurant serving Polish cuisine at moderate prices in a former ballroom decorated in the Art Nouveau style. Some rooms offer a view of Słowacki Theatre.

Saski

Sławkowska 3. **Map** 1 C4 (6 D2).
C 421 42 22. **Rooms:** 62. 1 H
24 H Y H AE, V, MC,
DC, JCB.

The cheapest of all the hotels situated close to Market Square (one-minute walk). The walls, façade, a 100-year-old lift and part of the reception area all date from the *belle époque*. Some rooms are without bath. The restaurant is run by Chinese.

Polski "Pod Białym Orłem"

Pijarska 17. **Map** 1 C4 (6 E1).
C 422 11 44. **Rooms:** 54. 1
H 24 TV AE, V, MC,
DC, JCB. www.podorlem.com.pl

An old hotel much neglected during the communist regime and now reviving former good traditions. A prime location opposite the remnants of the city's wall, next to St Florian's Gate. It returned to private ownership some years ago.

Elektor

Szpitalna 28. **Map** 2 D4 (6 E2).
C 423 23 17. **Rooms:** 21. 1
H 24 TV Y H
AE, V, MC, DC, JCB.
www.hotelelektor.com.pl

A town house situated near the Słowacki Theatre which has been painstakingly refurbished and converted into this very expensive luxurious hotel. It is a favourite with businessmen and VIPs rather than tourists. The Crown Prince and Princess of Japan stayed here. The suites are decorated in the style of 19th-century private apartments and can easily be adapted for the needs of business people to include the necessary electronic equipment. The restaurant is good and less expensive.

Francuski

Pijarska 13. **Map** 1 C4 (6 D1).
C 422 51 22. **Rooms:** 42. 1
H TV Y H
AE, V, MC, DC, JCB.
www.orbis.pl

Possibly the most renowned hotel in Cracow. When it opened in 1910 it was regarded as one of the most luxurious places in Europe. All possible technological inventions, such as a vacuum cleaner (the first in Poland) and a pneumatic tube system connecting rooms to reception, were introduced. The doorman spoke eight languages and this was regarded as the norm. Despite two world wars and nearly 50 years of communism, the Francuski (French) Hotel has retained much of this welcoming atmosphere and splendour. The doorman, however, is not a polyglot and the "pneumatic post" no longer exists. The hotel features in literary works by Leopold Tyrmand, Antoni Słonimski and others. Situated close to the remnants of the city's wall and St Florian's Gate, it is an ideal place for those with a fat wallet.

Grand

Sławkowska 5/7. **Map** 1 C4 (6 D2).
C 421 72 55. **Rooms:** 60. 1
H TV Y H
AE, V, MC, DC, JCB.
www.grand.pl

Built at the turn of the 20th century, the Grand slightly predates the Francuski Hotel. Elements of Art Nouveau decoration can still be seen in the restaurant, which is covered with a glass roof and embellished with crystal mirrors. Much more

For key to symbols *see p170*

of this decoration would have survived if not for refurbishment carried out at a snail's pace after World War II. Those interested in Polish literature may care to note that the Grand was a setting for Henryk Worcell's autobiographical novel *Enchanted Stations (Zakręte rewiry)*. The film version, starring Marek Kondrat and Roman Wilhelmi, was actually filmed in the Czech Republic as the Grand was undergoing refurbishment at the time. In the 1920s the Grand's café was a favourite haunt of Cracow's elite: professors, journalists and physicians met here. Market Square is within a two-minute, slow-paced walk.

Pod Różą

Floriańska 14. **Map** 1 C4 (6 E2).
422 12 44. **Rooms:** 53.
AE, V, MC. www.hotel.com.pl

This hotel was established in the first half of the 19th century and was called the Russia.n The name was soon changed. A historic, elegant and comfortable place, only a minute from Market Square.

KAZIMIERZ QUARTER

Mini

Plac Wolnica 7. **Map** 4 D2.
430 61 00. **Rooms:** 4.
AE, V, MC, DC, JCB. www.minihotel.krakow.pl

With only four rooms (a single, double, triple and a suite) this hotel is mini indeed. It occupies just one storey of an old town house in Wolnica Square, formerly the centre of the Kazimierz Quarter. It is superbly located opposite the Renaissance Town Hall of Kazimierz (housing today the Ethnographical Museum) and close to the beautiful Gothic Church of Corpus Christi. There is no in-house restaurant, but a Vietnamese bar and restaurant are in the same building, on the ground floor and in the cellars.

Alef

Szeroka 17. **Map** 4 E1. 421 38 70.
V, MC. www.alef.pl

An elegant five-suite hotel or pension, housed above a non-kosher Jewish restaurant of the same name. Fine decoration reminiscent of pre-war interiors stirs up a nostalgia for bygone days. Many period features. The lack of television sets in the rooms is intentional.

WESOŁA, KLEPARZ, AND BISKUPIE

Europejski

Lubicz 5. **Map** 2 D4 (6 F1).
423 25 10. **Rooms:** 53.
AE, V, MC, DC, JCB.

This is the best hotel in the Main Railway Station area. A choice of rooms is available, including a suite which overlooks the courtyard and is decorated in the style of 19th-century private interiors.

Hotel Wyspiański

Weterplatte 15/16. **Map** 2 D4 (6 F3).
422 95 66. **Rooms:** 160.
AE, V, MC, DC, JCB. www.hotel.wyspianski.pl

This ugly building situated very close to the Planty gardens dates from the period of Socialist Realism. In the past noisy school groups stayed here, but the hotel is now open to individuals, with single and double rooms with a bathroom.

Polonia

Basztowa 25. **Map** 2 D4 (6 E1).
422 12 33. **Rooms:** 70.
V, MC, DC, JCB. www.hotel-polonia.com.pl

One of several hotels set in historic houses, Polonia was established in 1917 and has recently been modernized. The three suites with 19th-century furnishings are recommended. In the city centre, close to the top historic sights.

PIASEK AND NOWY ŚWIAT

Fortuna

Czapskich 5. **Map** 1 B4 (5 B3).
422 31 43. **Rooms:** 30.
AE, V, MC, DC, JCB.

Not so long ago a college run by the Piarist Fathers was housed in this old and spacious building. It is now a hotel with a restaurant under Chinese management. A three-minute walk will take you to the Jagiellonian University campus and Market Square is five minutes away.

Pensjonat Rycerski

Plac Na Groblach 22.
Map 1 B5 (5 C4). 422 60 82.
Rooms: 16.
AE, V, MC, DC, JCB.

A rather small hotel benefiting from its location by the Vistula, close to Wawel Hill, with wonderful views. The ground-floor restaurant has disappointing decoration and furnishings; Cracow's cuisine deserves a better setting. A perfect hotel for fans of the Piwnica Pod Baranami Cabaret. Its leader, Piotr Skrzynecki, lived nearby for many years. Regarded by many as a charming place, Na Groblach Square featured in the Cabaret's hit song. A ten-minute walk to Market Square.

Logos

Szujskiego 5. **Map** 1 B4 (5 B1).
632 33 33. **Rooms:** 49.
AE, V, MC, DC, JCB. www.hotel-logos.pl

One of the recent additions to the list of places where you can stay in Cracow, the Logos is a rare example of modern architecture blending in well with its historic surroundings. Only 600 m (650 yards) from Market Square.

Cracovia

Al. Focha 1. **Map** 1 A5 (5 A3).
422 86 66. **Rooms:** 314.
AE, V, MC, DC, JCB.

When it was built in the 1960s this was one of the best modern hotels in the country. Despite frequent refurbishment, the Cracovia is no longer synonymous with the best in hotel standards but remains popular with its many regular guests. This is the best place for *kremówki*, a delicious French pastry filled with custard, and the last of only two restaurants in Cracow to serve *maczanka*, a local speciality. The hotel is situated by one of Cracow's most attractive places, the Błonia open fields. These former pastures saw grand cavalry parades before Word War II and, more recently, Holy Masses said by the Pope to millions of the faithful. The National Museum is close by. A five-minute walk along Piłsudski Street will take you to the centre of the Old Town.

FURTHER AFIELD

Piast Student Hotel

Piastowska 47. 637 49 33.
Rooms: 50.
@ piast@bratniak.krakow.pl.

This student hotel should not be mistaken for the Piast Motel. The two places have nothing in common. This Piast is set up within a student hall of residence of the same name, located in the student village. Rooms are available for guests throughout the year. There is one bathroom and toilet for every two double rooms. In summer, when students are away on holiday, the entire hall becomes a hostel. A number of other halls are also transformed into hostels offering the cheapest accommodation in Cracow. In summer this is an enjoyable place to stay. The student village throbs till the early hours and bars and discos in the area are always full of young people speaking a variety of languages. They arrive from all over the world either as tourists or to study Polish at summer schools.

Korona

Kalwaryjska 9. **Map** 4 D3.
[656 15 66. **Rooms:** 20. ⬚ [1]
[♨] [24] [♥] [≋] [♿] AE, V, MC. [ZŁ][ZŁ]
[W] www.korona.krakow.pl

This relatively low-priced hotel, housed together with the Korona Sports Club, is located in the Pogórze quarter on the opposite bank of the Vistula from the Old Town. Sports facilities, including a swimming pool, fitness gym and sports hall, will be welcomed by those who enjoy exercise.

    If you cross the Piłsudski Bridge you will find yourself in the majestic Kazimierz Quarter, rich in Jewish heritage. Wolnica Square, featuring the old Renaissance Town Hall of Kazimierz, is only a five-minute walk away. On foot, it takes 15 minutes to reach Wawel and half an hour to Market Square.

Perła

Zakopiańska 180B. **[** 267 31 92.
Rooms: 12. ⬚ [1] [♨] [24] [TV] [≣]
[♿] [P] [♥] [Y] [¶¶] [♣] [≋] AE, V, MC.
[ZŁ][ZŁ]

A newly built, comfortable hotel situated near Borkowska Mount on the periphery of the city, on the Cracow-Zakopane road. It is best suited to people travelling by car, although it can also be reached by public transport, including bus and tram (a tram stop is within a ten-minute walk). A car journey to the city centre should normally take no more than 15 minutes, but the outward drive can take much longer, particularly over the weekend, owing to frequent traffic jams and congestion on the route towards Zakopane.

Wisła

Reymonta 22. **[** 633 49 22.
Rooms: 25. ⬚ [1] [24] [TV] [P] [ZŁ][ZŁ]

A large hotel set up within the Wisła Sports Club. It offers basic accommodations but all rooms

have a bathroom. Relatively cheap. Close to the Błonia fields and Jordan Park.

Demel

Głowackiego 22. **[** 636 16 00.
Rooms: 62. ⬚ [1] [♨] [24] [TV] [≋] [♥]
[♣] [♥] [♿] [≋] [P] [♥] [Y] [¶¶] [♣]
[≋] AE, V, MC, DC, JCB. [ZŁ][ZŁ]
[W] www.demel.com.pl

A newly built, large and modern hotel. It is located just outside Bronowice, on the outskirts of the city. By Cracow's standards it is far from the city centre. The Old Town is, however, just a ten-minute journey by tram from nearby Podchorążych Street. The beer bar run by the Viennese Ottakringer Brewery is a local attraction. The name of the hotel brings pleasant memories to the Austrians who associate it with the pâtissier Demel, the famous supplier of cakes to the Habsburg court.

Ibis

Przy Rondzie 2. **Map** 2 F3.
[421 81 88. **Rooms:** 219. ⬚ [1] [♨]
[24] [TV] [≋] [♣] [♣] [♿] [≋] [♥] [Y]
[¶¶] AE, V, MC, JCB. [ZŁ][ZŁ]
[W] www.ibishotel.com.pl

This is a new tourist-class hotel built by the Austrians and under French management. Its location by the busy Mogilskie Roundabout is unpleasant, but it is only a ten-minute journey by tram to the historic city centre. It offers relatively inexpensive rooms of a similar standard. The restaurant forms part of the open-space lounge and reception area.

Novotel

Armii Krajowej 11. **[** 637 50 44.
Rooms: 304. ⬚ [♨] [24] [TV] [≋] [≣]
[≋] [♣] [♣] [♿] [≋] [P] [Y] [¶¶] [♣]
AE, V, MC, DC, JCB. [ZŁ][ZŁ]

This hotel used to belong to the Holiday Inn chain. After its licence expired the hotel changed its name and is now under new management. Situated on the outskirts of Cracow but only 15 minutes' journey by bus from the city centre. Rooms have recently been refurbished. Those on the top floors offer beautiful views over the Wolski Wood and Kościuszko Mound. The hotel houses a casino (roulette, black-jack). A perfect place for gamblers.

Wanda

Armii Krajowej 15. **[** 637 16 77.
Rooms: 80. ⬚ [♨] [24] [TV] [≋] [♥]
[♣] [♿] [≋] [P] [♥] [Y] [¶¶] [♣]
[≋] AE, V, MC, DC. [ZŁ][ZŁ][ZŁ]

A comfortable motel close to the Novotel (formerly Continental) Hotel, built in the 1980s. In-house restaurant and grill bar. The hotel organizes summer folk evenings in its garden during which regional music groups, dressed in traditional costumes, play for the enjoyment of overseas tourists while local cuisine and spirits are served.

Piast

Radzikowskiego 109. **[** 636 46 00.
Rooms: 162. ⬚ [1] [♨] [24] [TV] [≋]
[♣] [♿] [≋] [♥] [Y] [¶¶] [♣] [≋] AE, V,
MC, DC, JCB. [ZŁ][ZŁ][ZŁ][ZŁ]
[W] www.hotelpiast.pl

A motel-like hotel situated by Radzikowskiego Roundabout. It is a good starting point for the Cracow-Katowice motorway and the road to Olkusz. The Krak motel and campingsite are next door. The city centre is a 15-minute drive away or 25 minutes by bus or tram.

Pod Kopcem

Al. Waszyngtona 1 (Washington Av.)
[427 03 11. **Rooms:** 11. ⬚ [♨]
[24] [TV] [♥] [♣] [♿] [P] [♥] [Y] [¶¶] [♣]
[≋] AE, V, MC, DC, JCB. [ZŁ][ZŁ][ZŁ][ZŁ]

An unusual location in the former Austrian fortress at the foot of the Kościuszko Mound. Under new management following recent refurbishment carried out by RFM Radio. The RFM leases the grounds surrounding the mound from the city and broadcasts from the old fortress. The rooms and terrace offer a memorable view over Cracow. On a good day the view can even extend as far as the Tatra Mountains.

Sofitel

Konopnickiej 28. **Map** 3 C3.
[261 92 12. **Rooms:** 279. ⬚ [1]
[♨] [24] [TV] [≋] [≣] [≋] [♥] [♣] [♿]
[≋] [P] [♥] [Y] [¶¶] [♣] [≋] AE, V, MC,
DC, JCB. [ZŁ][ZŁ][ZŁ][ZŁ][ZŁ]
[@] rez.krsofitel@orbis.pl.

The Forum was built during the communist era, inefficiently and over a long period, as a flagship hotel. Although times have changed, the Forum remains the largest of Cracow's top-class hotels. It is situated by the Vistula, next to the Japanese Centre of Art and Technology. The top-floor café offers a magnificent view over Wawel and the city centre. A shopping arcade, restaurant, night-club, casino, swimming pool and tennis courts are all available. You can also stroll along the Vistula. Due to the large number of conference and function rooms, the hotel is a frequent venue for exhibitions and promotions.

For key to symbols see p170

RESTAURANTS, CAFÉS AND BARS

CRACOW HAS ALWAYS been known as a good place for eating out. Even during the communist era, when restaurants were uninviting places with very little on offer, visitors from other parts of the country were surprised to find in Cracow a multitude of busy cafés serving tea in fine china, espresso coffee, fresh crisp rolls and eggs *à la Viennoise* for breakfast. The traditional politeness of

Ice cream of many flavours

waiters was even more surprising. After the collapse of communist Poland the best was yet to come. Hundreds of new places opened in the 1990s. A number of restaurants have been returned to their former owners, who spare no effort in reviving old traditions and quality service. Places serving Middle Eastern, Chinese, Vietnamese, Korean, French, Greek, Mexican and Italian food can all be found in Cracow.

SOMETHING FOR EVERYONE

VISITORS TO CRACOW who are short of time and travelling on a budget may choose to eat in a canteen or fast-food bar where they can have a three-course meal for only 10 zł. It is often a good traditional Polish meal. Such places, however, close early (usually late afternoon or early evening, or when the food has been sold out).

A *pretzel*, known in Cracow as a bagel, from a street vendor can often do for a snack. It is a local speciality, traditionally coated with salt crystals or poppy seeds, and recently also with sesame seeds. Boiled corn on the cob and broad beans are offered by street vendors throughout the year and in late autumn roasted chestnuts as well.

Fast food is also available from well-known chains such as McDonald's, Kentucky Fried Chicken and Pizza Hut, but this is less varied and more expensive. Hamburgers in Polish bars are less expensive than the international brands. In some places you will find street vendors selling grilled sausages. The best sausages are sold near the Market Hall

The Wentzl Restaurant *(see p190)*

in Grzegórzecka Street, where they are available until 3 o'clock in the morning.

Those who enjoy good food in a pleasant atmosphere will not be disappointed in Cracow. Most of Cracow's restaurants have a nice location and are housed in period interiors or medieval cellars, all painstakingly restored and furnished tastefully. Evenings and weekends tend to be particularly busy and it often happens that there are more customers than tables. Booking a table in advance is, therefore, advisable.

EATING AT NIGHT

THE MAJORITY of restaurants in Cracow close around midnight but if you happen to be hungry early in the morning there are alternatives to buying food in one of the shops which are open round the clock. The Greek restaurant Dionisos in Dominikański Square is open

"Pod Aniołami" Restaurant *(see p188)*

24 hours. A bar in Kramy Dominikańskie (Dominican Stalls) in Stolarska Street is also open round the clock, serving burgers and chips.

The Main Railway Station (Dworzec Główny PKP), with its bars and restaurants, is another place open 24 hours. They are unusual for Polish station bars because of their pristine cleanness and the good food on offer.

The Endzior Bar in Nowy Square in Kazimierz district opens at 5am. You will enjoy their fantastic spare ribs served with cabbage, pea soup and *schnitzels*, in the company of their usual customers – coal merchants, stall-holders, street traders and porters.

It is worth noting that most restaurants remain open until the last customer leaves, so you may stay as long as you place orders.

PRICES AND TIPS

Prices of food in Cracow's restaurants are below the national average for restaurants in cities. While some critics say that the relatively low prices reflect the stinginess of the Cracovians, market research suggests that this is a result of wages which are lower than in Warsaw and other parts of Poland. Certainly 100 zł per person will suffice for a three-course meal without alcohol even in the most expensive places. Naturally, if you do wish to

Chimera Restaurant *(see p189)*

drink alcohol with your food, this will add a substantial amount to your bill. All alcohol, especially imported wines and spirits, is subject to excise duty and taxed heavily. Not to mention the mark-up added by the restaurant.

Credit cards are becoming ever more popular and should be readily accepted by all the larger restaurants and those located on the main tourist trails. Signs on windows or doors indicate which cards are accepted by the establishment.

All over Poland a customary tip amounts to ten per cent of the bill, but in Cracow if you give less no one will feel offended.

VEGETARIAN FOOD

Polish culinary customs have changed enormously since the borders opened up with the fall of communism. Mass tourism abroad has brought Poles into contact with the cuisines of many foreign countries and new trends in the eating habits of the West. Easy access to foodstuffs that were previously unavailable has also contributed to these changes. For most people, meat still plays a central role in their diet, but vegetables and fruit are becoming ever more popular. The majority of restaurants in Cracow serve some vegetarian dishes.

Chef in the Wierzynek Restaurant

Traditional local dishes, such as *pierogi* (dumplings) filled with sauerkraut, wild mushrooms, cheese or fruit, as well as all kinds of pancakes, omelettes and *kneдle* (potato dumplings), are very popular. A choice of many colourful and tasty salads is available in all restaurants. Beetroots, carrots, cabbage, cauliflower, celeriac and leeks are the old favourites. Broccoli, aubergines, celery, endives and courgettes have recently been introduced to Polish cuisine. Vegetarian food is available not only from most ethnic restaurants but also from salad bars, which are very popular and also serve freshly pressed fruit and vegetable juices. In some restaurants you can make your own choice of salad ingredients.

One of the period rooms at the Noworolski Café in the Cloth Hall

The well-stocked bar at the modern Demel Hotel

Cracow's Best: Restaurants

THERE are many restaurants in Cracow that serve ethnic food, but tourists tend to look for traditional local cuisine. The restaurants listed in this guide offer a choice. Some places described here have a long culinary tradition, and contribute to Cracow's atmosphere. If you wish to sample this ambience a visit to these restaurants is a must.

Cyrano de Bergerac
Cyrano serves French cuisine and is regarded as one of the best of its kind in Poland (see p190).

Old Quarter

Piasek and Nowy Świat

Chimera
A favourite haunt of Cracow's artistic circles. Traditional Polish cuisine is served in an interior modelled on an old burgher's house (see p189).

Hawełka
A full-length portrait of Emperor Franz Joseph is a reminder here of old Galician traditions. A good place for an inexpensive, traditional meal (see p189).

Wawel Hill

Wentzl
This legendary restaurant re-opened after a long break. A Central European menu, inspired by old Austro-Hungarian recipes, attracts an ever growing number of customers (see p190).

VISTULA

0 metres   500
0 yards   500

Pod Aniołami
Beautiful Gothic cellars provide a museum-like setting for this restaurant which offers Polish cuisine with many dishes from the highlands. You may see them being prepared in a clay oven (see p188).

Paese

This tavern-like Corsican restaurant serves fresh seafood, the best in town. This is a very popular place which is almost always busy (see p188).

Orient Express

Fantastic desserts and a choice of delicious dishes typical of countries on the route of the Orient Express are offered here. The interior is modelled on a train carriage (see p188).

Alef

This non-kosher Jewish restaurant is situated in the centre of Kazimierz. Steven Spielberg and his crew dined here while filming Schindler's List (see p191).

Chłopskie Jadło

A big success story for Polish cuisine in recent years, traditional peasant food is served in a country-style setting (see p188).

A Dong

This is the best Chinese-Vietnamese restaurant in Cracow, and one of the best of its kind in Poland (see p191).

Wesoła, Kleparz and Biskupie

Okół and Stradom Quarters

Kazimierz Quarter

What to Eat in Cracow

Smoked ham and kessler

CRACOW has retained much of its own culinary traditions. Nearly 200 years of Austro-Hungarian occupation has left its mark on the type of food enjoyed by the Cracovians. Goulash and pepper casseroles are more popular here than in other parts of Poland. The Tatra Mountains are not far away and some specialities of the highlands, such as the delicious *oszczypek* and *bundz* cheeses, are readily available in Cracow.

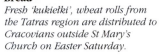

'Kukiełki' rolls   **Wholemeal bread**

Bread
Fresh 'kukiełki', wheat rolls from the Tatras region are distributed to Cracovians outside St Mary's Church on Easter Saturday.

Oszczypek
This ewe's cheese from the Tatras region is white, or yellowish, if smoked.

Ewe's Cheese and Lard Spread
Ewe's cheese and lard with crisp crackling, spread on wholemeal bread, are popular starters.

CURED MEAT AND SAUSAGES
Some villages around Cracow produce sausages using old recipes. The Lisiecka sausage made in Liszki deserves its fame. Cold-smoked kesslers and pork are also delicious.

Smoked kessler   **Lisiecka sausage**

Beetroot Soup
The popular barszcz (borsch) can be served with broad beans or potatoes.

Żurek
This soup is served with hard-boiled quail's eggs and ewe's buttermilk.

Wild Mushroom Soup
This is best made from boletus mushrooms and served with home-made pasta.

Baked potatoes

Roast lamb

Roast Lamb
A leg of lamb is marinated prior to roasting and served with baked potatoes.

Wild Duck Cracow Style
Wild duck stewed with wild mushrooms is usually served with pearl barley.

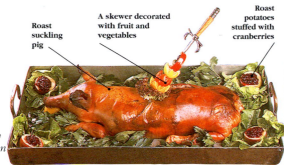

Roast suckling pig

A skewer decorated with fruit and vegetables

Roast potatoes stuffed with cranberries

Goulash
This paprika-spiced beef stew is closer to the Viennese version than the Hungarian recipe.

Roast Suckling Pig
A whole roasted piglet stuffed with barley and spices is a Polish speciality.

Golonka
A pork knuckle can be boiled, roasted or stewed in beer.

Trout
This freshwater fish is always popular, served with vegetables and potatoes.

Kiszka
Country-style black pudding is usually served with stewed sauerkraut.

Fruit Cup
Wild raspberries and blackberries picked in woodlands are full of flavour.

Apple Pie
Sour apples spiced with cinnamon are used for this pie.

Cheesecake Cracow Style
This popular cake is made with white curd cheese, eggs and raisins.

What to Drink in Cracow

I N CRACOW, as indeed anywhere in Poland, you may
try many different brands of exquisite vodkas, both
clear and flavoured. Beer is becoming ever more
popular and its production is growing rapidly.
There are many bars in Cracow that offer a large
selection of beers, especially beers brewed in Poland.
Poland does not produce quality wines but shops
and restaurants offer a large selection of brands
imported from all over the world, especially from
throughout Europe and the New World.

VODKA

V ODKA distilled from
potatoes or grain is a
Polish speciality. Such brands
as clear *Wódka Wyborowa*
and dry but flavoured
Żubrówka are both
world famous. The
variety of vodka
brands produced in
Poland may be
bewildering. Clear
Cracovia, which has
been produced in
Cracow for
some years, is
very popular.
Starka is
definitely the
oldest brand
among quality
vodkas. For
centuries *starka*
was made from
unrectified grain
spirit, which
was aged for at
least six years
in reused oak wine-casks.
The casks used to be buried
for ageing, but this is no longer
the case. Cracow *Starka* was
once regarded as the "queen"

**Starka
krakowska
vodka**

Cracovia, one of the best Polish
clear vodkas

**Dzięgielówka, a dry vodka
flavoured with angelica root**

of all *starkas*, but has lost
this status. Polish distilleries
have been decentralized, but
have retained the recipes
imposed during communist
rule. Above all the lack of an
appellation contrôlée has
resulted in the fact that, if you
buy a *Starka krakowska*
(Cracow starka), be prepared
to accept that it may have
been produced elsewhere.
(Another example is the
renowned Goldwasser liqueur

which was unique to Gdańsk
but is now produced in
Poznań.) *Starka bankietowa*
is aged for longer and is
definitely one of the best. It
is sold in crystal-glass bottles
and is a luxurious drink
difficult to find elsewhere.

Good kosher plum
vodka is distilled in
Poland. *Śliwowica
łącka* is the best and
most famous of all
plum vodkas.
Paradoxically, it is
produced illegally
owing to the lack of
proper regulations. It
is home-made in the
small Łącko village in
the mountain region,
some 70 km (43 miles) south
of Cracow. Śliwowica Łącka is
not available from off-licences
(liquor stores) but is offered in
many households in Cracow.

**A vodka
glass**

**Amaretto
liqueur**

**Plum Łąck
brandy**

**Passover Plum
vodka**

**Senator
vodka**

**Krakus
vodka**

**Harnaś
vodka**

Żywiec logo with the date of establishment

A dancing couple in traditional costumes from the Cracow region

Żywiec Beer Label
Many brands of beer are produced by the Żywiec Brewery, but bottles with the couple dressed in traditional Cracow costumes sell best.

Light Brackie Beer from Żywiec

Krakus Beer from Żywiec

Beer from the Okocim Brewery

Beer

POLISH BREWERIES have developed rapidly in recent years. The production of quality beer has grown and been modernized. Figures show that Poles are drinking

Pre-1939 advertisement of the Okocim Brewery

more and more beer and less strong alcohol.

Beers from Okocim and Żywiec are traditionally the most popular in Cracow. Cracovians are conservative and still very aware that both breweries were established in Galicia. The Okocim brewery was founded by the Goetz family who were raised to the rank of hereditary barons by Emperor Franz Joseph. The Żywiec brewery was set up and owned, until World War II, by the Habsburg Archdukes. The grim paradox was that this Żywiec branch of the Habsburgs, who took up Polish citizenship after World War I, had their brewery confiscated by the Nazis after they refused to sign the *Volkslist*. After World War II the communists nationalized Żywiec as a former German property. Heineken, the Dutch brewer, acquired a majority

holding in the enterprise a few years ago, and the brewery is now one of the most technologically advanced in Europe.

Wine

ALTHOUGH VINEYARDS were cultivated in the Cracow area quite successfully, they disappeared in the 15th century. Large quantities of quality wine were produced until World War II in the Zaleszczyki region on the then Romanian border. Today only a few vineyards can be found near Zielona Góra in the far west of the country, which means that Poland's wine production is negligible. Any visitor to Cracow wishing to drink wine will find a large selection of imported wines both in shops and restaurants. Wine comes from many countries, including France, Italy, Spain and Austria, as well as California, Australia, Chile and New Zealand. Hungarian wine, however, is to be recommended in Cracow. This is not only because of its budget price. For centuries Cracow was a place where Tokay wines were stored for ageing, in barrels housed in large cellars beneath Market Square, before being exported all over the world.

Non-Alcoholic Drinks

MINERAL water, sparkling and still, is the most popular non-alcoholic drink. Many brands of mineral water come from the springs in the mountain foothills or highlands not far from Cracow. Fruit juices are also popular. Apple and blackcurrant juices are Polish specialities.

Apple juice

Blackcurrant juice

Choosing a Restaurant

WHILE SELECTING RESTAURANTS for the listings below, good food and value for money were the main criteria. Some more expensive restaurants, beyond the means of the average Pole, are also included. These restaurants are renowned for their excellent cuisine and represent the best that Cracow has to offer.

Restaurant	Price	Attractive Location	Outdoor Eating	Live Music	Late Opening	Highly Recommended	Polish Cuisine
WAWEL HILL *(see p188)*							
Na Wawelu	zł zł zł	●					■
OKÓŁ AND STRADOM QUARTERS *(see p188)*							
Vega Vegetarian Bar	zł			●			
Pod Baranem	zł zł						■
Taco	zł zł	●			■		
Baba Ryba	zł zł zł			●			■
Chłopskie Jadło	zł zł zł			●	■	●	■
Orient Express	zł zł zł	●	■		■	●	
Paese	zł zł zł	●			■	●	
Pod Aniołami	zł zł zł	●	■		■	●	■
OLD QUARTER *(see pp188–191)*							
Jadłodajnia 'U Stasi'	zł					●	■
Akropolis	zł zł		■		■		
Cechowa	zł zł						■
El Paso	zł zł	●			■		
Gospoda CK Dezerter	zł zł	●			■	●	
Hawełka	zł zł	●			■	●	■
Piwnica Pod Ogródkiem	zł zł		■	●	■		
Pizzeria Cyklop	zł zł						
Sphinks	zł zł	●					
Szuflada	zł zł				■		
Café Restaurant Europejska	zł zł zł	●	■		■	●	
Cherubino	zł zł zł	●				●	
Chimera	zł zł zł	●				●	■
Da Pietro	zł zł zł	●	■		■		
Francuski Restaurant	zł zł zł				■		■
Krew i Roza	zł zł zł	●	■	●	■	●	■
Lemon	zł zł zł	●	■	●		●	
U Szkota	zł zł zł	●			■		
Amarone	zł zł zł zł	●			■	●	
Cyrano de Bergerac	zł zł zł zł	●	■		■	●	
Elektor	zł zł zł zł	●			■		■
Hawełka-Tetmajerowska	zł zł zł zł	●			■	●	■
Wentzl	zł zł zł zł	●	■	●	■	●	■
Wierzynek	zł zł zł zł	●	■		■		■
KAZIMIERZ QUARTER *(see p191)*							
Alef	zł zł zł	●	■	●	■	●	
Restauracja Norymberska	zł zł zł	●	■				
Szeroka	zł zł zł	●	■				
PIASEK AND NOWY ŚWIAT *(see p191)*							
CK Browar	zł zł		■	●	■		■

ATTRACTIVE LOCATION
A restaurant in a historic or unusual building.

LATE OPENING
Last orders taken after 11pm.

OUTDOOR EATING
Outside tables available, weather permitting.

POLISH CUISINE
A large selection of Polish dishes is available.

		ATTRACTIVE LOCATION	OUTDOOR EATING	LIVE MUSIC	LATE OPENING	HIGHLY RECOMMENDED	POLISH CUISINE
FURTHER AFIELD *(see p191)*							
Margit	zł zł		■				■
Mesa kapitana Cooka	zł zł		■			●	■
U Ziyada	zł zł	●	■				
A Dong	zł zł zł				■	●	
Karczma Pod Blachą	zł zł zł	●	■	●			■
Villa Decius	zł zł zł zł	●	■	●	■		

USING THE LISTINGS

(See pp188–191)

- ☐ Open
- ● Closed
- Ⅴ Vegetarian dishes available
- ♫ Live music
- ▦ Outdoor eating
- ★ Highly recommended

 Credit cards accepted
AE American Express
DC Diners Club
MC MasterCard/Access
V Visa
JCB Japanese Credit Bureau

Price categories for a three-course meal per person, including tax and service and a 0.25 litre carafe of wine or beer in Złoty:

zł under 20
zł zł 20 – 40
zł zł zł 40 – 75
zł zł zł zł over 75

WAWEL HILL

Na Wawelu

Wzgórze Wawelskie 9. **Map** 3 C1
(5 C5). 🛈 411 65 98. 🕐 noon–8pm.
🍴 AE, V, MC, DC, JCB. 📷 🍷
ⓩⓩ

The only restaurant on Wawel
Hill, housed in a building
constructed by the Austrians in the
early 19th century. A flagship
restaurant of the Rotary Club, this
is a must for foreign VIPs visiting
Cracow. Disappointing interior.

There are French dishes on the
menu, introduced by a French
chef who worked here for a
number of years. A carpaccio of
perch-pike and a classic
Châteaubriand served with Colbert
tarragon sauce, are both highly
recommended. A large selection
of French wines. Expensive.

You can stay as long as you
wish but must arrive before 8pm
when the Wawel main gate closes.

OKÓŁ AND STRADOM
QUARTERS

Vega Vegatarian Bar

Św. Gertrudy 7. **Map** 2 D5 (6 E4).
🛈 422 34 94. 🕐 10am–9pm daily.
🍴 V, MC. 🎵 Ⓥ ⓩ

The first truly vegetarian place in
Cracow. Vegetables, tofu and soya
dishes, bran cakes and home-
made juices, tables by candlelight,
live classical music at weekends.

Pod Baranem

Św. Gertrudy 21. **Map** 3 C1 (6 D5).
🛈 429 40 22. 🕐 11am–10pm daily.
🍴 AE, V, MC, DC, JCB. ⓩⓩ

A rather small, smart restaurant
situated opposite the Royal Hotel,
serving traditional Polish cuisine
and big portions. Try the tasty,
boneless roast chicken with a
bread, liver and dill stuffing.
Delicious dried-fruit compote is
served free with each order.

Taco

Poselska 20. **Map** 1 C5 (6 D4).
🛈 421 54 41. 🕐 noon–11pm daily.
📷 🍴 AE, V, MC, DC, JCB. ⓩⓩ

Texan cuisine, as in the El Paso
restaurant (see p189). Always full
of young people and students.
Extra hot chili on request.

Baba Ryba

Św. Agnieszki 1. **Map** 3 C1.
🛈 421 85 20. 🕐 noon–10pm
Sun–Thu, noon–midnight Fri and Sat.
🎵 🍷 ⓩⓩⓩ

At the same address as Chłopskie
Jadło and in adjoining rooms, this
restaurant serves fresh- and
saltwater fish. The furnishings
imitate the interior of a sailing ship
with uncanny realism, including
the sound of waves. As far as the
menu is concerned you will be
spoilt for choice. A variety of
herring-based dishes and smoked
eel are all excellent.

Chłopskie Jadło

Św. Agnieszki 1. **Map** 3 C1. 🛈 421
85 20. 🕐 noon–10pm Sun–Thu, noon–
midnight Fri–Sat. 🎵 ★ ⓩⓩ

A rustic interior modelled on a
peasant cottage, inside a 19th-
century tenement house. There is
another branch of this restaurant
in Głogoczów on the Cracow-Zakopane road, which won the "Teraz
Polska" (best Polish products) award.

This Polish culinary success
story of recent years is reflected in
the menu, featuring traditional,
country-style cuisine. Home-made
bread, lard spread, stuffed cabbage
(gołąbki) and wild mushroom soup
with pasta, as well as a variety of
dumplings and pork spare ribs,
are the main favourites.

Orient Express

Poselska 22. **Map** 1 C5 (6 D4).
🛈 422 66 72. 🕐 1pm–midnight
daily. 📷 🍴 🍷 ★ 🍴 AE, V, MC,
DC, JCB. ⓩⓩⓩ

The interior of this restaurant is
modelled on an early 20th-century
train carriage. Pride of place goes
to the desserts. The Hungarian
Gundelpalacsinta (pancakes with
nut stuffing served with plain
chocolate and alcohol sauce),
pancakes with roasted almond
flakes and French chocolate
mousse are renowned. Before
your dessert try the Flemish-style
beef (beef and onions stewed in
beer, served on bread with Dijon
mustard) or a plaice baked with
tomatoes and garlic.

A good place for pet lovers, but
not so good for those who dislike
dogs. Expect to be welcomed by
the owners' French bulldog.

Paese

Poselska 24. **Map** 1 C5 (6 D3).
🛈 421 62 73. 🕐 1pm–until last
customer leaves, daily. 📷 🍴 Ⓥ ★
🍴 AE, V, MC, DC, JCB. ⓩⓩⓩ

A Corsican restaurant set up in
a rustic, tavern-like interior.
A popular meeting place for
Cracow's artists, politicians and
aristocrats. The visitors' book is
full of laudatory comments signed
by famous people from all over
the world. Leeks in bechamel sauce,
garlic soup and beef fillet with
Roquefort cheese are all worth

trying but fresh seafood is a must.
Belgian-style mussels accompanied by chips, Portuguese-
style baked sardines, and deep-
fried lobster French-style are all
served. The restaurant also has
a good selection of wines,
including Corsican wines at quite
reasonable prices.

Early booking is advisable,
especially for evenings and
anytime at weekends.

Pod Aniołami

Grodzka 35. **Map** 1 C5 (6 D4).
🛈 421 39 99. 🕐 1pm–midnight
Mon–Thu, 1pm–1am Fri–Sun. 🍴 V,
MC, DC, JCB. 📷 🍽 🍷 ★ ⓩⓩⓩ

The restaurant is housed in very
old, painstakingly restored cellars
which were used by medieval
alchemists. The walls are decorated
with old pots and pans, tapestries
and other bric-a-brac. Food is
prepared under a grill or in an oven
situated in one of the dining rooms.

Polish cuisine served here is
dominated by dishes from the
Podhale region in the foothills
of the Tatra Mountains, and
includes grilled smoked ewe's
milk cheese (oszczypek od
Mulicόw), rolls (kukiełki) and
żurek (a fermented, sour soup).
This restaurant makes you want to
return, owing to the menu and
young, friendly staff.

OLD QUARTER

Jadłodajnia "U Stasi"

Mikołajska 16. **Map** 2 D4 (6 E2).
🛈 421 50 84. 🕐 12:30pm–5pm,
Mon–Fri. 🍷 ⓩ

Pass the inner courtyard to enter
this small, very popular place
situated in a tenement house. You
pay as you leave, declaring what
you have eaten. Food, though
simple, has always been good
here even in the lean years.
Home-made dumplings (pierogi),
in summer stuffed with fruit, veal
roast and boiled beef with
horseradish sauce (sztuka mięsa)
take people back to childhood
memories of food prepared by
mother. The highest concentration
of professors per square metre!

Akropolis

Grodzka 9. **Map** 1 C5 (6 D3).
🛈 421 77 25. 🕐 10am–1am daily.
📷 🍽 ⓩⓩ

A Greek self-service bar.
Moussaka, stuffed peppers and
other Greek dishes are kept warm
on a long, illuminated counter.
Gyros (doner) and souvlaki
(kebab) are also served.

Generous portions. A good
place for those on the move.

Cechowa

Jagiellońska 11. **Map** 1 C4 (5 C2).
📞 421 09 36. ⏰ 11am–10pm daily.
🍽 🍴 AE, V, MC, DC, JCB. ⓩⓩ

This place is very popular with
Cracow's intelligentsia. The name
"Cechowa" means Guild. Above
the dado walls are the coats of
arms of Cracow's craft guilds.

Traditional Polish cuisine is
served here and includes *barszcz*
(beetroot soup), white sausage in
onion sauce, *pierogi* (dumplings),
sztuka mięsa (boiled beef with
horseradish sauce) and *schabowy*
(a fried pork chop coated with egg
and breadcrumbs) accompanied
by sauerkraut. Moderate prices.

El Paso

Św. Krzyża 13. **Map** 2 D4 (6 E2).
📞 421 32 96. ⏰ 1pm–11pm daily.
🍽 🍴 AE, V, MC, JCB. ⓩⓩ

Typically Texan cuisine, with
standard *chili con carne* but also
nachos, *tacos* and *burritos*. The
decoration has transformed this
interior into a cowboys' saloon.
The Tequila tastes particularly
good here, being served with salt
and a piece of lime and not, as in
other bars in Poland, with lemon. A
number of brands of Mexican
beer are served, including the
popular Corona.

Gospoda CK Dezerter

Bracka 6. **Map** 1 C4 (6 D3). 📞 422
79 31. ⏰ 9am–midnight daily. 🍽 ★
🍴 AE, V, MC, DC, JCB. ⓩⓩ

This place has an Austro-
Hungarian atmosphere. Czech
beer is served from the barrel.
Rosół (bouillon) with liver
dumplings, bread with goulash, as
well as appetizing dumplings with
a choice of stuffing including
cheese, sauerkraut and
buckwheat, are served here.

Hawełka

Rynek Główny 34. **Map** 1 C4 (6 D2).
📞 422 47 53. ⏰ noon–11pm daily
🍽 🍷 ★ AE, V, MC, DC, JCB. ⓩⓩ

The tradition of good food served
here goes back to the 19th century,
when Antoni Hawełka (Havelka)
opened to the public a breakfast
room at the back of his shop in
Cracow, then part of Galicia,
selling imported goods. The place
was soon transformed into a
restaurant and gained considerable
fame throughout the Empire. It
was nationalized after World
War II and fell into neglect like
everything else.

Revived following the collapse
of communism, the place is still
"looked after" by His Imperial
Majesty Franz Joseph gazing from
his full-length portrait. This is an
ideal place for a nostalgic yet
quick and inexpensive meal. The
żurek and goulash soups, duck
Cracow-style (wild duck served
with wild mushrooms and pearl
barley), sauerkraut dumplings and
pepper casserole with a Viennese
dumpling, along with the
"compulsory" half a litre of beer,
are all to be recommended.

A place called Havelka can also
be found in Vienna and this
boosts the pride of the Cracovians.
The Viennese Art Nouveau café
was established by Leopold
Havelka, a relative of Antoni.

Piwnica Pod Ogródkiem

Jagiellońska 6. **Map** 1 C4 (5 C2).
📞 421 60 29. ⏰ 1pm–until last
customer leaves, daily. 🍽 🍴 🎵 V
🍷 🍴 AE, V, MC, DC, JCB. ⓩⓩ

This pub is housed in the cellars,
but in summer has also a lovely
and very popular outdoor eating
area within the inner courtyard.
Normandy pancakes, *galettes*,
made of buckwheat flour and with
all sorts of fillings, are the
speciality here. A good selection
of beers and spirits. Live music at
the weekends.

Pizzeria Cyklop

Mikołajska 16. **Map** 1 C4 (6 E2).
📞 421 66 03. ⏰ 11.30am–10pm
daily. 🍴 AE, V, MC. V ⓩⓩ

This place specializes in pizzas
baked in a wood-fired oven as
well as grilled meat and salads.
Reasonable prices.

Sphinks

Rynek Główny 26. **Map** 1 C4 (6 D2).
📞 423 11 44. ⏰ 11am–11pm daily.
🍽 V 🍴 V, MC. ⓩⓩ

One of the Sphinks chain of
restaurants, this fast food outlet
offers a quick bite at reasonable
prices, and is perfect if you are in a
hurry. Located right in the centre of
things in Market Square, it is very
convenient for all the sights in the
Old Quarter. The menu includes
pizzas, spicy meat dishes, salads
and chicken and chips, so would
probably please any children in
your party.

Szuflada

Wiślna 5. **Map** 1 C4 (5 C3).
📞 423 13 34. ⏰ 11am–1am daily.
🍴 AE, V, MC, DC, JCB. ⓩⓩ

This place is rightly called "sur-
restaurant". This is due to its
interior decoration influenced by
the Surrealist art of Salvador Dalí,
Max Ernst and Kazimierz Mikulski.
The cuisine, unfortunately, does
not show this level of refinement.
A large selection of spirits.

Café Restaurant Europejska

Rynek Główny 35. **Map** 1 C4 (6 D2).
📞 429 34 93. ⏰ 8am–midnight
daily. 🍽 🍴 V ★ 🍴 AE, V, MC,
DC, JCB. ⓩⓩⓩ

This used to be one of the most
popular cafés in town, decorated
in the Art Nouveau style.
Following refurbishment it has
retained its original character but
additionally acquired an enormous
English bar featuring a golden
coffee-machine. The café serves
a breakfast of a soft boiled egg
in a glass, fresh rolls, cream
and coffee accompanied by a
newspaper. Beef *carpaccio*, other
grilled meats and fish can be
ordered for lunch or dinner,
and pancakes *à la Gundel* for
dessert. In summer a garden café
is set up by the Europejska.

Cherubino

Św. Tomasza 15. **Map** 1 C4 (6 D2).
📞 429 40 07. ⏰ noon–midnight
daily (11pm Sun) 🍴 V, MC, DC, JCB.
🍽 V 🍴 ★ ⓩⓩⓩ

A beautiful interior in which
Tuscan and Polish dishes are
served. There is fantastic pasta,
which is always served *al dente*.
In addition, meat is prepared
under a grill that is placed in the
dining room.

Chimera

Św. Anny 3. **Map** 1 C4 (5 C2).
📞 423 21 78. Restaurant ⏰ noon–
10pm daily (11pm Sat & Sun). 🍽 V
🍷 🍴 AE, V, MC, DC, JCB. ★
ⓩⓩⓩ **Salad bar** 🍽 🍴 V ⓩⓩ

The Chimera restaurant was
opened on the ground floor as
an addition to an existing salad
bar, trading under the same name
and ownership, which was housed
in the Gothic cellars. The bar is
very popular with vegetarians,
students and the local English-
speaking community, while
the Chimera restaurant is a
favourite haunt of artists,
journalists and businessmen.

The bar offers a large selection
of salads, fruit and vegetable
juices, and in winter, jacket
potatoes baked in the fireplace.
Several kinds of asparagus dishes
can be ordered in season. Evening
concerts of Renaissance and
other music take place here.
On Sundays, plays for children
are staged. A number of tables
are pleasantly arranged on
the patio for outdoor dining.

The restaurant serves roasts of
suckling pig, lamb and goat, as
well as borsch (beetroot soup)
with *kulebiak* (cabbage in pastry)
and exquisite *nalewka* (home-
flavoured vodka).

For key to symbols *see p187*

Da Pietro

Rynek Główny 17. **Map** 1 C4 (6 D3).
【 422 32 79. ○ 12.30am–midnight daily. ▦ ♨ ▨ AE, V, MC, DC, JCB. ⓩⓩⓩ

Housed in Gothic and Renaissance cellars, this Italian restaurant is named after the late Piotr Skrzynecki.

Good but not too exciting cuisine. Salmon *carpaccio* and that of beef loin, creamed spinach with garlic dotted with whipped cream, *vitello tonnato* (marinated veal served cold with a sauce, such as tuna or anchovy) are all good. Grilled meat, pizza and Italian wines are on the menu.

Francuski Restaurant

Pijarska 13. **Map** 1 C4 (6 D1).
【 422 51 22. ○ 6–24 daily. ▮ ▨ AE, V, MC, DC, JCB. ⓩⓩⓩ

This air-conditioned restaurant at the Francuski Hotel serves Polish and French cuisine, including a snail pot, quails cooked in the old-French style and a speciality named after Maria Walewska, Napoleon's mistress. Good food and a unique *fin de siècle* atmosphere makes this restaurant one of the favourite places for socializing.

Krew i Roza

Grodzka 9. **Map** 1 C5 (6 D4). 【 429 61 87. ○ noon–midnight daily. ▦ ▦ ▮ ▨ AE, V, MC, DC, JCB. ⓩⓩⓩⓩ

This popular and traditional restaurant is conveniently located for sightseeing between Market Square and the Royal Castle. The chef specializes in hearty dishes such as wild game, roasted pork with plums, stuffed trout and other old Polish favourites.

The best time to visit is on Friday evenings, when there is live music from a variety of local bands. Unsurprisingly, this place is usually packed.

Lemon

Floriańska 53. **Map** 2 D4 (6 E1).
【 292 16 86. ○ noon–midnight daily. ▦ ▮ ★ ⓩⓩⓩ

Pass through a courtyard to enter this finely decorated restaurant serving Serbian food. On warm summer days the sliding glass doors open to form a large patio. There is a centrally situated grill. Plaits of dried paprika and garlic decorate the walls. The menu features many Balkan specialities, such as *ghibanitza* (cheese in pastry), *plyeskavitza* (grilled meat), *ayvar* (spread made from peppers, aubergines and grilled garlic). Two kinds of Croatian *rakhia* complement the wine list.

U Szkota

Mikołajska 4. **Map** 2 D4 (6 E2).
【 422 15 70. ○ noon–midnight daily. ▮ ▨ AE, V, MC, DC, JCB. ⓩⓩⓩ

This cosy restaurant with a fireplace is situated in cellars. In keeping with its Scottish theme the waiters wear tartan and there are a number of Scottish dishes on the menu, including haggis. When it comes to choosing what to drink, Scotch whisky is naturally recommended. A large selection of brands is available here, as well as American bourbons and Irish whiskeys.

Amarone

Floriańska 14. **Map** 1 C4 (6 E2).
【 422 12 44. ○ noon–until the last customer leaves, daily. ▦ Ⓥ ★ ▨ AE, V, MC, JCB. ⓩⓩⓩ

This Italian restaurant belongs to the Pod Różą Hotel. You may also use the entrance in St Thomas Street (Św. Tomasza). The interior decoration is adventurous by Cracow standards and combines modern design with historic architecture. The inner courtyard is covered with a glass roof.

The cuisine is unusual and includes *carpaccio* of pigeon, as well as good pasta and desserts. House wines are available.

Cyrano de Bergerac

Sławkowska 26. **Map** 1 C4 (6 D1).
【 411 72 88. ○ 9am–11pm daily. ▦ ▦ ▮ ★ ▨ AE, V, MC, DC, JCB. ⓩⓩⓩⓩ

A world-class French restaurant housed in beautiful medieval cellars. It has two elegant and cosy dining rooms, and a lovely and quiet patio is used in summer. The master chef, Pierre Gaillard from Lyon, trained under the famous Paul Bocuse, nicknamed the Ambassador of French gastronomy. The dishes served here are truly poetic and include: superb home-made *foie gras* (a pâté made from fattened liver of geese or duck) served either hot or cold in a delicious lemon and honey sauce; morel turnovers, *garbure soupe béarnaise* with pieces of goose; a variety of fish dishes made from pike-perch, turbot, burbot and mullet. First-class wine cellar. Expensive but well worth the price.

Elektor. Elektor Hotel

Szpitalna 28. **Map** 2 D4 (6 E2).
【 423 23 17. ○ noon–midnight daily. ▦ Ⓥ ▨ AE, V, MC, DC, JCB. ⓩⓩⓩⓩ

The restaurant was the talk of the town during the brief visit of the Crown Prince and Princess of Japan to Cracow. The couple stayed in the Elektor Hotel in 1994. The Princess enjoyed baby new potatoes, served with butter and fresh dill, so much that she ordered them every day.

If potatoes do not appeal to your taste you may chose another dish from the menu of "low-fat" traditional Polish and foreign foods. There is a good selection of wines, which are also available from the wine-bar in the cellar.

Hawełka-Tetmajerowska

Rynek Główny 34. **Map** 1 C4 (6 D2).
【 422 47 53. ○ noon–4pm and 6pm–until the last customer leaves, daily. ▦ ▮ ★ ▨ AE, V, MC, DC, JCB. ⓩⓩⓩⓩ

On the first floor of this tenement house is the Tetmajer Hall, named after the artist Włodzimierz Tetmajer who painted the decorative frieze depicting the legend of Master Twardowski. The hall houses an elegant and very expensive restaurant.

The menu is not extensive but includes choice Polish dishes. The house caviar from Siberia comes in little jars featuring Hawełka's own label, whose design has remained unchanged for more than a century. Hawełka was appointed supplier to the imperial court in Vienna. Perfect service, house-wine cellar.

Wentzl

Rynek Główny 19. **Map** 1 C4 (6 D3).
【 429 57 12. ○ noon–until the last customer leaves, daily. ▦ ▦ ♫ ▮ ★ ▨ AE, V, MC, DC, JCB. ⓩⓩⓩⓩ

This celebrated restaurant, established in the late 18th century, bears the name of its first owner. It was nationalized after World War II and renamed, strangely enough, as "Under the Icon". The new name referred to the large Baroque image of the Virgin Mary decorating the façade. The house was the only one in Market Square to have survived the great fire of 1850. The image also survived. According to an old saying, great news can be trumpeted in Cracow either from above the icon (meaning from the bugle-tower of St Mary's) or from under the icon, meaning the Wentzl restaurant.

Wentzl was once famous for a local speciality, *maczanka*. The dish consisted of pork served on bread with onion and caraway sauce. The restaurant re-opened recently after a long break. The menu features a number of Austro-Hungarian recipes, including *Wiener schnitzel*, Hungarian-style pike-perch, goulash soup, pancakes *à la Gundel* and, of course, *maczanka*. Live jazz is played here at weekends. You can also try out the revolving dance floor, which is unique in Cracow.

Wierzynek

Rynek Główny 15. **Map** 1 C4 (6 D3).
📞 292 10 88. ⏰ 10am–11pm daily.
❄ 🍴 🎵 ♦ *AE, V, MC, DC, JCB.*
ZŁ ZŁ ZŁ ZŁ

The place is reputed to have been the venue for a banquet hosted in 1364 by a Cracow burgher, Mikołaj Wierzynek, for five European sovereigns. The restaurant was actually established in 1945 as the Wierzynek Inn. It was soon nationalized and transformed into a flagship restaurant for visiting foreign VIPs.

KAZIMIERZ QUARTER

Alef

Szeroka 17. **Map** 4 E1. 📞 421 38 70.
⏰ 10am–until the last customer leaves, daily. ❄ 🍴 🎵 ♦ ★ V, MC. ZŁ ZŁ ZŁ

Alef is a non-kosher Jewish restaurant in an old and delightful house in Kazimierz. On the same street is the restaurant's other outlet, housed at No. 6 in the former *mykva* (baths). On your first visit *gefilte fisch* (stuffed carp), stuffed goose necks, *tchoolent*, stuffed vine leaves and goose liver fried with almonds and raisins are musts. Evening concerts of ethnic music, including gypsy and Russian love songs.

Restauracja Norymberska

Krakowska 27. **Map** 4 D2.
⏰ noon–11pm daily. ❄ 🍴 ♦
AE, V, MC, DC, JCB. ZŁ ZŁ ZŁ

Cracow's links with Nuremberg were established long ago. Twinned restaurants exist in both cities. The one in Cracow is housed in the Nuremberg House. *Golonka*, a boiled pork knuckle accompanied by cabbage and served with Nuremberg Tucher beer, is the speciality here.

Szeroka

Szeroka 39. **Map** 4 E1. 📞 422 67 90.
⏰ noon–10pm daily. ❄ 🍴 V ♦
♦ *AE, V, MC, DC, JCB.* ZŁ ZŁ ZŁ

Szeroka is the only Jewish restaurant in Cracow to be monitored by the rabbi so that it fulfils kosher food requirements. Minced herrings, roast duck and Passover Slivovitz (plum vodka) are all musts here. A kosher fast-food bar is housed on the ground floor of this house managed by the Nissenbaum Foundation. The bar is very popular with groups of tourists from Israel.

PIASEK AND NOWY ŚWIAT

CK Browar

Podwale 6. **Map** 1 B4 (5 C2).
📞 429 25 05. ⏰ 10am–2am daily.
🍴 🎵 ♦ V, MC, DC, JCB. ZŁ ZŁ

This is the only establishment in Cracow, and possibly one of two existing in Poland, where you can drink, in a mug, unpasteurized beer brewed on site. Delicious! The licensee is Austrian, so it should not come as a surprise that visitors are "greeted" by Emperor Franz Joseph, depicted in a large portrait hanging by the entrance to the enormous cellars (the Elefant department store is above). The acronym CK in the name means in Polish "royal and imperial" and is associated with everything Austro-Hungarian. The restaurant serves hot starters to go with draught beer, as well as roast pork with *knedle* (potato dumplings) and cabbage, and other specialities.

FURTHER AFIELD

Margit

Chłopickiego 3. **Map** 2 F3. 📞 411 53 31. ⏰ 10am–10pm daily. V 🍴
♦ V, MC, DC, JCB. ZŁ ZŁ

This restaurant in a house with a garden is located in a residential estate built before World War II for the military elite. Polish and European cuisine is served here, and pizza baked on site is a speciality. Decent food.

Mesa kapitana Cooka

Zamoyskiego 52. **Map** 4 D4.
📞 656 08 93. ⏰ noon–10pm daily.
V 🍴 ♦ ★ ♦ *AE, V, MC, DC, JCB.* ZŁ ZŁ

One of a very few good restaurants in the Podgórze quarter located on the opposite bank of the Vistula from the Old Town. It specializes in fish and seafood. Food is good and tempting and prices equally so. Garlic pancakes with bran and salmon are delicious. In summer, tables are set up outdoors in a very pleasant garden.

U Ziyada

Jodłowa 13. 📞 421 98 31.
⏰ Restaurant noon–9pm daily. Café 8am–midnight daily. ❄ 🍴 ♦
AE, V, MC, DC, JCB. ZŁ ZŁ

The view offered from this restaurant-cum-café, situated on top of high, white cliffs above the Vistula, is quite extraordinary: it

extends over the river and the Tyniec Abbey and Bielany Monastery. U Ziyada is housed in a most unusual round house built in 1928 by Adolf Szyszko-Bohusz, the architect and restorer of Wawel Castle. Next door is a building erected during the war by the Germans. It is modelled on the Alpine residences of Adolf Hitler. Both buildings are today managed by the Kolegium Polonijne of the Jagiellonian University. The restaurant is run by a Kurd, Ziyad, whose acquaintances include the city's dignitaries. A rare opportunity to taste Kurdish specialities, as well as Polish cuisine.

A Dong

Brodzińskiego 3. **Map** 4 E3.
📞 656 48 72. ⏰ 11am–11pm. V
★ ♦ *AE, V, MC, DC, JCB.* ZŁ ZŁ

Exquisite cuisine. Without question the best restaurant serving Chinese and Vietnamese food in Cracow. Among other specialities is a highly recommended variant of *fondue*. It is a seafood dish which you prepare yourself in a special pan, heated over a log fire, boiling various sea creatures in stock. Duck and crisp, fried frog legs in batter and stuffed octopus are all delicious.

Karczma Pod Blachą

Piastowska 22. ⏰ 11am–10pm daily.
❄ 🍴 🎵 ♦ *AE, V, MC, DC, JCB.* ZŁ ZŁ ZŁ

Housed in an authentic 18th-century inn in Cichy Kącik near Błonia, this restaurant caters mainly for foreign tourists travelling in groups and interested in local folklore.

Traditional, country-style Polish cuisine based on old recipes is served here. The *gramatka*, for example, is a beer soup served with curd cheese. In the summer you can delight in eating outdoors in the garden. Mallows growing along a wooden fence give this place a truly rustic character. Customers enjoy drinking vodka and listening to country music while they wait for their meat, grilled on a log fire. Pretty expensive.

Villa Decius

28 lipca 17a. 📞 425 33 90.
⏰ noon–1am daily. ❄ 🍴 V ♦
🎵 ♦ *AE, V, MC, DC, JCB.* ZŁ ZŁ ZŁ

A luxurious restaurant housed in the beautiful Renaissance Villa Decius. The villa belonged to an Italian courtier to Zygmunt the Old, Justus Decius. It was recently painstakingly restored.

International Italian, French and Polish cuisine is served here while music of the Renaissance is played live.

For key to symbols *see p187*

Cafés and Bars

CRACOW'S CAFÉS are an important part of everyday life and often institutions in their own right. It would be unthinkable to deny a Cracovian his or her daily 15 minutes or so spent chatting with a friend or reading a newspaper in a café. The majority of cafés have regular customers, who come year in, year out to their chosen place, every day except at of weekends.

CAFÉS

SITUATED IN THE VERY HEART of the city, the **Noworolski** is one of the longest established cafés. It is housed in the Cloth Hall, with its entrance facing the Mickiewicz Monument. It dates back to the turn of the 19th century. The interior, modelled on Viennese cafés, has preserved its original appearance. A visit to the **Jama Michalika** *(see p114),* renowned for the Zielony Balonik (Green Balloon) Cabaret, is a must. However, the Art Nouveau rooms offer a feast for the eye rather than the palate. They are now often deserted, possibly because of a total ban on smoking (smoke would damage the historic interior).

The **Pożegnanie z Afryką** (Out of Africa) is the best place for lovers of good coffee. The coffee served here will satisfy even the most demanding customer. Situated in St Thomas Street (Św. Tomasza), it is a coffee bar and shop. A variety of brands are available here, which can be prepared in small espresso machines. The smell is so fantastic that even a connoisseur will not be able to resist the temptation. There are many outlets of Pożegnanie z Afryką in other cities throughout Poland but the company started in Cracow and has its headquarters here.

The **Café Larousse** is a tiny place, ideal for a romantic date. The walls of this lovely café are all papered with pages taken from 19th-century editions of the well-known French dictionary. If you want to travel back in time and see how a patisserie looked in the early 19th century, then **Redolfi** in Market Square is the place to visit, to see the original period furnishing. This café was established by a Swiss man, Lorenzo Paganino Cortesi, in 1823, but the name Redolfi refers to its second owner, also a Swiss. Lunch is also served here.

The **Maska** is a favourite haunt with celebrities, especially from the theatre and film circles. It is housed in the cellars of the Stary (Old) Theatre and is decorated in Art Deco style. The Maska was co-founded some years ago by the well-known actor, Tadeusz Huk. The film and theatre director Andrzej Wajda is one of those who have a permanent reservation here. Take a break from eyeing the stars to sample the delicious roast garlic and a drink called "Teraz Polska" (Poland Now). This famous cocktail imitates the colours of the Polish flag.

Delicious canapés served on bread from the highlands and tea with home-made raspberry syrup are just two specialities of the **Café Camelot**. The walls here are decorated with pictures by the celebrated Polish naive artist Nikifor. The **Dym** (Smoke) is next door, serving delicious Pischinger cake as well as beer and spirits.

STREET CAFÉS

MOST of the eating establishments in Market Square open street bars and cafés in the spring and summer. The square is thus transformed into a huge open-air café for thousands of customers.

The **Bambus** (Bamboo) Café, situated in front of the Palace of the Rams, is very popular during the day. The street café set up by the **Black Gallery** is very busy at night, sometimes till the early hours. An enormous parachute will protect you from rain, and the house drink Kamikaze, a deceptive mixture of Blue Curacao, vodka and lemon juice, may well help you not to notice any change in the weather.

If you decide to eat at one of the outdoor restaurant tables, expect a lunch rather than a full dinner menu. Dishes served outside are less elaborate. Bear in mind that the journey from the kitchen to the table is a long one and makes serving an exotic *flambé* lobster, for example, almost impossible.

All sorts of street buskers roam and play in and around the street cafés. They request gratuities but you are not obliged to give any. It is worth listening to the Gypsy band, with a partially paralysed fiddler in a wheelchair, who plays his violin holding it like a double-bass.

BARS

A NUMBER of new bars have opened in Cracow in recent years. They are often called pubs as in English. They are housed in cellars and are open till late. Live music is played in many. The **Free Pub** and **Roentgen** are open longest. They are both very popular with young people (but generally not teenagers) and artists. The Roentgen has a dental chair, in which you can sit and drink. Young people like to meet in the **Pod Papugami** (Parrots) where there is a disco.

The **Pod Złotą Pipą** is popular with more conservative customers. The place is nostalgically decorated in the Austro-Hungarian style and features many portraits of His Imperial Majesty Franz Joseph and the Empress Sissi. White sausage with cabbage and peas is served here, and to accompany this you may order authentic Czech Budweiser on draught. The **Klub Kulturalny** (Culture Club) has recently become very fashionable. The large cellars have a mosaic floor, which leads some to believe, after a few drinks, they are in Ravenna.

DIRECTORY

Albo Tak
Mały Rynek.
Map 2 D4 (6 E3).
421 11 05.

Arka Noego
Szeroka 2.
Map 4 E1.
421 71 66.

Arlekin
Rynek Główny 24.
Map 1 C4 (6 D2).
430 24 57.

Bambus Café
Rynek Główny 27.
Map 1 C4 (6 D2).
421 97 25.

Black Gallery
Mikołajska 24.
Map 2 D4 (6 E2).
421 00 30.

Bosto
Floriańska 33.
Map 2 D4 (6 E2).
421 16 93.

**Burzliwy
Poniedziałek**
Grodzka 4.
Map 1 C5 (6 D3).

Café Cabaret
Jabłonowskich 6.
Map 1 B4 (5 B4).
422 85 77.

Café Camelot
Św. Tomasza 17.
Map 1 C4 (6 D2).
421 01 23.

Café Larousse
Św. Tomasza 22.
Map 1 C4 (6 E2).

Café Molier
Szewska 4.
Map 1 C4 (5 C2).
292 64 00.

**Café
Numer 0**
Rynek Główny 6.
Map 1 C4 (6 D2).

Casa de la Pizza
Mały Rynek 2.
Map 1 C4 (6 E3).
421 64 98.

Dandy Café
Św. Tomasza 19.
Map 1 C4 (6 D2).
421 73 91.

Deja vu
Rynek Główny 9.
Map 1 C4 (6 D2).

Dom Wina
Pijarska 11.
Map 1 C4 (6 D1).

Dym
Św. Tomasza 13.
Map 1 C4 (6 D2).
423 18 74.

Free Pub
Sławkowska 4.
Map 1 C4 (6 D2).
413 03 66.

George
Lea 5a.
Map 1 A3.

Hamlet
Miodowa 9.
Map 4 D1 (6 F5).
422 12 11.

**Jama
Michalika**
Floriańska 45.
Map 2 D4 (6 E2).
422 15 61.

**Jazz Rock
Café**
Sławkowska 12.
Map 1 C4 (6 E1).
422 19 88.

John Bull
Mikołajska 2.
Map 2 D4 (6 E2).
423 11 68.

Kapsuła
Rynek Główny 6.
Map 1 C4 (6 D2).

**Kawiarnia
Noworolski**
Rynek Główny 1,
Cloth Hall.
Map 1 C4 (6 D2).
422 47 71.

**Klub
Kulturalny**
Szewska 25.
Map 1 C4 (5 C2).
429 67 39.

Krzysztofory
Szczepańska 2.
Map 1 C4 (6 D2).
422 93 60.

Lamus
Karmelicka 54.
Map 1 B3.
633 37 24.

Le Fumoir
Sławkowska 26.
Map 1 C4 (6 D2).
429 54 28.

Manggha
Starowiślna 10.
Map 2 D5 (6 E3).
422 85 61.

Maska
Jagiellońska 1.
Map 1 C4 (5 C2).
429 60 44.

Milano
Praska 18.
266 64 83.

Osorya
Jagiellońska 5.
Map 1 C4 (6 D2).
292 80 20.

**Piwnica
pod Ogródkiem**
Jagiellońska 6.
Map 1 C4 (5 C2).
421 60 29.

**Pod Białym
Orłem**
Rynek Główny 45.
Map 1 C4 (6 D2).
421 57 97.

Pod Chochołami
Plac św. Ducha 1.
Map 2 D4 (6 E2).
422 45 75 w. 54.

Pod Papugami
Szpitalna 1.
Map 2 D4 (6 E2).
421 93 07.

Pod Papugami
Św. Jana 18.
Map 1 C4 (6 D2).
422 82 99.

**Pod Złotą
Pipą**
Floriańska 30.
Map 2 D4 (6 E2).
421 94 66.

**Pożegnanie
z Afryką**
Św. Tomasza 21.
Map 1 C4 (6 E2).
644 47 45.

Prohibicja
Grodzka 51.
Map 1 C5 (6 D4).
422 86 41.

Ratuszowa
Rynek Główny 1.
Map 1 C4 (6 D2).
421 13 26.

Redolfi
Rynek Główny 38.
Map 1 C4 (6 D2).
423 05 79.

Roentgen
Plac Szczepański 3.
Map 1 C4 (5 C2).

Santos
Grodzka 65.
Map 3 C1 (6 D5).
423 14 87.

Stare Mury
Pijarska 21. **Map** 2 D4 (6 E1).
421 38 98.

Strawberry
Św. Tomasza 1.
Map 1 C4 (6 D2).
422 73 42.

Sylaba
Sławkowska 10.
Map 1 C4 (6 D1).

U Literatów
Kanonicza 7.
Map 1 C5 (6 D4).
421 86 66.

U Louisa
Rynek Główny 13.
Map 1 C4 (6 D2).
421 80 92.

Vis-a-vis
Rynek Główny 29.
Map 1 C4 (6 D2).
422 69 61.

Windsor
Rynek Główny 25.
Map 1 C4 (6 D2).
421 98 94.

Zdarzenie
Plac Mariacki 7.
Map 1 C4 (6 D2).
421 84 86.

SHOPS AND MARKETS

CRACOW HAS ALWAYS been a favourable place for merchants. Recent reforms have stimulated trade. Unlike in other Polish cities, most of the prewar buildings in Cracow have remained in private hands. After 1989 the number of new shops opening surged. House owners opened shops themselves or let premises out. A profusion of shop-signs appeared on façades, inner courtyards and basements. Quality

A wooden statue of Christ

soon took over and big Western names also began to appear. Today one can hardly tell the difference between a Cracow shop and its Viennese or Parisian counterpart. The area around Market Square is especially good for shopping. It offers a variety of elegant shops, little traffic and many cafés. Markets and street stalls offer a different kind of shopping and a lively atmosphere. There is something for everyone.

SHOPPING HOURS

IN POLAND, unlike in many Western European countries, there is no law regulating the hours of trade. The shop owner decides when to open and close his shop and this is regarded as a condition of a free-market economy. Grocers open in Cracow at 6 or 7 o'clock in the morning and close at 7pm at the earliest. Many remain open until 10pm or longer, and a dozen or so shops are open 24 hours. Other shops are generally open between 10am and 7pm on weekdays but on Saturdays close at 2 or 3pm. All shops within the Planty green belt tend to trade on Sundays for similar periods to those on Saturdays. All shops are customarily open on the Sunday preceding Christmas and Easter Day. Supermarkets are at their busiest on Friday afternoon and evening.

Pictures for sale, displayed on the wall near St Florian's Gate

The great number of tourist shops in the centre attract customers all the time regardless of the day of the week but Saturdays are possibly the busiest.

HOW TO PAY

CASH IS THE MOST popular form of payment throughout Poland, but most shops in the centre

of Cracow accept major credit cards, as indicated by stickers displayed in their windows. Supermarkets and department stores also accept credit cards as well as cheques, but the latter must be issued by a Polish bank. All prices are inclusive of VAT which can be claimed back on the Polish border if the goods were bought in shops with labels TAX FREE.

DEPARTMENT STORES AND SHOPPING CENTRES

JUBILAT, built in the mid-1970s, is the largest department store in Cracow. The food department is on the ground floor, and on the other floors you may find household goods, furniture and electrical appliances, clothes, shoes and cosmetics, as well as toys and books. The "Galeria Centrum", another departament store is located

A collectors' fair in Market Square

by Market Square. The large Krakchemia shopping centre was built after 1989. It houses two enormous halls. Food, shoes, clothes, cosmetics and kitchenwares are sold in one of them and items for the home and garden in the other. Just out of town, but well served by a bus route, is the Nico store. It sells Italian clothes and shoes.

The Mozart Shopping Centre was established recently next to the Billa supermarket. Mozart has many small fashion and shoe boutiques, as well as chemists (drug stores) served by an escalator.

The large Herbewo store is housed in a building which dates from the inter-war years. Its name originates from the then famous manufacturer of the most popular cigarette holders and other products.

Dolls in regional costumes sold in the Cloth Hall

Jewellery shop on Floriańska Street

MARKETS AND FAIRS

CRACOW'S MARKETS are never called bazaars as in other Polish towns. Here the term bazaar has a pejorative connotation. In Cracow one goes to the 'square' to buy fruit and vegetables, cheese, meat, fish or other produce from the stall-holders.

The Old Kleparz market is the nearest to the city centre. The New Kleparz market sells not only food but also flowers and clothes, while every Tuesday and Friday you will find stalls

selling brooms, clay pots and wickerware. The market in Grzegórzecka Street by the Market Hall is the biggest and full of stalls selling meat, fruit and vegetables. On Sundays you have the added attraction of book and antique stalls.

The unique atmosphere of the New Market in Kazimierz was used to good effect in the filming of *Days and Nights (Noce i dnie)*, a Polish film after a well-known novel by Maria Dąbrowska of the same title. The late 19th-century round butchers stalls, which are centrally located, are still in use. These stalls are surrounded by vegetable and fruit stands. On Sundays this place becomes an extensive flea market, where among other things you can buy famous Harris tweed jackets from Scotland and woollen coats and Tyrolean

tunics from Austria. The Tomex Market in Nowa Huta is dominated by sellers from the former Soviet Union. The so-called Tandeta Market sells mostly clothes. Although *tandeta* means rubbish in Polish, this term is used in Cracow to mean an ordinary clothes market and has no derogatory meaning.

SALES

SEASONAL SALES have been introduced, only a couple of years ago, by a number of larger shops and, in terms of selection of goods and prices, are not as attractive as those in the West. Goods are no longer reduced because they are imperfect or no longer in fashion, as used to be the case, but because of promotions, end of season sales or the arrival of new collections.

A flower stall in Market Square

Shopping in Cracow

I F YOU ARE A WESTERN VISITOR you can expect to be able to find everything in Cracow you can buy at home. It is no longer necessary to bring items of everyday use. On the other hand you should not expect luxury Western merchandise, such as perfumes, alcohol, designer clothes and shoes and other branded items, to be cheaper in Poland. You may, however, find bargains in shops and galleries selling handicrafts, silver jewellery, contemporary paintings and prints, as well as leather goods, bric-a-brac and coffee-table books.

BOOK AND RECORD SHOPS

T HERE ARE MANY excellent bookshops in Cracow. Some of them, like the **Galeria 17** situated in the Hetmański Arcade in Market Place, are open till very late. This surprises visitors but is typical of Cracow, where the way of life is still heavily influenced by artists, professors and students.

The **Empik** (formerly the Odeon) in Market Square is a mega-bookstore occupying several storeys, selling different types of publications, as well as records, cassettes and stationery. There is another branch of Empik, selling the same sorts of products, on Bora Komorowskiego.

For visitors with more literary tastes, the prestigious **Znak** bookshop in Sławkowska Street has a large selection of foreign titles. Academic books and fiction can be bought at the **Ossolineum** and Elefant bookshops. The **Księgarnia Muzyczna** in Market Square specializes in music books, scores and recordings. The shop of the **Polskie Wydawnictwo Muzyczne** (Polish Music Publishers) has a similar assortment with an emphasis on classical music. Among many shops in the centre selling CDs and cassettes, the one in Poselska Street offers a particularly good selection of jazz and classical recordings. It also has a useful sale-or-return section. The music shop found in Mikołajska Street specializes in jazz.

ANTIQUES

C RACOW is possibily the best place in Poland for antiques because the city was saved from destruction during World War II and Cracovians did not have to migrate. Foreigners are advised that exporting pre-1945 antiques from Poland is illegal without special permission, which is very difficult to obtain *(see p210)*. As far as valuable works of art are concerned, as well as those which form part of the cultural heritage, such as paintings, furniture, jewellery, old prints, rare books and maps, this law is rigorously observed, but less so in the case of objects of lesser value and bric-a-brac, which are plentiful in Cracow.

Antique dealers are mainly located within the area around the Planty gardens. Occasional antique markets take place in Market Square. Every Sunday, sellers of collectors' items and books put up their stalls by the Market Hall in Grzegórzecka Street. They are worth visiting.

FOLK ART

T HE ANNUAL Folk Art Fair in Market Square takes place in September. Dozens of stalls are set up, selling sculpture, earthenware, woven rugs and wood carvings made in various parts of Poland.

The stalls in the **Cloth Hall** offer a large selection of crafts and are a must for the tourist. You will find here colourful, embroidered traditional costumes of the Cracow and Podhale regions, as well as walking sticks from the highlands, with an axe-like handle (a favourite souvenir with children); chess sets and jewellery boxes, devotional statues and Jewish objects all carved in wood; paper cut-outs, painted Easter eggs and much more.

CRAFTS AND CONTEMPORARY ART

T HE STANDS in the Cloth Hall also sell silver jewellery, amber *objets d'art*, leather items and fabrics for the home. Shopping in this Renaissance hall has the added bonus of sustaining a trading tradition that goes back to the 16th century. The old and charming **Kramy Dominikańskie** (Dominican Stalls) also specialize in crafts. The **Galeria Osobliwości** (Gallery of Curiosities) in Sławkowska Street sells rare and unusual objects. The **Calik** Gallery is famous for Christmas decorations and attracts customers from all over the world.

Cracow is a good centre for Polish contemporary art, which is enjoying an ever greater demand. Works by contemporary artists can be found in the **Starmach Gallery, Zderzak, Space Gallery, Glass and Ceramics Gallery, Dominik Rostworowski Gallery, Stawski Gallery, Kocioł Artystyczny** and many others. The open-air gallery by St Florian's Gate is the place for lovers of images of sunsets and sunrises, galloping horses or large-scale nudes. This kind of painting is displayed on the city wall throughout the year. Fans of satirical drawings by **Andrzej Mleczko** will find a visit to his gallery in St John's Street (Św. Jana) a must.

CLOTHES AND SHOES

J EANS CAN BE FOUND in abundance in almost any clothes shop and those who prefer the well-known brands can go to the shops of **Levi Strauss, Mustang, Diesel, Wrangler** or Lee. There are also shops that sell the leading brands of sports shoes: **Adidas, Reebok** and **Nike**. Benetton and the **House of Carli Gry** have fashion selections for the young. Designer menswear is available from **Pierre Cardin**. Polish brands, such as **Vistula** and **M.W. Prestige**, offer less expensive suits for men, and **Wólczanka** specializes in shirts.

Cora caters for ladies who like to buy home brands, but those of a more cosmopolitan taste may prefer to choose **Paradise**, which sells clothes and shoes from both leading foreign brands and designers.

The **Zebra** and **Olivier** chain of shops are best for Italian shoes and the **Nico** store is great for Italian fashion for the whole family – men, women and children.

Food Shops

There are no supermarkets in the centre of Cracow. The Delikatesy general grocery store next to the Hawełka Restaurant is the largest in Market Square. Its selection of alcoholic drinks is particularly good. Apart from a number of small shops close to Market Square there are several self-service ones, such as **Dominik**. The large supermarkets such as **Géant, Hit, Hypernova, Krakchemia, Tesco** and **Billa** are located away from the centre and cater for shoppers who come by car. There are supermarkets on most of the housing estates, catering for local needs.

Most Cracovians purchase their fruit and vegetables from local stalls and markets. The Old Kleparz market is closest to the city centre and only a few minutes' walk away. The selection of coffee brands available from the charming **Pożegnanie z Afryką** (Out of Africa) is hard to beat. Julius Meinl's famous Viennese coffee is only available from the Meinl supermarket in the Azory (Azores) housing estate. The little and delightfully decorated **Pod Aniołami** (Angels) shop sells exquisite

cold meats prepared according to old Polish recipes, *bundz* and *oszczypek* cheese from the highlands, as well as country-style bread baked in log-fired ovens. Wines are also sold here but the largest selection can be found in the off-licence (liquor store) In Vino Veritas, as well as in the drinks department at the **Billa** supermarket. Those who favour strong spirits may choose the **Polmos** shop, where they can not only buy but also sample drinks at the bar.

Lovers of chocolate will be welcomed in the **Wawel** shop in Market Square, selling goods from the local sweet factory, Zakłady Przemysłu Cukierniczego. Many patisseries throughout Cracow offer a wonderful selection of cakes and pastries. The best doughnuts can be bought at Michałek and nougat at Cichowski. The shop in the Cracovia Hotel *(see p176)* is famous for *kremówki*, a puff pastry cake filled with custard. Note that what is known as *kremówka* in Cracow, in Warsaw is called *napoleonka*.

Other language differences between Mazovia and Lesser Poland include the names given to fruits of the forest. Blueberries are called *borówki* in Cracow and Galicia, and *czarne jagody* in the Warsaw region. All berries, including those non-edible, are called *jagody* in Cracow; *brusznice* is the name given to small red berries, which are called *borówki* in Warsaw, but in both regions *żurawiny* is the name for cranberries.

There are further differences in bread terminology which will probably confuse first-time visitors to the city. A long white loaf of bread called *weka* in Cracow is known as Wrocław bread in Warsaw.

Cosmetics

All chemists (drug stores) and supermarkets sell basic cosmetic goods, but expensive international brands are best purchased

from specialist shops where expert advice is also available. **Guerlain** and Yves Rocher have their own outlets and beauty clinics.

Well-known foreign brands of perfumes, such as Gucci, Biagotti, Trussardi, Bulgari, Carolina Herrera and Burberrys are available from the large **INA Center** shop. A good selection is also offered by hotel shops.

Pharmacies

The majority of drugs are available from Polish chemists on prescription only. Prescriptions issued by overseas doctors are generally accepted without any problem. Non-prescription drugs and medicines are readily available. In the city centre there are many chemists in the following streets, among others: **Szczepańska, Grodzka** or **Dunajewskiego**. A number of chemists are open 24 hours and their addresses are displayed in all the chemists' shop windows. A 24-hour telephone service (422 05 11) will provide you with the addresses of pharmacies that are open 24 hours, as well as the nearest hospitals with accident and emergency units.

Florists

Cracow would not be Cracow without the city flower-stalls by the Mickiewicz statue in Market Square. On the day of the great poet's birthday, these street vendors have made it a tradition to lay flowers at the base of the statue. They also make a gift of flowers to visiting foreign VIPs. On warm days you can buy flowers till late into the evening. There are many flower stalls to be found in New Kleparz market. The florist's shop, Niezapominajka (Forget-me-not), is well known. You can also buy bunches of flowers in numerous 24-hour shops and petrol stations.

DIRECTORY

DEPARTMENT STORES

Billa
Mackiewicza 17.
📞 415 39 01.

Galeria Centrum
Św. Anny 2.
Map 1 C4 (5 C2).
📞 422 98 22.

Géant
Bora Komorowskiego 37.
📞 617 06 00.

Hit
Wielicka 259.
📞 657 74 44.

Jubilat
Al. Krasińskiego 1–3.
Map 1 B5 (5 B4).
📞 422 30 33.

Krakchemia
Pilotów 6.
📞 411 21 33.

BOOKSHOPS

Columbus. Multi-language Bookshop
Grodzka 60.
Map 1C5 (6 D4).
📞 431 20 98.

Empik
Sienna 2.
Map 1 C4 (6 D2).
📞 429 45 77.

English Book Centre
Plac Matejki.

Galeria 17
Rynek Główny 17.
Map 1 C4 (6 D2).
📞 421 93 05.

Kossakówka. Bookshop and Gallery
Pl. Kossaka 4.
Map 1 B5 (5 B4).
📞 422 85 14.

Księgarnia Muzyczna
Rynek Główny 36.
Map 1 C4 (6 D2).
📞 422 98 59.

Music Corner
Św. Jana 18.
Map 1 C4 (6 D2).
📞 423 21 42.

Ossolineum
Św. Marka 12.
Map 2 D4 (6 E2).
📞 422 58 44.

Polskie Wydawnictwo Muzyczne (Polish Music Publishers)
Al. Krasińskiego 11a.
Map 1 B5 (5 A4).
📞 422 70 44 ext. 113.

Znak
Sławkowska 1.
Map 1 C4 (6 D2).
📞 422 45 48.

RARE AND SECOND-HAND BOOKS

AB
Rynek Główny 43.
Map 1 C4 (6 D2).
📞 421 69 03.

Antykwariat księgarski
Stolarska 8/10.
Map 1 C5 (6 D3).
📞 422 62 88.

Bibliofil
Szpitalna 19.
Map 2 D4 (6 E2).
📞 422 18 61.

Krakowski Antykwariat Naukowy
Św. Tomasza 8.
Map 1 C4 (6 D2).
📞 421 21 43.

Rara Avis
Szpitalna 7.
Map 2 D4 (6 E2).
📞 422 03 90.

ANTIQUES

Antique
Św. Tomasza 19.
Map 1 C4 (6 D2).
📞 421 79 44.

Connaisseur
Rynek Główny 11.
Map 1 C4 (6 D2).
📞 421 02 34.

Desa
Floriańska 13.
Map 1 C4 (6 D2).
📞 422 27 06.

Desa
Mikołajska 10.
Map 2 D4 (6 E2).
📞 422 49 33.

Galeria 17
Rynek Główny 17.
Map 1 C4 (6 D2).
📞 421 33 74.

Sopocki Dom Aukcyiny
Rynek Główny 45.
Map 1 C4 (6 D2).
📞 429 12 17.

FOLK ART

Cloth Hall
Rynek Główny 1/3.
Map 1 C4 (6 D2).

CRAFTS AND CONTEMPORARY ART

Mleczko Gallery (Autorska Galeria Andrzeja Mleczki)
Św. Jana 14.
Map 1 C4 (6 D2).
📞 421 71 04.

BWA
Pl. Szczepański 3A.
Map 1 C4 (5 C2).
📞 422 40 21.

Calik
Rynek Główny 7.
Map 1 C4 (6 D2).
📞 421 77 60.

Dominik Rostworowski Gallery
Św. Jana 20.
Map 1 C4 (6 D2).
📞 423 21 51.

Galeria Osobliwości
Sławkowska 16.
Map 1 C4 (6 D1).
📞 429 19 84.

Galeria Związku Polskich Artystów Plastyków (Gallery of the Association of Polish Artists)
Floriańska 34.
Map 2 D4 (6 E2).
📞 422 74 86.

Glass and Ceramics Gallery
Grodzka 29.
Map 1 C5 (6 D4).
📞 421 44 19.

Kocioł Artystyczny
Mikołajska 6.
Map 2 D4 (6 E2).
📞 292 00 29.

Krakowska Szkoła Malarstwa
Sławkowska 14.
Map 1 C4 (6 D1).
📞 421 25 34.

Kramy Dominikańskie
Stolarska 8/10.
Map 1 C5 (6 D3).
📞 422 19 08.

Pryzmat
Łobzowska 3.
Map 1 C3 (5 C1).
📞 422 28 04.

Space Gallery
Floriańska 13.
Map 1 C4 (6 D2).
📞 421 89 94.

Starmach Gallery
Wegierska 5.
Map 4 E3.
📞 656 43 17,
656 49 15.

Stawski Gallery
Miodowa 15.
Map 4 D1 (6 F5).
📞 421 80 46.

Zderzak
Floriańska 3.
Map 1 C4 (6 D2).
📞 429 67 43.

CLOTHES AND SHOES

Adidas
Szewska 21.
Map 1 C4 (5 C2).
📞 422 66 84.

Cora
Zwierzyniecka 22.
Map 1 B5 (5 B4).

Diesel
Szewska 22.
Map 1 C4 (5 C2).

House of Carli Gry (Jackpot & Cottonfield)
Rynek Główny 36.
Map 1 C4 (6 D2).
📞 292 74 87.

Floriańska 38.
Map 1 C4 (6 D2).
📞 422 61 86.

Levi Strauss
Floriańska 9.
Map 1 C4 (6 D2).

Mustang
Szewska 14.
Map 1 C4 (5 C2).

M.W. Prestige
Karmelicka 14.
Map 1 B4 (5 C1).
📞 422 28 68.

Nico
Modlnica 214.
📞 637 03 95.

Nike
Szewska 20.
Map 1 C4 (5 C2).

Olivier
Szewska 9.
Map 1 C4 (5 C2).
📞 422 28 19.

Paradise
Floriańska 18.
Map 1 C4 (6 D2).
📞 421 87 51.

Pierre Cardin
Św. Jana 12.
Map 1 C4 (6 D2).
📞 423 11 02.

Reebok
Grodzka 26.
Map 1 C5 (6 D4).
📞 422 28 08.

Troll
Floriańska 31.
Map 2 D4 (6 E2).
📞 422 41 42.

Wólczanka
Pl. Mariacki.
Map 1 C4 (6 D2).
📞 421 83 16.

Wrangler
Sienna 1.
Map 1 C4 (6 D2).
📞 421 92 89.

Vistula
Szpitalna 3.
Map 2 D4 (6 E2).
📞 422 09 55.

Zebra
Szczepańska 7.
Map 1 C4 (5 C2).
📞 422 46 05.

COSMETICS

Guerlain
Św. Jana 20.
Map 1 C4 (6 D2).
📞 422 39 45.

INA Center
Szpitalna 34.
Map 2 D4 (6 E2).
📞 421 55 83.
Szewska 15.
Map 1 C4 (5 C2).

FOOD SHOPS

Cracovia
Al. Focha 1.
Map 1 A5 (5 A3).
📞 422 13 43.

Delikatesy
Rynek Główny 34.
Map 1 C4 (6 D2).
📞 422 01 16.

Dominik
Pl. Dominikański 2.
Map 1 C5 (6 D3).
📞 422 90 80.

Hypernova
Witosa 7.
📞 654 58 07.

Julius Meinl-Major
Dobrego Pasterza 67.
📞 412 75 34.
Włoska 2.
📞 655 76 71.
Wybickiego 10.
📞 633 43 99.

Michałek
Krupnicza 6.
Map 1 B4 (5 C2).
📞 422 47 05.

Pod Aniołami
Grodzka 35.
Map 1 C5 (6 D4).
📞 421 39 99.

Pożegnanie z Afryką
Św. Tomasza 21.
Map 2 D4 (6 D2).
📞 644 47 45.

Tesco
Kapelanka 54.
Map 3 A3.
📞 293 21 00.

Wawel
Rynek Główny 33.
Map 1 C4 (6 D2).
📞 423 12 47.

OFF-LICENCES (LIQUOR STORES)

Baryłeczka
Szczepańska 9.
Map 1 C4 (5 C2).
📞 429 62 67.

Dom Wina
Starowiślna 66.
Map 2 D5 (6 E3).
📞 431 03 68.

Polmos
Starowiślna 26.
Map 2 D5 (6 F3).
📞 423 11 18.

Vis-Pol
Lea 90a.
📞 637 95 47.

PHARMACIES

Dunajewskiego 2.
Map 1 B4 (5 C2).
📞 422 65 04.

Grodzka 34.
Map 1 C5 (6 D4).
📞 421 85 44.

Szczepańska 1.
Map 1 C4 (6 D2).
📞 422 92 93.

Apteka Na Kazimierzu
Krakowska 49.
Map 4 D2.

Europa
Karmelicka 56.
Map 1 B3.

Mały Rynek
Mały Rynek 6.
Map 1 C4 (6 E2).
📞 421 90 89.

Pod Słońcem
Rynek Główny 42.
Map 1 C4 (6 D2).

Pod Świętym Hubertem
Krakowska 1.
Map 4 D2.
📞 422 19 98.

Pod Złotą Głową
13, Market Square.
Map 1 C4 (6 D3).
📞 422 41 90.

Pod Złotym Słoniem
Pl. Wszystkich Świętych 11.
Map 1 C5 (6 D3).
📞 422 91 39.

FLORISTS

BeA
Sławkowska 20.
Map 1 C4 (6 D1).

Kamelia
Pl. Wszystkich Świętych 11a.
Map 1 C5 (6 D3).
📞 422 76 45.

Konwalia
Zwierzyniecka 23.
Map 1 B5 (5 B4).
📞 422 93 52.

Margareta
Długa 74.
Map 1 C2.
📞 633 78 63.

ENTERTAINMENT IN CRACOW

Cracow is the cultural capital of Poland and there are many reasons for that claim. Local theatres are among the best in the country and often host leading international companies. The Szymanowski Philharmonic Orchestra and Choir and the Capella Cracoviensis have high reputations. There are many concerts and festivals of classical music organized in the magnificent interiors of historic houses and churches. The history of Cracow's cabarets goes back some 100 years,

Open-air concert

attracting both domestic and foreign audiences. The intense nightlife can be compared to that offered by Italian or Spanish cities. You only have to walk a couple of minutes to find a variety of music clubs, discotheques and bars. They are usually housed in Gothic or Renaissance cellars and are open until very late or even till the early hours of the morning. They will leave you with unforgettable memories. Theatre, film, music and ballet festivals take place throughout the year.

USEFUL INFORMATION

Full listings of cultural events in Cracow appear in the *Karnet – Krakowskie Aktualności Kulturalne* monthly, published by the Centrum Informacji Kulturalnej (Cultural Information Centre) in Polish and English. For the electronic version of the *Karnet* see their website on: http://karnet.euro.net.pl. or: e-mail@karnet.euro.net.pl. Current listings and reviews of cinemas, theatres and other events, as well as a guide to restaurants, discos and clubs (live music) are published on Friday in the *Gazeta Wyborcza* supplement entitled *Co jest grane?* (What's on?). Listings also appear in local newpapers on a daily basis. *Kraków, What, Where, When* is published monthly in

A Bücklein Theatre performance

English and contains listings in German, French, Spanish and Japanese. *The Kraków Insider* is published solely in English.

BOOKING TICKETS

Tickets for all major events can be purchased from the Cultural Information Centre. This is the best place to make enquires how and where to buy tickets or make an

advanced booking. Staff at the Centre speak English, French, German and Italian. Booking is also possible through travel agents and hotel receptions. Seats for the Philharmonic Hall and the theatres are available from their respective box offices, which also take advance bookings. Cinema tickets can be booked over the phone. Bear in mind that some performances require booking months in advance.

TICKET PRICES

Ticket prices have increased considerably in recent years but are still cheaper than in the West. Theatre seats are more expensive in Cracow compared to anywhere else in Poland, and in greatest demand. Average prices vary from 25 to 40 zł per person. Cinema tickets cost between 13 and 20 zł. Museum tickets are good value; in some museums the entrance is free on one day of the week.

NIGHT TRANSPORT

Bus and tram day routes stop around 11pm. Trams do not resume before 5am. Night buses operate according to a timetable displayed at bus stops. Tickets can be purchased from the driver. Taxis are a better option. A radio-taxi booked over the phone is cheaper than one at a taxi-

Musicians wearing costumes of the Cracow region

rank but you can rely on all the taxis waiting at the ranks in the city centre. Most taxi drivers are honest, but it is best to avoid the taxi rank by the Main Railway Station. If you require a taxi while in the Main Railway Station area, use the radio-taxi rank situated at roof level above the platforms (use the platform stairway).

FESTIVALS

THE CITY plays host to a multitude of cultural festivals; the only problem is to choose the most interesting. The International Festival of Alternative Theatre will appeal to theatre fans, the International Short Film Festival to film lovers, the Cracow Spring Ballet Festival to ballet aficionados, the International Festival of Music in Old Cracow to admirers of classical music, while enthusiasts of brass instruments may attend the International Music Festival of Military Bands.

WALKS AND OPEN-AIR EVENTS

THE TRADITION of open-air fairs goes back in Cracow to at least the early part of the 19th century when folk festivals were organized on the Błonia fields, then located out of town. One of the attractions was to try to climb a pole smeared in soap, a flask of alcohol and sausages attached to the top of the pole awaiting the successful climber. The poles have disappeared since but the Błonia are still a venue for public events, of either a national or light entertainment nature. Two great cavalry parades in the inter-war years, attended by Marshals Józef Piłsudski and Edward Rydz Śmigły respectively, took place here. The masses celebrated on these fields by Pope John Paul II, and attended by

millions of the faithful, are commemorated by a granite block brought here from the Tatra Mountains. All kinds of concerts, festivals and fairs take place at the Błonia.

The Jordan Park, situated opposite the Błonia fields, is very popular with mothers with toddlers. Doctor Henryk Jordan, a Cracow physician, introduced the idea of playing fields which are now found throughout the country and are named after this celebrated physician. The Jordan Park in Cracow was the first ever public playground for small children.

The Wolski Wood (Las Wolski) is not far from Cracow and offers many walking routes *(see pp164–5)*. For Cracovians it is one of the favourite destinations for a day out, but the zoo *(see p165)* is also popular. On weekends and public holidays there is no access to the zoo by car, so use bus or taxi services. On weekdays a charge is made to enter the zoo by car.

A pillar advertising cultural events

Summer concerts in the open air are organized in the Wawel Castle courtyard, in the gardens of the Archaeological Museum and in Radio Kraków's amphitheatre as well as in the courtyard of the Collegium Iuridicum and on a temporary stage in Market Square.

"Pod Baranami" Cinema

OUT OF TOWN TRIPS

A NUMBER of appealing sights are located within close proximity of Cracow. A trip to the Ojców National Park *(see p154)*, one of the smallest but most beautiful of Polish national parks, is an unforgettable experience. White limestone rocks, such as Hercules's Club, have most unusual forms; there are many indigenous plants and a fine Renaissance castle in Pieskowa Skała *(see p150)*.

The Salt Mines at Wieliczka *(see p154)* have been included by UNESCO on their World Heritage List. The mines and the underground sanatorium housed here are unique. Niepołomice has a recently restored 14th-century castle and the remnants of an ancient forest where bison are bred. The Benedictine Abbey in Tyniec *(see p155)* is beautifully located on the Vistula and worth visiting.

The Operetta theatre in the former military riding school theatre

Entertainment in Cracow

CRACOW IS FAMOUS for its cultural traditions. The underground Rapsodyczny Theatre was established here during World War II and in 1956 Tadeusz Kantor founded the world-famous Cricot 2 Theatre. The Stary Theatre gained its fame through productions directed by Konrad Swinarski. The Pod Baranami Cabaret and other cabarets in Cracow continue the best of traditions that go back to the Zielony Balonik at the beginning of the 20th century. An evening out in a cabaret or nightclub is highly recommended, and boredom is out of the question in this cultural city.

FOREIGN-LANGUAGE PERFORMANCES

CRACOW does not have a theatre performing in a foreign language on a permanent basis. The annual Festival of French-Speaking Theatre takes place in May and attracts many companies from French-speaking countries. The city occasionally hosts foreign theatre companies from all over the world. They perform in their own languages.

A number of bodies, such as the Austrian Consulate, French Institute, Goethe Institute, Italian Cultural Centre and Japanese Centre of Art and Technology, are all actively involved in artistic patronage. They usually organize events in the languages of their countries and information about these events can be obtained from the Cultural Information Centre.

THEATRE

THE FIRST professional theatre company was established in Cracow in 1781. Today there are many theatres. The most renowned is **Stary Teatr** (Old Theatre). The best actors, directors and set designers work for the Stary Teatr whose performances are mostly based on Polish classics and Romantic literature.

The **Słowacki Theatre** shares the same traditions and types of plays. The building, modelled on the Opéra Garnier in Paris, opened in 1893. Its splendid Art Nouveau interior features a curtain designed by Siemiradzki. As an added bonus, spectators may watch the performance from the box originally used by the Austro-Hungarian Emperor, Franz Joseph and his wife Sissi.

The **Krakowski Teatr, Scena Stu** gained fame through unconventional performances, sometimes staged in the open air, and other grand productions. In their main venue in Krasiński Avenue classics predominate. Benefit performances celebrating theatre stars are broadcast by television and have became classics in their own right.

The **Ludowy Theatre** in Nowa Huta has had its ups and downs. Today it has a young cast who perform not only in Nowa Huta but also in two other venues in Cracow, namely in the cellars beneath the Town Hall and in Kanonicza Street. The **Bagatela Theatre** specializes in light satirical productions. The **Teatr Lalki i Maski Groteska** generally performs for children but has also staged a number of plays for adults. The productions of the world-famous **Cricot 2** theatre practically ceased following the death of Tadeusz Kantor. The student **Teatr 38** performs only occasionally.

OPERA AND BALLET

THE OPERA of Cracow has no permanent seat and performs in the Słowacki Theatre. This situation is possibly a consequence of the old tradition of attending opera performances in Vienna or the Lemberg (now L'viv) Opera's guest appearances in Cracow.

The **Operetta** is housed rather unusually in the former Austrian riding school. The productions here include Galician all-time favourites by Kalman, Lehar and the Strausses.

The Cracovians have some sort of resistance towards ballet. Even leading foreign companies perform to half-deserted theatres and there is not a single independent ballet company in the city.

Two festivals, namely the annual Cracow Spring Ballet Festival, which takes place in May and June, and the International Ballet Festival, both aim at improving the situation.

CABARET

CABARET ARTISTS are in a much better position in Cracow than ballet dancers and can always rely on good audiences and sell-outs. Following the death of Piotr Skrzynecki, the founder of the **Piwnica pod Baranami**, the future of this cabaret has not yet been decided but the majority of the artists believe it should continue. And this is indeed the case despite the irregularity of performances and often incomplete cast. Individual appearances by the Piwnica's stars are more frequent.

The **Loch Camelot** is artistically affiliated to the Piwnica and also performs in cellars. Very popular is the **Piwnica pod Wyrwigroszem**.

Lovers of classic, satirical texts of the **Jama Michalika** Cabaret may still attend a performance here. In the surroundings of Art Nouveau objects and caricatures dating from the early 20th century, they may listen to Tadeusz Boy-Żeleński's verses. The original decadent ambience of this place is, however, difficult to recreate. The present menu lacks absinthe and there is a total ban on smoking.

CINEMAS

KIJÓW is the largest cinema in Cracow. It is a venue for a number of festivals, including the short-film festival and that dedicated to commercials. Food and drinks are available on the first floor. A truly Parisian-style multiplex is situated at the junction of St John's (św. Jana) and St Thomas (św. Tomasza) Streets. It comprises the **Apollo, Sztuka, Aneks Sztuki** and **Reduta Sztuki** cinemas. Cafés can be found in all of them. The Reduta Sztuki is said to be the most prestigious and expensive cinema in Poland.

The small **Pod Baranami** Cinema, housed in the Palace of the Rams, is very popular. Its prime location is an added bonus. After a show, walk a few steps to enjoy a drink in the Piwnica pod Baranami bar. Among other cinemas worth recommending are the **Uciecha, Atlantic, Wanda** and **Mikro**.

CLASSICAL MUSIC

THE MOST PRESTIGIOUS concert hall in Cracow is the **Szymanowski Philharmonic Hall**. Classical music is, however, best enjoyed in historic houses. Among the many venues are the Wawel Castle, the National Museum in the Cloth Hall and the **Music Academy**, as well as churches, such as St Mary's, St Catherine's and the Holy Cross. In summer, concerts are also organized in the arcades of the Wawel Castle, Collegium Maius's courtyard, in the former prison of St Michael (now the Archaeological Museum), and in the Radio Kraków amphitheatre, housed in the former Tarnowski Palace. Organ recitals in the Romanesque Benedictine Abbey in Tyniec near Cracow, are renowned.

MUSIC CLUBS

ANY JAZZ FAN visiting Cracow should have pencilled in his diary the address of the **Jazz Club u Muniaka**.

Here on Fridays and Saturdays Janusz Muniak, one of Poland's most celebrated jazzmen, plays to the accompaniment of other musicians. Jazz concerts take place at the **Harris Piano Jazz Bar, Extreme Club, Pod Jaszczurami** and **Jazz Club Kornet** (traditional jazz) as well as Piwnica pod Baranami. Apart from jazz, the **Klub U Louisa** provides blues music and during the break you can surf the Internet using one of several terminals provided.

The **Rotunda-Orlik** and **Pod Jaszczurami** student clubs are also venues for rock groups, blues bands and student cabaret songs. Live music, and rock in particular, can be heard in a number of pubs such as **Klinika 35** or **Jazz Rock Café**.

NIGHTCLUBS AND DISCOS

THE BEST PLACE for techno music is the **Krzysztofory**, while the **Bar Rózowy Stoń** will attract fans of classic disco.

The **Wolność FM** music club is the largest and most modern, with the latest state-of-the-art Western equipment. It specializes in house, dance and soul music. It may be of interest to visitors that this building used to house a cinema, and, during World War II, a Gestapo torture chamber. The **Equinox, Pod Papugami** and **Pasja** discos are also popular.

The **Emergency Club** caters for fans of avant-garde hip hop, grunge and acid jazz music. Lovers of music of the sixties will enjoy the **Bosto** club which offers a small dance floor. The front end of a Syrena car, mounted in the wall, is a reminder of this unforgettable period.

If you feel exhausted after having a wild time in a disco, the **Roentgen, Free Pub** and **Black Gallery** are good places to relax in.

Cracow's nightclubs do not have any specific hour at which they close. In summer,

especially, a club-goer can simply leave a club and go straight to work.

SPORTS

AS FAR AS sports facilities are concerned Cracow has much to offer. Two neighbouring sports clubs, **KS Cracovia** and **TS Wisła**, are the oldest and most popular in Poland. Both clubs have swimming pools open to the public.

The artificial lake in Kryspinów is a good place for both beach lovers and windsurfers. The lake's water is clean. A supervised swimming area can be found in the Nad Zalewem Recreation Centre. There is a charge for the use of the centre and the lake's beaches. The sports grounds in the Jordan Park are a good place for badminton players. Other sports clubs include **Korona, Olsza** and **Zwierzyniecki**.

Tennis courts are available at **Centrum tenisowe, Klub tenisowy „Kosłówek"** and **Hotel Piast**. The courts at the Olza and Zwierzyniecki sports centres are open all year round. Horse-riding facilities are available at the University Riding Club, the **Ewelina Riding Club** and at a number of stables located on the outskirts of the city and further afield. The Korona Club, located in the highlands, also offers a covered swimming pool, fitness and sauna facilities.

In recent years, even the Cracovians have shown an interest in healthy living. Sauna, sun bed and health and beauty clinics have been opened in all parts of the city, as have fitness clubs such as **Metamorfoza, Relax Body Club** and **A & J**.

Anyone interested in an active lifestyle can take advantage of Błonia, the expansive field in the middle of the town. Bridge and chess clubs will appeal to those who prefer more cerebral activities. Billiards can be played in a number of places throughout the city.

DIRECTORY

BOOKING TICKETS

**Cultural
Information
Centre**
Św. Jana 2.
Map 1 C4 (6 D2).
☏ 421 77 87.

FOREIGN AND INTERNATIONAL INSTITUTES

**The British
Council**
Rynek Główny 26,
Map 1 C4 (6 D3).
☏ 428 59 30.

**Consulate General
of the Republic
of Austria**
Cybulskiego 9.
Map 1 B4 (5 A2).
☏ 421 99 00.

**The Manggha
Japanese Centre
of Art and
Technology**
Konopnickiej 26. **Map** 3 B1.
☏ 267 27 03.

Institut Français
Storlarska 15.
Map 1 C5 (6 D3).
☏ 424 5350.

Goethe Institut
Rynek Główny 20.
Map 1 C4 (6 D3).
☏ 422 69 02.

**Istituto Italiano
di Cultura**
Grodzka 49.
Map 1 C5 (6 D5).
☏ 421 89 46.

**International
Cultural Centre**
Rynek Główny 25.
Map 1 C4 (6 D3).
☏ 421 77 59, 421 86 01.

THEATRE

Bagatela
Karmelicka 6.
Map 1 B4 (5 C2).
☏ 422 45 44.

Cricot 2
Kanonicza 5.
Map 1 C5 (6 D4).
☏ 421 32 66.

Groteska
Skarbowa 2.
Map 1 B4 (5 A2).
☏ 633 37 62.

KTO
Gzymsików 8.
☏ 633 89 47.

Ludowy
Os. Teatralne 34.
Map 1 B4 (5 C2).
☏ 644 27 66.

**Opera
i Operetka**
Lubicz 48. **Map** 2 F3.
☏ 422 78 07.

Im. J. Słowackiego
Pl. Świętego Ducha 1.
Map 2 D4 (6 E1).
☏ 422 45 75.

Stary
Jagiellońska 1.
Map 1 C4 (5 C2).
☏ 422 40 40.

**Stowarzyszenie
Teatralne „Łaźnia"**
Paulińska 28.
Map 3 C2.

STU
Al. Krasińskiego 16.
Map 1 A5 (5 A4).
☏ 422 27 44.

Zależny
Kanonicza 1.
Map 1 C5 (6 D4).
☏ 421 71 36.

CABARET

Café Cabaret
Św. Jana 2.
Map 1 C4 (6 D2).

Jama Michalika
Floriańska 45.
Map 2 D4 (6 E2).
☏ 422 15 61.

Loch Camelot
Św. Tomasza 17.
Map 1 C4 (6 D2).
☏ 423 06 38.

**Piwnica
pod Baranami**
Rynek Główny 27.
Map 1 C4 (6 D2).
☏ 421 25 00.

**Piwnica pod
Wyrwigroszem**
Św. Jana 30.
Map 1 C4 (6 D2).
☏ 431 18 00.

CINEMA

Apollo
Św. Tomasza 11a.
Map 1 C4 (6 D2).
☏ 421 89 50.

**Ars: Sztuka, Aneks
Sztuki, Reduta Sztuki**
Św. Jana 6. **Map** 1 C4 (6 D2).
☏ 421 41 99.

Atlantic
Stradomska 15.
Map 3 C1 (6 E5).
☏ 422 15 44.

Kijów
Al. Krasińskiego 34.
Map 1 A5 (5 A3).
☏ 422 30 93.

Mikro
Lea 5. **Map** 1 A3.
☏ 634 28 97.

Paradox
Krowoderska 8. **Map** 1 C3.
☏ 422 52 44.

Pasaż
Rynek Główny 9,
(Market Square).
Map 1 C4 (6 D2).
☏ 422 71 13.

Pod Baranami
Rynek Główny 27,
(Market Square).
Map 1 C4 (6 D2).
☏ 423 07 68.

Sfinks
Ós. Górali 5.
☏ 644 27 65.

Świt
Os. Teatralne 10.
☏ 644 27 72.

Tęcza
Praska 52.
☏ 266 90 80.

Uciecha
Starowiślna 16.
Map 2 D5 (6 F4).
☏ 422 00 77.

Wanda
Św. Gertrudy 5.
Map 2 D5 (6 E4).
☏ 422 14 55.

Wrzos
Zamojskiego 50.
Map 4 D3.
☏ 656 10 50.

CLASSICAL MUSIC

**Akademia
Muzyczna**
Św. Tomasza 43.
Map 2 D4 (6 E2).
☏ 423 20 78.

**Capella
Cracoviensis**
Zwierzyniecka 1.
Map 1 B5 (5 C3).
☏ 421 45 66, 422 94 77.

**Centrum Kultury
„Dworek
Białoprądnicki"**
Papiernicza 2.
☏ 415 02 00, 415 02 03.

Filharmonia
Zwierzyniecka 1.
Map 1 B5 (5 C3).
☏ 422 09 58.

Radio Kraków SA
Szlak 71. **Map** 2 D2.
☏ 632 52 00.

**Sinfonietta
Cracovia**
Papiernicza 2.
☏ 415 02 00, 415 00 97.

Willa Decjusza
28 lipca 17a.
☏ 425 36 44, 425 36 38.

MUSIC CLUBS

Extreme Club
Oleandry 1.
Map 1 A5.
☏ 634 34 12.

**Harris Piano
Jazz Bar**
Rynek Główny 28.
Map 1 C4 (6 D2).
☏ 421 57 41.

**Jazz Club
u Muniaka**
Floriańska 3.
Map 1 C4 (6 D2).
423 12 05.

Jazz Klub Kornet
Al. Krasińskiego 19.
Map 1 A5 (5 A4).

Jazz Rock Café
Sławkowska 12.
Map 1 C4 (6 D2).
422 19 88.

Klinika 35
Św. Tomasza 35.
Map 2 D4 (6 E2).
429 20 88.

**Piwnica
pod Baranami**
Rynek Główny 27.
Map 1 C4 (6 D2).
422 44 02.

**Piwnica
pod Wyrwigroszem**
Św. Jana 30.
Map 1 C4 (6 D2).
431 1800.

Pod Jaszczurami
Rynek Główny 8.
Map 1 C4 (6 D3).

U Louisa
Rynek Główny 13.
Map 1 C4 (6 D3).
421 80 92.

NIGHTCLUBS
AND DISCOS

Bar Rózowy Stoń
Szpitalna 38.
Map 2 D4 (6 E2).
422 14 16.

Black Gallery
Mikołajska 24.
Map 2 D4 (6 E2).
421 18 63.

Bosto
Floriańska 33.
Map 1 C4 (6 D2).
421 16 93.

**Emergency
Club**
Łazarza 9a.
Map 2 E5.

Equinox
Sławkowska 13/15.
Map 1 C4 (6 D2).
421 17 71.

Free Pub
Sławkowska 4.
Map 1 C4 (6 D2).
413 03 66.

Krzysztofory
Szczepańska 2.
Map 1 C4 (6 D2).
422 93 60.

Night Club Hades
Starowiślna 60.
Map 4 E2.

Pasja
Szewska 5.
Map 1 C4 (5 C2).
423 04 83.

Pod Papugami
Św. Jana 18.
Map 1 C4 (6 D2).

Roentgen
Pl. Szczepański 3.
Map 1 C4 (5 C2).

Wolność FM
Królewska 1. **Map** 1 A2.
423 47 05.

SPORTS CLUBS

Korona
Kalwaryjska 9/15.
Map 4 D3.
656 15 66.

KS Cracovia
Kałuży 1. **Map** 1 A5.
422 77 02.

Olsza
Siedleckiego 7.
421 10 69.

TS Wisła
Reymonta 22.
410 15 00.

Zwierzyniecki
Na Błoniach 1.
425 18 46.

TENNIS
COURTS

Centrum tenisowe
Na Błoniach 1.
425 31 71.

Gołaski Sport
Królowej Jadwigi 220.
425 39 00.

Hotel Piast
Radzikowskiego 109.
636 46 00.

**Klub tenisowy
„Kozłówek"**
Spółdzielców 13.
655 55 54.

KS Wieczysta
Chałupnika 16.
413 84 66.

Nadwiślan
Koletek 20.
Map 3 C1.
422 21 22.

Olsza
Siedleckiego 7.
421 10 69.

Tenis servis
Al. Jana Pawła II 37.

SWIMMING
POOLS

Borek Fałęcki
Jagodowa.
268 14 17.

Clepardia
Mackiewicza 14.
415 16 74

Krakowianka
Bulwarowa 1.
644 14 21 (summer
only), 411 40 88..

Polfa
Eisenberga 2.
411 40 88.

Wisła
Reymonta 22.
Map 1 A4.
610 15 29.

BILLIARDS
AND SNOOKER
CLUBS

**Bila Café
Club**
Studencka 15.
Map 1 B4 (5 B2).
422 09 74.

Café Bilard
Kazimierza Wielkiego 6.
Map 1 A2.
423 43 14.

HORSEMANSHIP

Decjusz
Al. Kasztanowa 1.
425 24 21.

**Ewelina Riding
Club**
Jezynowa 9.
643 52 22 (after
2pm).

**Krakowski Klub
Jazdy Konnej**
Kobierzyńska.
262 14 18.

Krakus
Kąpielowa 51.
267 32 46.

Pegaz
Dobczyce, Ogrodowa 12.
271 10 18.

Pegaz
Łowińskiego 1.
425 80 88.

Pod żubrem
Niepołomice,
Targowa 5.
281 19 96.

Stary Młyn
Wilczkowice 50.
411 10 91.

HEALTH,
FITNESS AND
SAUNA CLUBS

A & J Fitness Club
Miodowa 21.
Map 4 D1.
421 95 34.

Euro Fitness Club
Biskupia 18.
Map 1 C3.
633 01 13.

Metamorfoza
Stolarska 13.
Map 1 C5 (6 D3).
421 91 48.

Relax Body Club
Mogilska 70.
Map 2 F3.
411 03 60.

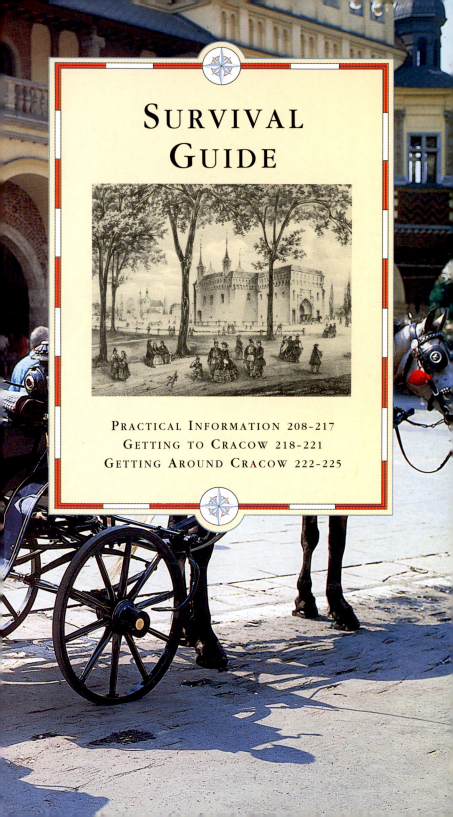

SURVIVAL
GUIDE

PRACTICAL INFORMATION

Cracow is the most popular Polish city with visitors. They come here in great numbers. Much has been done in recent years to improve services for visitors. Balice airport has been modernized and is now second within Poland to Warsaw's Okęcie. The number of hotels has increased substantially both in the city centre and on the outskirts, but is still insufficient to satisfy current require-

Polish Tourist Information logo

ments. Hundreds of restaurants, bars and nightclubs have opened. The season lasts all year round in Cracow, but summer is particularly busy. Booking a hotel well in advance is necessary, otherwise finding accommodation on arrival may prove extremely difficult. If you think about going to the theatre book your ticket early to avoid disappointment. Good performances sell out quickly.

Orbis Tourist Office sign

TOURIST INFORMATION

THE MAIN TOURIST Information office is situated in the Cloth Hall on Market Square. Maps, plans and brochures are available from hotels. Electronic displays with information on the availability of hotels can be found at the Main Railway Station and Balice Airport. The PTTK (Polish Tourist Organization) bookshop in Jagiellońska Street specializes in maps and guides to Poland.

The Polish Travel Office, Orbis, has agents in major cities around the world and travel, accommodation and car rental arrangements can be made through them prior to your arrival in Cracow. Enquiries concerning events, their programmes and booking, can be made

by phoning, faxing or e-mailing the Cultural Information Centre in Cracow.

TIPS FOR VISITORS

THE STAFF at hotels and restaurants generally speak English and German. Although learning foreign languages is becoming ever more popular in Poland you may experience some difficulty in communicating while in town, at a post office or at shop.

Drivers speaking foreign languages work for radio-taxi companies so you may, for example, request an English-speaking driver. All taxis serving the taxi-rank at the airport accept credit card payment. There is, therefore, no need to exchange money at the airport immediately after your arrival. Spring and summer are the best times to visit Cracow. The city is then transformed into an enormous open-air café.

Cultural Information Centre

Street cafés and restaurants around Market Square do not close until very late at night. You will certainly enjoy eating in the surroundings of Market Square, the largest Gothic and Renaissance square in Europe, and sharing this experience with thousands of others.

OPENING HOURS

THE OPENING HOURS of the museums and galleries listed in this guide are given individually for each sight. Most state museums and galleries are closed on Mondays. Private galleries of contemporary art are generally closed on Sundays. The opening times vary depending on the day of the week, but late openings are generally on Thursdays. Opening hours are the same throughout the year.

Churches generally remain open from the first to the last service without closing at midday but there are some variations. Visitors are not allowed to sightsee during services. Food stores are generally open between 6 or 7am and 7pm, but there

Street cafés in Market Square

Horse-drawn cab in Market Square

are no strict rules about the opening hours, which are at the owner's discretion. Other shops tend to be open between 10am and 7pm. Many shops are open on Sundays. Enquiries about shops (including pharmacies) and customer services can be made by calling 632 34 12 or 634 30 20, between 9am and 6pm, Monday to Friday. If you are not certain where to buy a specific item call the above number.

Banks generally open at 8am and close at 6pm on weekdays. The hours are 8am to 1 or 2pm on Saturdays. Banks, shops, restaurants and other public institutions do not close for lunch.

LISTINGS MAGAZINES AND TICKETS

A FULL LISTING of Cracow's events appears in the *Karnet* monthly magazine, published by the Cultural Information Centre in English and Polish. The *Kraków Insider* is a good source of

Cracow's listings magazines

information for English-speaking visitors. This magazine, published four times a year, has listings, useful tips, reviews and an excellent food section. The *Kraków. What, Where, When?* and *Miesiąc w Krakowie* are two monthly magazines available from hotels and tourist information desks. Local newspapers list events on a daily basis.

Admission charges to museums and galleries' permanent collections are modest but may be increased substantially for a temporary show. Reduced rates are available for children, students and senior citizens. Overseas students should have a valid international student card to qualify for a discount.

SIGHTSEEING

G UIDED SIGHTSEEING tours of Cracow are strongly recommended. A guide who can drive you round in a small electric *meleks* vehicle is a good choice. The *meleks* rank is situated in Market Square by the Church of St Adalbert. The driver-guides speak English, French and German and their best language is indicated by a sticker on the *meleks*. A bike or horse-drawn cab is another option and both these modes of transport have their ranks in Market Square.

The Orbis Travel Office specializes in out of town excursions. Oświęcim (Auschwitz), Zakopane, Wieliczka, Ojców and Pieskowa Skała are among the most popular destinations. An Orbis guide can also be hired for a tour of the town. Out of town excursions are also organized by the PTTK Tourist Organisation. Top sightseeing spots, such as Wawel Castle and Wieliczka, have their own guides.

A number of tourist agents cater for both individual and group visitors, providing all the necessary help for those who wish to stay in and around Cracow.

DIRECTORY

TOURIST INFORMATION AND AGENTS

Tourist Information and Accommodation Centre
Pawia 8. **Map** 2 D4 (6 F1).
℡ 422 60 91.
w www.jordan.pl

Cultural Information Centre
Św. Jana 2. **Map** 1 C4 (6 D2).
℡ 421 77 87.
@ karnet@krakow 2000.pl

Fregata Travel
Szpitalna 32. **Map** 2 D4 (6 E2).
℡ 422 41 44.
w www.fregatatravel.pl

Polish Tourist Promotion Agency
Pl. Wszystkich Świętych 8.
Map 1 C5 (6 D3).
℡ 422 71 27

Orbis Polish Travel Office
Pl. Szczepański 2.
Map 1 C4 (5 C1).
℡ 422 30 44.
@ incoming @orbistravel.krakow.pl

Rynek Główny 41.
Map 1 C4 (6 D2).
℡ 422 43 35.

PTTK. Polish Tourist Organization
Westerplatte 5. **Map** 2 D4 (6 F2).
℡ 422 26 76.

Waweltur
Pawia 8.
Map C D4 (6 F1).
℡ 422 19 21.
w www.waweltour.com.pl

More Practical Information

Telecommunications Centre in Market Square

VISITORS WITH DISABILITIES

Facilities for people with disabilities are still limited in Cracow. Some pedestrian crossings have a low-edge pavement and the number which are equipped with a sound message for the blind is on the increase. Wheelchair access and special lifts are available at the Main Railway Station. Such facilities can also be found in a number of museums, including the National Museum's Main Building and the Japanese Centre for Art and Technology, as well as in some cinemas and public institutions. Access to the latter is generally restricted for the disabled, but the Main Post Office and the Telecommunications Centre in Market Square both offer easy access. A number of hotel rooms are available for the disabled. Some buses have low-level entry floors. Moving around Cracow in a wheelchair is problematic owing to the lack of contoured pavements and the number of cars parked in pedestrian areas.

Several organizations assisting the disabled exist in Cracow, but there is only one taxi company which offers a service for individuals in a wheelchair. People are generally very helpful, however.

YOUNG PEOPLE AND STUDENTS

Those who are entitled to the ISIC (International Student Identity Card) are advised to apply for it before arriving in Cracow. The card entitles the holder to reduced rates in museums and galleries and at International Youth Hostels.

Students with a valid ISIC card can purchase rail tickets on international routes at a reduced rate, but must buy tickets on public city transport at the normal rate. Youth hostels in Cracow accept IYHF cards.

You will also find that some shops and pizza outlets, as well as places of entertainment and hostels, offer reduced rates to Euro<26 holders. This card is available to those who are 26 years old or younger.

ISIC International Student Card and the Euro<26 Card

CUSTOMS REGULATIONS

To enter Poland all visitors require a valid passport. The citizens of most European and many other countries do not reguire a visa. If in doubt, check with your local Polish embassy. There are no restrictions on items for personal use brought into Poland, but a limit applies on the amount of alcohol and cigarettes. It is essential to obtain a certificate before entering Poland with firearms. Gifts up to the value of US$100 are duty free. To export antiques, works of art such as contemporary paintings, permission or licences must be sought from the local authority: Urząd Miasta Krakowa, 3-4 Wszystkich Świętych, Tel: 422 34 52, or go to www.krakow.pl.

RELIGIOUS SERVICES

There are nearly 100 Roman Catholic churches in Cracow. Holy Masses are said every Saturday, Sunday and feast day, as well as during the week. There are also churches of other religious denominations in Cracow.

PUBLIC TOILETS

Until recently, the lack of public lavatories used to be a real hindrance. Today, the situation has much improved. The largest lavatories are in the Cloth Hall, in the Planty gardens by Sienna and Reformacka streets, and at the coach car park by the Wawel. Toilets are readily available in restaurants, bars and cafés throughout the city.

LOST PROPERTY

To recover lost property is, unfortunately, rarely possible but it is always worth trying the lost property office, which has two outlets. One is situated in the local government (Urząd Miasta) building at 10, Powstania Warszawskiego Street; the other, in the MPK Transport Office at 3, Brozka Street, Tel: 254 10 10. To claim an item left behind on a train, try the Main Railway Station, office no. 162.

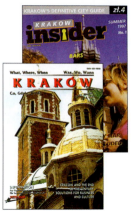

Cracow's English-language listings magazines

NEWSPAPERS, TV AND RADIO

FOREIGN PAPERS are available from hotel shops, selected newsagents and bookshops. National newspapers such as *Gazeta Wyborcza* and *Rzeczpospolita*, the local *Dziennik Polski* and *Gazeta*

Krakowska, and the tabloid *Superexpress* are the most popular newspapers in Cracow. The *Dziennik Polski* and *Gazeta Wyborcza* have the best classified sections. The listings magazines *Kraków Insider, Kraków What, Where, When?, Karnet* and *Miesiąc w Krakowie* are published in Polish and English and are available from hotels, newsagents and bookshops.

Polish television offers an ever larger selection of programmes which are broadcast directly, through cable or satellite. The Polish state television, Telewizja Polska, broadcasts on two channels, has a local Cracow channel and the satellite channel Polonia. Private channels include Polsat, Polsat 2, TVN, RTL 7 and TV 4.

The most popular radio stations include RMF FM, Trójka, Radio Kraków and Radio Zet. The following stations and frequencies are available: Radio Alfa – 102.4

FM, Radio Bis – 89.4 FM, Radio Blue – 97.7 FM, Radio TOK FM– 102.9 FM, Jazz Radio – 101 FM, Radio Maryja – 90.6 and 100.7 FM, Radio Plus – 106.1 FM, PR I (Polish Radio One) – 104.8 kHz, PR II – 89.4 FM, PR III (Trójka) – 99.4 FM, Radio Kraków – 101.6 FM, Radio RAK – 100.5 FM, Radio RMF FM – 96 FM, Radio Wanda – 92.5 FM, Radio WaWa – 107 FM, Radio Zet – 104.1 FM.

ELECTRICAL APPLIANCES

THE VOLTAGE in Poland is 220 volts. Plugs are the same as in most countries in Europe.

TIME

CRACOW is one hour ahead of GMT and six hours ahead of Eastern Standard Time. Summer time is observed throughout Poland from late March until late October.

DIRECTORY

INFORMATION FOR THE DISABLED

Polish Association for the Blind
Joselewicza 3.
Map 6 F5.
[422 80 05.

Polish Association for the Deaf
Św. Jana 18.
Map 1 C4 (6 D2).
[422 39 94.

Polish Society for the Prevention of Disability
Dunajewskiego 5.
Map 1 C4 (5 C1).
[422 28 11.
[W] www.fundacja-sm.malopolska.pl

Taxi Service for the Disabled
Radio Taxi
[96 33, 96 88.

CONSULATES

Austria
Cybulskiego 9.
Map 1 B4 (5 A2).
[421 99 00.

France
Stolarska 15.
Map 1 C5 (6 D3).
[422 33 90.

Germany
Stolarska 7.
Map 1 C5 (6 D3).
[421 89 80.

Hungary
Św. Marka 7/9.
Map 2 C4 (6 D1).
[422 56 79.

Russian Federation
Westerplatte 11.
Map 2 D4 (6 F2).
[422 26 47.

Ukraine
Krakowska 41.
Map 4 D2.
[429 60 66.

United Kingdom
Św. Anny 9.
Map 1 B4, 5 C2.
[421 70 30.
[@] ukconsul@sonly.pl

United States of America
Stolarska 9.
Map 1 C5 (6 D3).
[424 51 00.

PLACES OF WORSHIP

Augsburg Evangelical Church of St Martin
Grodzka 58.
Map 3 C1 (6 D4).
[423 00 31.

Baptist Church
Wyspiańskiego 4.
Map 1 A2.
[633 23 05.

Bethlehem Pentecostal Church
Lubomirskiego 7a.
Map 2 E3. [421 08 29.
[@] bethlehem@poozta.onet.pl

Evangelical Methodist Church
Długa 3.
Map 4 E1.
[422 80 37.

Polish Autocephalic Church
Szpitalna 24.
Map 1 D4 (6 E2).
[422 72 62.

Polish-Catholic Church
Friedleina 8. **Map** 1 B1.
[633 82 82.

Pentecostal Church of God
Przybyszewskiego 36.
[637 70 62.

Remu'h Synagogue
Szeroka 40.
Map 4 D1.
[422 12 74.

Seventh-Day Adventist Church
Lubelska 25.
Map 1 C2.
[633 34 69.

Personal Security and Health

Logo of the Town Wardens

CRACOW is one of the safest cities in Poland. Although the number of reported crimes is generally on the increase, Cracow is a quiet place and visitors can feel safe in all parts of the city. Pollution, a big problem for Cracovians until recently, is showing some signs of improvement. General safety rules apply here as everywhere, so beware of pickpockets, do not leave any property visible in the car, and use guarded car parks. Anyone suffering a minor health problem should seek advice at a pharmacy, while hotels can usually arrange a doctor's visit.

A typical blue and white Police car

PERSONAL SECURITY

DURING THE NIGHT the dark, poorly lit Planty Gardens in the city centre are a place for occasional crimes. This is despite frequent police patrols in the area. A 24-hour police station is situated next to the Palace of the Rams in Market Square. Due to its large window, it is known as the "police shop". The housing estates in Nowa Huta have a bad reputation and are one source of Cracow's skinheads. Pickpockets tend to operate in the markets. Dishonest gamblers here tempt naive players, promising big wins in card or dice games. To recover money lost through such gambling is practically impossible.

Pickpockets are notorious in trams and buses so keep a close eye on your bag or rucksack, and carry it in a safe way. Passports, ID cards and wallets, car keys and other valuable items should never be carried in a back pocket or the external pockets of a rucksack. A solitary pickpocket is rare. They usually operate in gangs, and a sudden push or other distraction caused by them is hardly ever accidental.

Valuables should never be left unattended in the car. Car break-ins are a big problem in Cracow. If you can remove the radio and take it with you, you may save your windows from being smashed. A car alarm offers no protection against professional thieves, so guarded parking may be a good option. A number of guarded car parks are available in the centre. Figures released by police show that the Polonez, Mercedes, VW Golf, Audi and BMW cars are the most frequent targets.

POLICJA

Police sign

POLICE AND SECURITY SERVICES

THE POLICE are assisted in Cracow by other services that include town wardens and private security guards. Serious crime should be reported to a uniformed policeman at a police station. Major police stations are indicated on the map of Cracow *(see pp230–233)*. The national police force is allowed by law to carry arms and arrest a suspect. Blue and white police cars are used for patrolling the streets. Officers on the beat are also common. City wardens are unarmed and have no power of arrest. They mostly perform traffic wardens' duties and fine the owners of illegally parked vehicles. A traffic policeman will impose a severe fine for exceeding the speed limit and will deal even more severely with a drunken driver. Anyone who drives under the influence

Policeman

Policewoman

Town warden

Ambulance

of alcohol within the Cracow region is arrested and charged and will have to appear before a magistrate's court the following day. The court will decide upon the penalty and driving ban period. The level of alcohol in the blood must not exceed 0.02%, so if you drink at all, it is best not to drive. In the event of a serious road accident you are required by law to call an ambulance and the fire brigade. You are also required to contact the traffic police.

Private security agencies are generally responsible for security in large shops and public buildings, as well as during public events. Their security guards wear black uniforms and should always carry identification badges.

A pharmacy sign

A pharmacy window

MEDICAL SERVICES

BOTH STATE and private health care is available in Cracow. First aid is provided free of charge. Other treatment may be subject to a fee. Payment is generally required in advance. It is advisable to have insurance coverage. The ambulance service is on call 24 hours a day and should be contacted in case of an accident or emergency. Hospital casualty units are indicated on the map in the Street Finder Section (*see pp230–235*). Treatment of the most minor cases is available at the 24-hour pharmacies.

Foreign visitors may seek medical assistance in local hospitals. They should carry a passport for identification and be able to pay for treatment. Confirmation of payment should always be requested and obtained. As a result of international agreements, citizens of the following countries are entitled to free hospital treatment while in Poland: Belarus, China, the Czech Republic, Denmark, Finland, Mongolia, Sweden, Tunisia, Ukraine, United Kingdom and countries of the former Yugoslavia.

POLLUTION

THE PROBLEM of pollution in Cracow was at the top of the local agenda until the late 1980s. The emissions from industrial plants constructed after World War II, of which the Sendzimir, formerly Lenin, Steelworks were the largest, systematically polluted the city. Coal stoves used in heating the old tenement houses in the centre, as well as Cracow's location in a valley, added to the problem. By the 1970s pollution had damaged the gilt dome of the Zygmunt Chapel in the Cathedral. Along with the collapse of communism, heavy industry fell into decline. New technologies, more concerned with the environment, were introduced. Industrial chimneys were equipped with filters. Thanks to the efforts of George Bush, special funds were designated by the government of the United States to help reduce the low-level pollution caused by domestic stoves. Coal has been replaced by an electric heating system. Coal containing a high level of sulphur is no longer in use. The air is monitored for chemical pollution and information about its current level is displayed electronically above the entrance to 22, Market Square.

DIRECTORY

EMERGENCY SERVICES

Ambulance
📞 999.

Police
📞 997.

Fire
📞 998.

MEDICAL ASSISTANCE

Telephone Directory for Hospital Emergency Services and 24 hour Pharmacies
📞 422 05 11 (24 hrs).

24-Hour Pharmacies
Galla 26.
📞 636 73 65.

Nowa Huta
Os. Centrum A, blok 3.
📞 644 17 36.

Kalwaryjska 94. **Map** 4 D4.
📞 656 18 50.

OTHER SERVICES

Vehicle Assistance
📞 981, 96 37.

Personal Helpline
📞 633 71 37 (4–10pm).

Wake-Up Service
📞 917.

Banking and Local Currency

PKO Bank logo

FINANCIAL TRANSACTIONS are easy in Cracow. For foreign visitors there are many bureaux de change in the city centre, offering more favourable exchange rates than the banks. Credit cards are accepted by many of Cracow's shops and restaurants. Signs displayed by the entrance to the establishment indicate which cards are accepted.

BANKS AND BUREAUX DE CHANGE

BANKS can be found throughout the city, both in and around the centre, as well as in the outskirts. Expect queues. Banks generally open at 8am and close at 6pm. Most banks have their own exchange service but better rates are offered by the independent bureaux de change *(kantor),* which do not charge commission. Foreign currency can also be changed at hotels (some have a 24-hour service), but rates are poorer. You should never enter into any deal with street "agents" as the money they offer may well be counterfeit. You will just cause a lot of trouble for yourself making any payments with counterfeit bank notes.

Bankomat cashpoint machine

CREDIT CARDS

CREDIT CARDS are becoming ever more popular in Poland. These are also issued by Polish banks. Credit card payments are accepted in hotels, the larger clubs and restaurants, car rental outlets and the more exclusive shops. Check with the staff whether credit cards are accepted and what hidden, if any, extras are involved, before entering into any transaction.

Bureau de change sign

Shops, restaurants and hotels normally indicate which cards they accept by displaying appropriate stickers on their windows. Some shops offer minimal discounts for credit card payments. Cards can be used in banks and at cashpoint machines *(bankomat)* to withdraw cash. A listing of cashpoint machines is available from larger banks. The American dollar remains the most popular foreign currency and in emergency payments in dollars can be made at petrol stations and in private shops.

Entrance to the PKO Bank in Market Square

DIRECTORY

BANKS

Narodowy Bank Polski
Basztowa 20.
Map 2 D3 (6 E5).
(618 58 00.

Bank Polska Kasa Opieki SA
Rynek Główny 31.
Map 1 C4 (6 D2).
(422 60 22.

Powszechna Kasa Oszczędności. Bank Państwowy
Wielopole 19.
Map 2 D5 (6 F4).
(421 55 55.

Rynek Główny 21.
Map 1 C4 (6 D2).
(422 40 76.

Powszechny Bank Kredytowy
Smoleńsk 33.
Map 1 B5 (5 B3).
(422 37 48.

Bank Przemysłowo-Handlowy
Rynek Główny 47.
Map 1 C4 (6 D2).
(422 20 66.

BUREAUX DE CHANGE

Change Office
Sławkowska 14.
Map 1 C4 (6 D2).
(421 66 88.

Dukat
Sienna 14.
Map 1 C4 (6 D2).
(421 41 59.

Euro-Kantor
Szewska 21.
Map 1 C4 (5 C2).
(421 55 65.

J.P.J.
Wielopole 3.
Map 2 D5 (6 E3).
(421 74 67.

Pod Arkadami
Grodzka 40.
Map 1 C5 (6 D5).
(421 50 21.

CURRENCY

THE POLISH UNIT of currency is the złoty (meaning golden), which is indicated by the abbreviation zł. One złoty equals 100 groszy, abbreviated gr. Pronounce zł as *zwo-te* and gr as *gro-she*.

10 złoty

20 złoty

50 złoty

100 złoty

200 złoty

Bank Notes
Polish bank notes come in denominations of 10, 20, 50, 100 and 200 zł. They portray Polish sovereigns.

5 zł

2 zł

1 zł

50 gr

20 gr

10 gr

5 gr

2 gr

1 gr

Coins
Polish coins come in denominations of 1, 2, 5, 10, 20, 50 gr and 1, 2, 5 zł. They all feature on one side a crowned eagle, the emblem of Poland.

Communications

THE TELEPHONE SERVICE is provided in Poland by Telekomunikacja Polska S.A. and the Poczta Polska is the postal service. Queues are sometimes long at a post office. There are many public telephones in the centre and they are generally card operated. Some have access for the disabled.

USING THE TELEPHONE

TO MAKE a telephone call you may choose to use a public telephone or go through the operator service at the post office. Note that calling from a hotel room is much more expensive, so it is always better to find a public telephone at the hotel or in its vicinity.

There are no coin-operated public telephones in Poland. A card must be used instead and these can be purchased from newsagents and post offices. Telephone cards come in units of 25, 50 and 100. A local call will only use up a few units, but for long-distance calls a more expensive card is a good option.

Main Post Office

There is a uniform tariff for local and international calls, but inter-city calls are charged according to the time of day of the call. Peak time is from 8am to 6pm. Between 6pm and 10pm you will pay 25 per cent less, and between 10pm and 8am the charge is 50 per cent less than the peak tariff. Calls made over the weekend are also cheaper.

Polish Telecommunications sign

To make a telephone call lift the receiver and wait for a continuous dialling tone. Insert payment and dial the number. A vibrating sound may be heard at first while the connection is being made. If the connection is successful, a longer, intermittent tone will follow. A short, rapidly repeating tone indicates that the telephone number is engaged.

USING A PHONECARD-OPERATED TELEPHONE

1 Before using a new card, break off the top left-hand corner along the perforations.

2 Lift the receiver and await the dialling tone.

3 Insert the card in the direction indicated when WRZUĆ MONETĘ / INSERT CARD is displayed. The display will indicate the amount of KREDYT/CREDIT available.

4 Dial the number and await connection.

5 When you have finished the call, replace the receiver and remove the ejected card.

Break off this corner before inserting the card

TELEKOMUNIKACJA POLSKA S.A.

KARTA TELEFONICZNA

A 100-unit telephone card

100

Post office sign

ACCESSING THE INTERNET

CRACOW HAS plenty of public access to computers and the Internet. Free Internet access is often available at public libraries, but you may have to book in advance for a slot. Internet cafés (Kafejki Internetowe) usually charge by the minute for computer use, and charges build up quickly, especially when including the cost of printed pages. Internet access is cheapest during off-peak times. There are several Internet Cafés in the city including Centrum Internetowe (Rynek Glowny 9), Café Internet Clarus (ul.Golebia 4), Looz (ul.Mikolajska 13) and the Internet Café at the Main Academic Bookshop (Podwale 6).

MOBILE PHONES

MOBILE telecommunication is advancing in Poland at a prodigious rate. Poland is well covered and growing in mobile telephone coverage. If you have access to roaming facilities you should have no problem in using your mobile in Cracow. Remember to dial the Cracow area code when making local calls. For other locations in Poland dial the appropriate area code followed by the subscriber's number. Before leaving for Poland check with your service provider, who will be able to give you the latest information.

POSTAL SERVICES

THE POLISH Post Office offers a wide range of services and has numerous outlets in towns and villages throughout Poland. You will find a large number of postal counters in the centre of Cracow as well as in all the housing estates.

The Main Post Office, situated at the junction of Westerplatte and Wielopole streets, is the most popular. It is open longer than all the others and some counters are open 24 hours a day. You can send letters, telegrams and parcels as well as make national money transfers; use operator initiated calls, and send a fax or telex. Stamp collectors can buy from the philatelic counter. A *poste restante* (mail holding) service is also available. A computerized queue system is in operation. Take a numbered ticket (press the button) from the dispensing machine by the entrance. The electronic display in the main hall indicates the number of people in the queue. Wait for your number to appear then go to the indicated counter.

The Main Post Office has access for the disabled.

A post office housed in an old palace by the Main Railway Station

SENDING A LETTER

STAMPS can be purchased at post office counters and from selected newsagents. Some newspaper kiosks sell stamped envelopes and postcards only. Local letters should be posted in the green boxes and all other post in the red ones. Inland letters take from two to three days but international mail takes a week or maybe a little longer. However, mail to some European destination takes less time. Letters sent by express service will arrive sooner. Courier service is the fastest but very expensive. This service is available from the Main Post Office and the Main Railway Station post counter, as well as from DHL and other courier companies.

Urgent letters and small packets can be sent by PKP, the Polish State Railways. Trains which provide this

A letter box

service are indicated in the train time-table by the letter K. To use this service mark your parcel clearly and deliver it to the train conductor who will also take payment. The parcel must be collected from the conductor by the addressee at the destination station.

Inland letter and postcard stamps

DIRECTORY

USEFUL ADDRESSES

Main Post Office
Westerplatte 20.
Map 2 D5 (6 E3).

DHL
Balicka 79.
☎ *0801 345345*

TELEPHONE DIRECTORIES

- Local (Cracow) directory enquiries dial 911 or 913.
- National (Polish) directory enquiries dial 912.
- National and international operator dial 900.
- Cracow's area code, dial 12 from abroad, 01033 or 01044 within Poland (followed by area code).
- To call overseas dial 0 and wait for the tone, dial 0 again followed by the country code, followed by the area code (omit the initial 0) and the subscriber's number. Country codes: UK 44; Eire 353; Canada and USA 1; Australia 61; South Africa 27; New Zeland 64.

GETTING TO CRACOW

Cracow has good connections with other Polish and European cities. Polish roads are, unfortunately, dangerously busy and many require resurfacing or modernizing. There are only a few motorways and the network is growing slowly. Travelling by car may occasionally prove to be tiresome. Cracow is located only 80 km (50 miles) away from the

A Polish Airlines aeroplane

Chyżne crossing point on the Polish-Slovak border, less than 400 km (248 miles) from Budapest and 450 km (280 miles) from Vienna. Direct air routes from Cracow-Balice airport serve an ever increasing number of European and American cities, as well as Warsaw. The best connection to Warsaw is by train, with an average journey time of only two and half hours.

The logo of Polish Airlines

ARRIVING BY AIR

Cracow's John Paul II Airport in Balice offers direct flights to the following cities: Chicago, Frankfurt am Main, London, Milan, New York, Paris, Rome, Toronto, Vienna and Zurich. Among the air carriers using Balice are LOT, Austrian Airlines, Swissair, Eurolot, British Airways and Eurowing. In summer regular charter flights serve Tunisia, Turkey, Morocco and other destinations. The Cracow-Warsaw route is the only domestic flight.

Balice is the second largest airport in Poland in terms of the number of passengers using it. A flight to Warsaw is the shortest, taking only

50 minutes; a flight to Toronto takes nine hours 25 minutes. Flying time to Chicago and New York is more than eight hours, London is approximately two and half hours away, Paris two hours ten minutes, while Vienna is only one hour away. Travel agents offer air tickets to a number of other destinations throughout the world, but they are usually for indirect routes and require interconnecting flights or stopovers.

Balice Airport sign

TICKETS AND DISCOUNTS

Apex tickets are good value but restrictive. They require booking at least a week in advance and the dates of the outward and inward leg need to be fixed at the time you make the reservation. Reduced fares are available to children, students, senior citizens, families and groups.

A LOT Flight Attendant

BALICE AIRPORT

Balice airport is small but modern. It is situated west of the city and the journey time to the centre of Cracow is approximately 20 minutes. The present terminal was built in 1995. Apart from ticket and check-in desks, you have at your disposal a bureau de change, a small duty-free shop, a restaurant, a café, public phones, a newsagent and tobacco and souvenir shops. Car rental firms have their desks in the main lounge of Balice Airport. An electronic display indicates hotel availability in and around Cracow.

The lack of a large duty-free shop is a disadvantage, but this should improve in the near future.

Kraków-Balice Airport

Luggage trolley

GETTING INTO TOWN

Balice airport lies approximately 20 km (12.5 miles) west of the city centre. Two bus routes serve the centre and connect with the Main Railway Station or Balice Airport, or both. Bus 192 goes from Rondo Mogilskie through to the Main Railway Station and then on to Cracovia Hotel (*see p176*).

The 208 route has an hourly schedule, serving the Main Railway Station. From here, bus 208 passes via Warszawska Street, Słowacki Street, Mickiewicz Street, Czarnowiejska, Nowojki, Armiikrajowej and Balicka to Balice Airport.

A ticket for the bus must be purchased either from a newsagent at the airport or from the driver prior to commencing your journey. Large pieces of luggage are subject to an additional charge. At the terminal's main exit there is a taxi rank. Here you will find radio taxis which accept payment by credit card, so you need not change money at the airport if you do not have enough cash in the correct currency.

The journey into town should not usually take longer than 20 minutes by taxi but in the rush hour may take 30 minutes or even longer. The bus takes half an hour or so to get to town, but you should allow a little longer at rush hour times.

A bus connecting Balice Airport and Cracow city centre

DIRECTORY

Cracow-Balice Airport
411 19 55.

Cracow Main Railway Station
Pl. Kolejowy 1.
Map 2 D3 (6 F1).

AIRLINES SERVING CRACOW

Alitalia
Krupnicza 3.
Map 1 B4 (5 A2).
431 06 21.

Austrian Airlines
Krakowska 41.
Map 4 D2.
429 66 66
www.austrianairlines.pl.
krakow.office@aua.com

British Airways
Św. Tomasza 25.
Map 2 D4 (6 E2).
422 86 45,
422 86 21.

Lufthansa
Sienna 9.
Map 2 D5 (6 E3).
422 41 88.

LOT Polish Airlines
Basztowa 15.
Map 2 D3 (6 D1).
422 42 15.

EUROPEAN AIR NETWORK FROM CRACOW

Cracow has good air connections with a number of European cities. All the cities shown on the map are less than 2.5 hours away by air from Cracow.

London
Dresden
Warsaw
Paris
Frankfurt a. M.
Cracow
Zurich
Vienna
Milan
Rome

Cracow's Main Railway Station

ARRIVING BY RAIL

Y OU CAN GET to Cracow by train from almost any Polish city and town, as well as many other European cities. The extensive Polish rail network is operated by the PKP, the Polish National Railways. Trains tend to be faster then either car or coach journeys.

Train tickets are cheaper than in the West. Tickets may be purchased at the main and other rail stations. They are also available in advance from the Orbis Travel Office, 41 Market Square, which charges a small commission. If you intend to purchase your ticket on the day of travel then allow at least half an hour, or more, for possible queues or delays.

A seat reservation must be made for the InterCity and express trains. Trains which require seat reservations are indicated in the time-table by the letter R. Other trains with a stopping service *(osobowy)* and fast service *(pospieszny)* do not offer seat reservations. A place must be reserved in overnight couchettes (*kuszetka*, six persons to a compartment) and sleeping carriages (*sypialny*, two or three persons to a compartment). Any passenger travelling without a valid ticket or reservation is liable to be fined.

You may also buy a ticket from the train conductor but you must tell him that you have no ticket before commencing your journey. A ticket bought from the conductor is subject to a substantial surcharge.

Carriages offering comfortable sleeping facilities are attached to trains on all major long distance domestic routes and on all international connections. When on the train, and especially when boarding or alighting be wary of pickpockets. Do not leave your luggage unattended in the carriage.

Rail Conductor

INTERCITY AND EXPRESS TRAINS

W HEN TRAVELLING in Poland the InterCity trains are best. They are modern, fast, clean and comfortable.

There is a wider choice of express trains. Both types of service require a reservation to be made at the time of purchasing the ticket. A seat can also be reserved on the train through the conductor, subject to availability and an additional charge.

The InterCity and express trains have a restaurant or a bar but the cuisine they offer is dull and rather disappointing. A trolley service is in operation, offering hot and cold drinks and snacks. Complimentary coffee, tea or juice and a pastry are offered to passengers on InterCity trains.

RAILWAY STATIONS

D WORZEC GŁÓWNY is Cracow's main railway station and is located in the heart of the city. All international and the majority of domestic trains pass through this station. Trains stop for a couple of minutes or longer and some are ready at the platform well before departure time so there is plenty of time to get comfortable and settled. In the main hall are counters to purchase international and domestic tickets and ticket machines for local destinations, as well as the lost property office and the information desk. Two restaurants and three bars, plus a hairdresser, bank, pharmacy and a number of small shops can be found within the station. A bureau de change is next door and a post office nearby.

The station hall is closed for an hour at night for it to be cleaned. The hall and platforms are monitored by security cameras, which help to keep a check on petty criminals and pickpockets who operate in and around the station.

An InterCity train at Cracow's Main Railway Station

A platform at Cracow's Main Railway Station

There are other smaller stations in Cracow, including Kraków-Płaszów southeast of the centre. This station is served from the city centre by trams 3, 6, 9, 13 and 24, as well as bus routes 107, 143, 163, 174 and 184.

ARRIVING BY COACH

REGULAR COACH services operate from Cracow to many European cities. The main coach station, Dworzec Autobusowy, is located in the centre, opposite the Main Railway Station. Local, domestic and most international services operate from this station. When this station opened, it proved to be too small. Today even small towns in Poland have better facilities. Cracow's coach station is not very inviting, lacking modern lavatories, shops and other basic facilities. The few ticket desks are unable to cope with the demand and are permanently busy. Buying a ticket in advance or early in the morning are good options. Coach drivers sell tickets if there are unreserved seats. There is no surcharge for this service. The current situation will improve when the new coach station, which is under construction, opens next to the Main Railway Station, which is also undergoing modernization.

Private international coach operators use a coach rank in Bosacka Street, on the other side of the railway station. They also use other coach parks. The international coach timetable is on display at the Main Coach Station and enquiries can be made at the information desk in the ticket hall. Tickets for domestic services can be purchased in the same hall. Travel agents and coach operators sell tickets for international routes.

The PKS, Polska Komunikacja Samochodowa, is the main national coach operator for inter-city connections within Poland. Many old, mechanically inferior and dirty coaches are used on some domestic routes and the drivers are sometimes not as polite as they should be. Modern coaches are being introduced at a slow but gradually increasing rate. Privately owned companies provide many inter-city and long-distance services. A coach journey from Cracow to a distant city may take a very long time, owing to many stops on the way, some requiring a detour from the main road. Travelling by coach is generally cheaper than by rail.

Cracow's road sign

ARRIVING BY CAR

DRIVING LICENCES issued in other countries are generally valid in Poland. If you drive in Poland you must carry on you a valid driving licence and vehicle registration document, as well as the Green Card as confirmation of your international insurance cover. If you drive a hired car, an appropriate document stating this is also obligatory. A national sticker identifying the country in which the car is registered must be displayed on the vehicle. The wearing of seat belts is compulsory. Children under the age of twelve are not allowed to travel in the front of the car. Between 1 October and 1 March headlights must be on, day and night, regardless of the weather conditions.

Road signs at the Polish border indicate speed limits (in kilometres). Speed limits should be strictly observed. Drivers breaking the speed limit risk hefty fines of up to 500 zł. Foreign drivers are required to pay on the spot.

The permitted alcohol content in blood is so low in Poland (two parts per thousand) that drinking and driving should be avoided altogether. Routine checks by police are frequent.

Car thefts are on the increase. Luggage and other property should not be left in the car. It is safer to remove the car radio. Using a guarded car park, even if only for a short stay, is strongly recommended.

A "Polski Express" coach

GETTING AROUND CRACOW

CENTRAL CRACOW is small and compact so moving around on foot or by public transport is best. Children in particular will enjoy a sightseeing ride on one of Cracow's blue trams. This guide lists bus and tram routes which you can use to get to the sights described in the *Cracow Area by Area* section. Maps of Cracow's tram and bus systems can be found on the inside back cover. If you require

A house number

more detailed maps, these can be bought from newsagents, bookshops and tourist information desks. Sightseeing tours in a horse-drawn cab are very popular with visitors. A small electric *meleks* vehicle can also be hired for sightseeing. *Meleks* drivers are qualified guides and speak foreign languages. Both cabs and *Meleks* vehicles await passengers in Cracow's historic Market Square.

The busy square in front of the local government building

PUBLIC TRANSPORT

CRACOW is well covered by an extensive public transport network. Trams and buses are frequent on weekdays but less frequent on Saturdays, Sundays and public holidays. Rush hours are between 7–8am and 2–5pm. At night only buses operate. Many bus routes extend to the suburbs. A number of private firms operate minibus services within the inner and outer city and stop on request. Further information on bus and tram services can be found on pp224–5.

DRIVING IN CRACOW

THE HISTORIC centre of the city of Cracow is a pedestrian precinct and is divided into three zones. Market Square and the surrounding streets fall

within zone A. Access is restricted within this zone to emergency and city services, and between 6pm and 10am also to the city's commercial delivery vans. In zone B, an area which extends to the Planty green belt, access is additionally given to local residents and vehicles displaying a special permit. Zone C extends to the so-called Avenue of the Three Poets (Krasińskiego, Mickiewicza, Słowackiego), Dietla and Westerplatte

A stop and give way road sign

streets. There is no access restriction to any car within Zone C but you need to purchase a parking permit in order to park. Parking permits are available from most newsagents.
Long queues of traffic are characteristic of rush hours, especially on Friday afternoons as well as when Cracovians are returning from their holidays.
Road works and temporary road closures are real

TICKETS

One type of ticket is used for trams and buses. Tickets are purchased from newspaper kiosks and MPK ticket outlets. Several types are available: timed, daily, weekly and family tickets. A ticket must be validated after boarding by punching it in a ticket punching machine. Timed tickets are valid for one hour from the moment of punching and you can change routes as often as necessary within this hour. Daily tickets are valid from the time of punching till midnight. Weekly tickets require the holder to have an ID and are valid for all tram and bus routes, either ordinary or express. A family ticket, not transferable, covers two adults and two children and is valid over the weekend. Children under 4 and senior citizens over 75 travel free of charge. Children between the ages of 4 and 14 years, students, senior citizens and the disabled are entitled to reduced-fare travel, but must carry appropriate identification documents. Foreign visitors to Cracow are not entitled to travel on reduced-fare tickets.

To validate ticket, insert arrow end into punching machine

Nie dotyczy pojazdów:
- z identyfikatorem B,C
- w godz. 18-10 dla i na czas wyk. czynności ładunkowych
- z silnikiem elektr., taxi,CC, CD
- konwoju pieniędzy, służb porządkowych, obsługi techn... pomocy medycznej na czas wyk. czynności
- komunikacji zbiorowej

Strefa B

No vehicles in zone B

WALKING IN CRACOW

The majority of historic sights, many museums and other tourist attractions, as well as restaurants and cafés, are located within the very centre of the Old Town, which is a pedestrian precinct. This is a relatively small area and can easily be seen and enjoyed foot. Signs indicating the directions to major sights are of great help to pedestrian visitors. Information plaques in several languages are displayed on historic buildings and by other sights.

Pedestrian crossing

Map of the Old Town with the Royal Route in red

hindrances to drivers who have to follow temporary diversion signs set up around the city. Cracow as yet has no ring road. Despite works being undertaken for some time now on a fast ring road round the city, only short stretches are presently in use.

The car is a convenient mode of transport during excursions to the suburbs and out-of-town locations. If you wish to escape the city centre, cars are available for hire from one of the many firms established in Cracow, but at a considerable cost.

No stopping

to the historic centre, only a few hundred metres from Market Square. This car park is, therefore, always busy and one of the most expensive. It is always easy to find a space at the large car park situated on the roof above the railway platforms at the Main Station. Other large guarded car parks can be found in Powiśle Street near Wawel, as well as in Rajska, Starowiślna and Straszewskiego streets.

Parking in Cracow is, by Western standards, still relatively easy and finding a guarded car park within walking distance of the historic centre should not be a problem.

WHEEL CLAMPS

ILLEGALLY PARKED vehicles may be clamped by a traffic warden. To have the clamp removed you have to call the warden. The

telephone number is given on the penalty notice which you will find attached to the windscreen. The text of this notice is printed in several languages. The warden will arrive and remove the clamp but you will have to pay the fine first.

Parking availability ("wolny" means "free")

PARKING

FINDING PARKING in the city centre may be difficult. Using a guarded car park (parking strzeżony) is a safe option. Parking on the pavement is allowed in Cracow but you have to leave at least one metre (3 ft) width free for pedestrians. The guarded car park in Szczepański Square is closest

A clamped, illegally parked car which can be removed from the street

Travelling by Tram

HORSE-DRAWN TRAMS were introduced to Cracow in 1895. Six years later they were replaced by electric trams. The trams you can see today are made up of either one, two or three carriages. Although they tend to be extremely busy during rush hours, trams are a fast mode of public transport, and are particularly convenient for the city centre. Visitors will find travelling by tram an excellent way to see Cracow. Trams serve the Main Railway Station, the centre and all major hotels, as well as residential quarters and many sights of interest.

A Cracow tram

Sign indicating a tram stop

All tram routes which serve the stop, along with a timetable for each, are displayed at each stop.

Tram routes serving the stop

Time-table

TRAM TICKETS

TRAM AND BUS tickets are the same *(see p222)*. A ticket should be purchased prior to boarding the tram. You may also buy a ticket from the driver when the tram is stationary at a stop and if you have the correct change. Trams are sometimes full and to reach the driver may be difficult. A ticket is a little more expensive if bought from the tram driver.

The ticket must be validated, or punched, immediately after boarding the tram. As on the buses, a ticket which has not been punched is not valid.

A single-fare ticket is valid for an unlimited single journey. A daily ticket should be validated (punched) only once, on your first journey, and is valid on all trams and buses until midnight. Weekly and monthly tickets must not be punched.

A map inside the carriage shows all the stops and connections on the route.

Tram time-tables are displayed at all stops. Trams start at 5am and run until 11pm, with a frequency varying from a few minutes to around twenty minutes. There is no night tram service. In some carriages you must press a button to open the door.

TICKET INSPECTORS

ON CRACOW'S TRAMS, tickets are occasionally inspected. The inspectors of MPK, Cracow's transport company, operate in plain clothes but carry an ID with a photograph. A passenger without a valid ticket is liable to a fine which is several times the price of a normal single fare. Travelling with an unpunched ticket can result in a fine, in the same way as travelling without a ticket. You may chose to pay on the spot or get a penalty ticket which must by paid at a post office. In the latter case the fine is higher. Foreign visitors must pay on the spot.

Instructions

Insert ticket here

Ticket punching machine

SAFETY TIPS

PICKPOCKETS operate on trams and buses. If you carry money or documents, take precautions. An open handbag or external pockets on a rucksack, coat or trousers are not safe places. Avoid ostentation when carrying a camera or laptop.

DIRECTORY
Cracow Transport Information ■ 910

A tram stop

Travelling by Bus

CRACOW IS WELL SERVED by buses which take passengers to all parts of the city and many suburban destinations. A variety of blue, red and multicoloured Ikarus, Jelcz and Scania buses, some modern, some a little bit older, operate on the dozens of different routes. Smoking is forbidden on all the city's buses and trams.

BUS TICKETS

BUS TICKETS are the same as those used on trams. If you change buses you need a new ticket for every subsequent leg of your journey, unless you carry a timed, daily or weekly ticket or a monthly pass. A detailed timetable is displayed at every bus stop and generally observed by drivers.

BUS ROUTES

BUS ROUTES indicated by a three-figure number operate a stopping service. Fast routes are operated by buses 501, 502 and 511. They serve selected stops only. The fare on a fast bus is 50 per cent more expensive than on a stopping service.

Bus frequency varies from every few minutes to approximately twenty minutes on week-days, but buses are less frequent on weekends and public holidays.

Buses indicated by a number above 600 operate a night service. Eight night bus routes link the city centre with the surrounding quarters. A night bus departs every hour and the fare is double the daily stopping fare.

Private minibus services operate on many routes within the city and in the suburbs. You can buy a ticket from the driver and it will cost you twice the fare of the MPK public transport. Most minibuses depart from the Main Railway Station. It is a fast and reliable service, especially convenient for Nowa Huta and other quarters outside the centre.

A Cracow bus

Travelling by Taxi

TAXIS are a convenient way of getting around Cracow, especially for visitors. To avoid being overcharged, however, it is best to use the services of the reliable radio taxis.

11pm, the second comes into effect on Sundays, public holidays and at night. The taxi fare increases as you leave the city limits. Requesting a receipt from the taxi driver will, in most cases, ensure that you will not be overcharged.

A City Taxi

TYPES OF TAXIS

TAXIS in Cracow vary in colour and make, and have different signs, depending on the company to which the drivers belong. All have an identification number clearly marked on the side of the car, as well as an illuminated 'Taxi' sign on the roof with the name of the company. Several taxi companies operate in Cracow; their fares are very similar to each other.

TAXI FARES

ON BOARDING a taxi an initial amount will be displayed on the meter; it will increase at a specified rate with each kilometre travelled. Payment is generally accepted by cash, but radio taxis which serve the Balice airport (and some other taxis) accept credit cards. There are two tariffs in use. The first tariff applies on weekdays from 5am to

STREET FINDER

MAP REFERENCES, given for each sight within its individual entry in this guide, relate to the map on the pages that follow. The same applies to the hotels *(see pp175–177)* and restaurants *(see pp188–191)* listed. The first figure indicates the map number, while the middle letter and the last number refer to the relevant grid. The key map on the right

Tourists in Cracow

shows Cracow divided into six parts which correspond to the maps that follow. All symbols used are explained in the key. You will find the Street Finder Index on pp228–229. Note that Polish is an inflected language and street names require different name endings (Jan Kowalski but Jana Kowalskiego Street).

Top sights and attractions are indicated on the maps.

KEY TO STREET FINDER

- Major sight
- Other sight
- Railway station
- Coach terminal
- Tram depot
- Bus stop
- Parking
- Tourist information
- Hospital
- Police station
- Boat pier
- Church
- Synagogue
- Post office
- Railway line
- One-way street
- Pedestrian street
- City wall

SCALE OF MAPS 1–4
0 metres   200
0 yards   200
1:14 000

SCALE OF MAPS 5–6
0 metres   150
0 yards   150
1:9000

0 kilometres   1
0 miles   0,5

A hurdy-gurdy man in Market Square

Stairs leading to the Decius Villa

Church of St Adalbert in Market Square

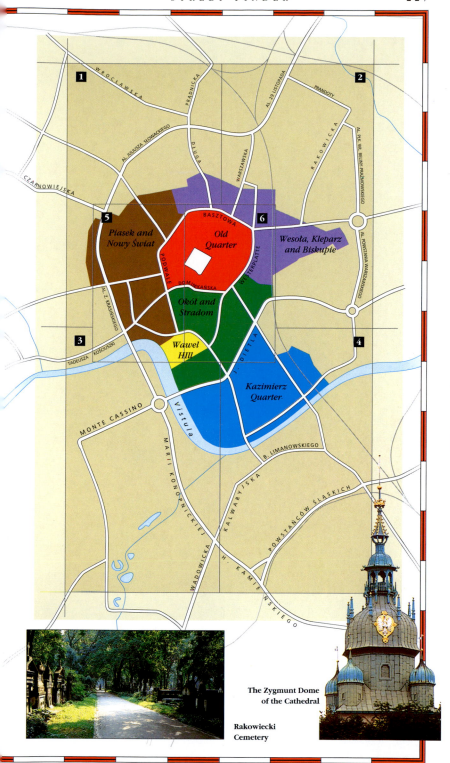

1

2

WROCŁAWSKA

PRĄDNICKA

AL. 29 LISTOPADA

PRANDOTY

AL. JULIUSZA SŁOWACKIEGO

DŁUGA

WARSZAWSKA

RAKOWICKA

AL. PŁK. WŁ. BELINY-PRAŻMOWSKIEGO

CZARNOWIEJSKA

AL. POWSTANIA WARSZAWSKIEGO

5

BASZTOWA

6

Piasek and
Nowy Świat

Old
Quarter

Wesoła, Kleparz
and Biskupie

PODWALE

WESTERPLATTE

DOMINIKAŃSKA

AL. Z. KRASIŃSKIEGO

Okół and
Stradom

3

Wawel
Hill

L. DIETLA

4

TADEUSZA KOŚCIUSZKI

Kazimierz
Quarter

MONTE CASSINO

VISTULA

MARII KONOPNICKIEJ

B. LIMANOWSKIEGO

KALWARYJSKA

POWSTAŃCÓW ŚLĄSKICH

WADOWICKA

H. KAMIEŃSKIEGO

**The Zygmunt Dome
of the Cathedral**

**Rakowiecki
Cemetery**

Street Finder Index

General Index

Acknowledgements

DORLING KINDERSLEY would like to thank the following people whose assistance has made the preparation of this book possible.

MANAGING EDITOR
Helen Townsend

MANAGING ART EDITOR
Kate Poole

SENIOR MANAGING EDITOR
Louise B. Lang

ART DIRECTOR
Gillian Allan

DESIGN AND EDITORIAL ASSISTANCE
Hilary Bird, Arwen Burnett, Eli Estaugh, Elly King, Ferdie McDonald, Gordon McLachlan.

DORLING KINDERSLEY wish to thank the following institutions, picture libraries and individuals for their kind permission to reproduce photographs of objects in their care and for the use of other photographic material:

Magdalena Maros the Director, and Krystyna Litewka at the Public Record State Office,
Krzysztof Zamorski, Director of the Jagiellonian Library,
Stanisław Waltoś the Director, Lucyna Bełtowska and Robert Springwald at the Collegium Maius,
Matejko House,
St Vladimir Foundation,
Katarzyna Bałus, Princes Czartoryski Foundation,
Jama Michalika,
Prelate Janusz Bielański, Cracow Cathedral and Cathedral Museum,
Church of the Bernardine Nuns,
Bernardine Church,
Father Mirosław Pilśniak, OP, Dominican Church,
Sister Wanda Batko, Church of the Felician Nuns,
Brother Bogumił Stachowicz, OFM, Franciscan Church,
Father Edward Stoch, SJ, Jesuit Church in Wesoła,
Capuchin Church,
Father Dr Bronisław Fidelus, Church of St Mary,
Father Jan Mazur, Paulite Church "On the Rock",
Church of St Anne,
Father Henryk Dziadosz, Church of St Barbara,
Church of St Florian,
Church of St Catherine,
Church of the Holy Cross,
Church of St Mark,
Church of St Peter and St Paul,
Church of St Vincent,
Wieliczka Salt Mine,
Father Dr Józef A. Nowobilski, the Metropolitan Curia and Archdiocesan Museum,
Balice Airport,
Archaeological Museum,
Andrzej Szczygieł, Director of the Museum of Cracow,
Anna Studnicka, National Museum,
Natural History Museum,

Zbigniew Święcicki the Director, and Mirosław Ciunowicz at the Polish Military Museum in Warsaw,
PAP Polish Press Agency,
Society of Physicians,
Pieskowa Skała Castle.

DORLING KINDERSLEY are grateful to the following individuals for their kind permission to reproduce their photographs:
Jacek Bednarczyk,
Olaf Beer,
Maja Florczykowska,
Michał Grychowski,
Stanisława Jabłońska,
Dorota i Mariusz Jarymowiczowie,
Beata i Mariusz Kowalewscy,
Grzegorz Kozakiewicz,
Wojciech Mędrzak,
Stanisław Michta,
Hanna i Maciej Musiałowie,
Tomasz Robaczyński,
Maciej Sochor,
Jan Zych.

All the dishes whose photographs feature in this guide were prepared in the restaurant Pod Aniołami. We wish to thank the owner, Jacek Łodziński for his help. We are also grateful to Marcin Duszyński, Madropol for his kind assistance.

PICTURE CREDITS
t=top; tc=top centre; tr=top right; cla=centre left above; ca=centre above; cra=centre right above; cl=centre left; c=centre; cr=centre right; clb=centre left below; b=bottom; bc=bottom centre; bl=bottom left; br=bottom right; c=centre=below; crb=centre right below;

ARCHAEOLOGICAL MUSEUM: 18clb, 18b, 19cr, 19cb, 19b, 38b;

CATHEDRAL MUSEUM: 20-21c, 22cla, 26cla, 40cl, 60ca, 62c;

COLLEGIUM MAIUS: 23cb, 29b, 106–107;

CZARTORYSKI MUSEUM: 39t, 41b, 112–113;

JAGIELLONIAN LIBRARY: 18–19c, 22clb, 24tl, 24cra, 24b, 28b, 28crb, 26br, 30cb, 148b;

MATEJKO HOUSE: 21cr;

MUSEUM OF CRACOW: 16, 17b, 25ca, 27cb, 32b, 33ca, 33cr, 38cr, 39cbr, 40tl, 92tr, 99br;

NATIONAL MUSEUM: 8–9, 20bc, 21tc, 22b, 23cr, 27br, 28bl, 28–29c, 29cr, 30tc, 30–31c, 31t, 31tr, 32cl, 32–33c, 35bl, 38tr, 38cl, 39tcr, 39c, 41t, 50cla, 51tl, 51br, 76c, 83l, 102tr, 102c, 103, 145l, 146–147;

NATURAL HISTORY MUSEUM: 41c.

PUBLIC RECORD STATE OFFICE: 22–23c, 22bl, 22t.

All other images ©Dorling Kindersley.
For further information see: www.dkimages.com

Phrase Book

SUMMARY OF PRONUNCIATION IN POLISH

ą a nasal *"awn"* as in *"sawn"* or *"an"* as in the French *"Anjou"* but barely sounded

c *"ts"* as in *"bats"*

ć, cz *"ch"* as in *"challenge"*

ch *"ch"* as in Scottish *"loch"*

dz *"j"* as in *"jeans"* when followed by **i** or **e** but otherwise *"dz"* as in *"adze"*

dź *"j"* as in *"jeans"*

dż *"d"* as in *"dog"* followed by *"s"* as in *"leisure"*

ę similar to *"en"* in *"end"* only nasal and barely sounded, but if at the end of the word pronounced *"e"* as in *"bed"*

h *"ch"* as in Scottish *"loch"*

i *"ee"* as in *"teeth"*

j *"y"* as in yes

ł *"w"* as in *"window"*

ń similar to the *"ni"* in *"companion"*

ó *"oo"* as in *"soot"*

rz similar to the *"s"* in *"leisure"* or, when it follows **p**, **t** or **k**, *"sh"* as in *"shut"*

ś, sz *"sh"* as in *"shut"*

w *"v"* as in *"vine"*

y similar to the *"i"* in *"bit"*

ź, ż similar to the *"s"* in *"leisure"*

EMERGENCIES

Help!	**pomocy!**	pomotsi
Call a doctor!	**zawołać doktora!**	zawowach doctora
Call an ambulance!	**zadzwonić po pogotowie!**	zadzvoneech po pogotovee
Police!	**policja!**	poleetsya
Call the fire brigade!	**zadzwonić po straż pożarną!**	zadzvoneech po stras posarnAWN
Where is the nearest phone?	**Gdzie jest najbliższa budka telefoniczna?**	gjeh yest nlbleezhsha boodka telefoneechna
Where is the hospital?	**Gdzie jest szpital?**	gjeh yest shpeetal
Where is the police station	**Gdzie jest posterunek policji?**	gjeh yest posterunek politsyee

COMMUNICATION ESSENTIALS

Yes	**Tak**	tak
No	**Nie**	n-yeh
Thank you	**Dziękuję**	jENkoo-yeh
No thank you	**Nie, dziękuję**	n-ycj jENkoo-yeh
Please	**Proszę**	prosheh
I don't understand.	**Nie rozumiem.**	n-yeh rozoom-yem
Do you speak English? (to a man)	**Czy mówi pan po angielsku?**	chi moovee pan po ang-yelskoo
Do you speak English? (to a woman)	**Czy mówi pani po angielsku?**	chi moovee panee po ang-yelskoo
Please speak more slowly	**Proszę mówić wolniej.**	prosch mooveech voln-yay
Please write it down for me.	**Proszę mi to napisać.**	prosheh mee to napeesach
My name is...	**Nazywam się...**	nazivam sheh

USEFUL WORDS AND PHRASES

Pleased to meet you (to a man)	**Bardzo mi miło pana poznać**	bardzo mee meewo pana poznach
Pleased to meet you (to a woman)	**Bardzo mi miło panią poznać**	bardzo mee meewo pan-yAWN poznach
Good morning	**Dzień dobry**	jen-yuh dobri
Good afternoon	**Dzień dobry**	jen-yuh dobri
Good evening	**Dobry wieczór**	dobri y-yechoor

Good night	**Dobranoc**	dobranots
Goodbye	**Do widzenia**	do veedzen-ya
What time is it..?	**Która jest godzina?**	ktoora yest gojeena
Cheers!	**Na zdrowie!**	na zdrov-yeh
Excellent!	**Wspaniale**	wspan-yaleh

SHOPPING

Do you have...? (to a man)	**Czy ma pan...?**	che ma pan
Do you have...? (to a woman)	**Czy ma pani...?**	che ma panee
How much is this?	**Ile to kosztuje?**	eeleh to koshtoo-yeh
Where is the... department?	**Gdzie jest dział z...?**	gjeh yest jawuh z
Do you take credit cards? (to a man)	**Czy przyjmuje pan karty kredytowe?**	chi pshi-yuhmoo-yeh pan karti kreditoveh
Do you take credit cards? (to a woman)	**Czy przyjmuje pani karty kredytowe?**	chi pshi-yuhmoo-yeh panee karti kreditoveh
bakery	**piekarnia**	p-yekarn-ya
bookshop	**księgarnia**	kshENgarn-ya
chemist	**apteka**	apteka
department store	**dom towarowy**	dom tovarovi
exchange office	**kantor walutowy**	kantor valootovi
travel agent	**biuro podróży**	b-yooro podroozhi
post office	**poczta, urząd pocztowy**	pochta, ooZHAWNd pochtovi
postcard	**pocztówka**	pochtoovka
stamp	**znaczek**	znachek
How much is a postcard to...?	**Ile kosztuje pocztówka do...?**	eeleh koshtoo-yeh pochtoovka do
airmail	**poczta lotnicza**	pochta lotneecha

STAYING IN A HOTEL

Have you any vacancies? (to a man)	**Czy ma pan wolne pokoje?**	chi ma pan volneh poko-yeh
Have you any vacancies? (to a woman)	**Czy ma pani wolne pokoje?**	chi ma panee volneh poko-yeh
What is the charge per night?	**Ile kosztuje za dobę?**	eeleh koshtoo-yeh za dobeh
I'd like a single room.	**Poproszę pokój jednoosobowy.**	poprosheh pokoo-yuh yedno-osobovi
I'd like a double room.	**Poproszę pokój dwuosobowy.**	poprosheh pokoo-yuh dvoo-osobovi
I'd like a twin room.	**Poproszę pokój z dwoma łóżkami.**	poprosheh pokoo-yuh z dvoma woozhkamee
I'd like a room with a bathroom.	**Poproszę pokój z łazienką.**	poprosheh pokoo-yuh z wazhenkAWN
bathroom	**łazienka**	wazhenka
bed	**łóżko**	woozhko
bill	**rachunek**	raHoonek
breakfast	**śniadanie**	shn-yadan-yeh
dinner	**kolacja**	kolats-ya
double room	**pokój dwuosobowy**	pokoo-yuh dvoo-osobovi
full board	**pełne utrzymanie**	pewuhneh ootzhiman-yeh
guest house	**zajazd**	za-yazd
half board	**dwa posiłki dziennie**	dva posheewuhkee jen-yeh
key	**klucz**	klooch
restaurant	**restauracja**	restawrats-ya
shower	**prysznic**	prishneets
single room	**pokój jednoosobowy**	pokoo-yuh yedno-osobovi
toilet	**toaleta**	to-aleta

EATING OUT

A table for one, please.	**Stolik dla jednej osoby proszę.**	stoolek dla yednay osobi proshehh
A table for two, please.	**Stolik dla dwóch osób proszę.**	stoolek dla dvooh osoob prosheh
Can I see the menu?	**Mogę prosić jadłospis?**	mogeh prosheech yadwospees

Can I see the wine list?	**Mogę prosić kartę win?**	mogeh prosheech karteh veen
I'd like...	**Proszę**	prosheh
Can we have the bill, please?	**Proszę rachunek?**	prosheh raHoonek
Where is the toilet?	**Gdzie jest toaleta?**	gjeh yest to-aleta

MENU DECODER

baranina	mutton, lamb
barszcz czerwony	beetroot soup
bażant	pheasant
befsztyk	beef steak
bigos	hunter's stew (sweet and sour cabbage with a variety of meats and seasonings)
bukiet z jarzyn	a variety of raw and pickled vegetables
ciasto	cake, pastry
cielęcina	veal
cukier	sugar
cukierek	sweet, confectionery
dania mięsne	meat dishes
dania rybne	fish dishes
dania z drobiu	poultry dishes
deser	dessert
flaki	tripe
grzybki marynowane	marinated mushrooms
herbata	tea
jarzyny	vegetables
kabanos	dry, smoked pork sausage
kaczka	duck
kapusta	cabbage
kartofle	potatoes
kasza gryczana	buckwheat
kaszanka	black pudding
kawa	coffee
kiełbasa	sausage
klopsiki	minced meat balls
lody	ice cream
łosoś	salmon
łosoś wędzony	smoked salmon
makowiec	poppy seed cake
naleśniki	pancakes
piernik	spiced honeycake
pierogi	ravioli-like dumplings
piwo	beer
prawdziwki	ceps (type of mushroom)
przystawki	entrées
pstrąg	trout
rolmopsy	rollmop herrings
sałatka	salad
sałatka owocowa	fruit salad
sok	juice
sok jabłkowy	apple juice
sok owocowy	fruit juice
sól	salt
śledź	herring
tort	cake, gâteau
wieprzowina	pork
wino	wine
woda	water
ziemniaki	potatoes
zupa	soup

HEALTH

I do not feel well.	**Źle się czuję**	zhleh sheh choo-yeh
I need	**Potrzebuję**	potzheboo-yeh
a prescription for...	**receptę na...**	retsepteh na
cold	**przeziębienie**	pshef-yENb-yen-yeh
cough (noun)	**kaszel**	kashel
cut	**skaleczenie**	skalechen-yeh
flu	**grypa**	gripa
hayfever	**katar sienny**	katar shyienny
headache pills	**proszki od bólu głowy**	proshkee od booloo gwovi
hospital	**szpital**	shpeetal
nausea	**mdłości**	mudwosh-che
sore throat	**ból gardła**	bool gardwa

TRAVEL AND TRANSPORT

| When is the next train to...? | **Kiedy jest następny pociąg do...?** | k-yedi yest nastENpni pochAWNg do |
| What is the fare to...? | **Ile kosztuje bilet do...?** | eeleh koshtoo-yeh beelet do |

A single ticket to ... please	**Proszę bilet w jedną stronę bilet do...**	prosheh beelet v yednAWN stroneh beelet do
A return ticket to ... please	**Proszę bilet w obie strony do...**	prosheh beelet v obye strony do
Where is the bus station?	**Gdzie jest dworzec autobusowy?**	gjeh yest dvozhets awtoboosovi
Where is the bus stop?	**Gdzie jest przystanek autobusowy?**	gjeh yest pshistanek awtoboosovi
Where is the tram stop?	**Gdzie jest przystanek tramwajowy?**	gjeh yest pshistanek tramvl-yovi
booking office	**kasa biletowa**	kasa beeletova
station	**stacja**	stats-ya
timetable	**rozkład jazdy**	rozkwad yazdi
left luggage	**przechowalnia bagażu**	pshel-Hovaln-ya bagazhoo
platform	**peron**	peron
first class	**pierwsza klasa**	p-yervsha klasa
second class	**druga klasa**	drooga klasa
single ticket	**bilet w jedną stronę**	beelet v jednAWN stroneh
return ticket	**bilet powrotny**	beelet povrotni
airline	**linia lotnicza**	leen-ya lotna-yeecha
airport	**lotnisko**	lotn-yeesko
arrival	**przylot**	pshilot
flight number	**numer lotu**	noomer lotoo
gate	**przejście**	pshaysh-cheh
coach	**autokar**	awtokar

NUMBERS

0	**zero**	zero
1	**jeden**	yeden
2	**dwa**	dva
3	**trzy**	tshi
4	**cztery**	chteri
5	**pięć**	p-yENch
6	**sześć**	shesh-ch
7	**siedem**	sh-yedem
8	**osiem**	oshem
9	**dziewięć**	jev-yENch
10	**dziesięć**	jeshENch
11	**jedenaście**	yedenash-cheh
12	**dwanaście**	dvanash-cheh
13	**trzynaście**	tshinash-cheh
14	**czternaście**	chternash-cheh
15	**piętnaście**	p-yEntnash-cheh
16	**szesnaście**	shesnash-cheh
17	**siedemnaście**	shedemnash-cheh
18	**osiemnaście**	oshemnash-cheh
19	**dziewiętnaście**	jev-yENtnash-cheh
20	**dwadzieścia**	dvajesh-cha
21	**dwadzieścia jeden**	dvajesh-cha yeden
22	**dwadzieścia dwa**	dvajesh-cha dva
30	**trzydzieści**	tshijesh-chee
40	**czterdzieści**	chterjesh-chee
50	**pięćdziesiąt**	p-yENchjeshAWNt
100	**sto**	sto
200	**dwieście**	dv-yesh-cheh
500	**pięćset**	p-yENchset
1,000	**tysiąc**	tishAWNts
1,000,000	**milion**	meel-yon

TIME

today	**dzisiaj**	jeeshl
yesterday	**wczoraj**	vchorl
tomorrow	**jutro**	yootro
tonight	**dzisiejszej nocy**	jeeshAYshay notsi
one minute	**jedna minuta**	yedna meenoota
half an hour	**pół godziny**	poowuh gojeeni
hour	**godzina**	gojeena

DAYS OF THE WEEK

Sunday	**niedziela**	n-yejela
Monday	**poniedziałek**	pon-yejawek
Tuesday	**wtorek**	vtorek
Wednesday	**środa**	shroda
Thursday	**czwartek**	chvartek
Friday	**piątek**	p-yAWNtek
Saturday	**sobota**	sobota

Cracow Trams and Buses